NEW AMERICAN VEGAN

New American Vegan
by Vincent Guihan
ISBN: 978-1-60486-079-5
LCCN: 2009912455
This edition copyright ©2011 PM Press
All Rights Reserved

PM Press
PO Box 23912
Oakland, CA 94623
www.pmpress.org

Layout by Daniel Meltzer
Cover art by Tofu Hound/John Yates

Printed on recycled paper by the Employee Owners of Thomson-Shore in Dexter, Michigan.
www.thomsonshore.com

Table of Contents

Chapter 3:

Get Saucy! 47

Recipes:

Getting Past the Recipes:

Chapter 4:

Side Dishes or Plate Partners?.........83

Recipes:

Getting Past the Recipes:
What Makes a Good Side
Dish, a Good Appetizer
& a Good Salad?

Chapter 5:

Seitan & Potatoes, and Other
Soon-to-Be-Traditional Favorites

Recipes:

Getting Past the Recipes:
Addressing the
Center of the Plate

Chapter 6:

When Vegan Desserts Attack!

Recipes:

Introduction:
How I Went Vegan, Why I Stay Vegan & Why the Food Is Central to My Life

I promise this will be a short introduction. I'm not an especially wordy person and I know you're buying this book for the recipes!

And yet, it all starts decades ago in a large Irish family in a very small town, Waterman, IL. My father was a janitor at Northern Illinois University (about twelve miles away in De Kalb). My back yard was our neighbor's cornfield. As a child, I thought De Kalb was huge. It had several fast food restaurants, a few grills, the works! My parents cooked only sporadically, even though the nearest fast-food restaurants were a twenty-minute car ride away. We moved to the southwest side of Chicago when I was eleven. Raised on TV dinners, burgers, pizza, and spaghetti, I spent much of my young adulthood nestled between the delicatessens, greasy spoons, and taquerias dotted around Cermak Road and Cicero Avenue, which helped to build my palate. Of course, I also made sure to provide my palate with serious depth by eating junk food in the bleachers at Cubs games (and the infrequent White Sox game, although I'm embarrassed to admit it) with father and my older brothers.

Today, I live in Ottawa, Canada—a city renowned (at least in Canada!) for its cosmopolitan flair in spite of its small size—where I eat a great number of things I can't even pronounce. Today, the two most common questions I get as a vegan are "Why are you vegan?" and "What do you eat?" This book answers both but with an emphasis on the latter, of course. I started becoming vegan when I was twenty-six by eliminating all animal products from my diet, and then over the next few months eliminating all of my leather, wool, silk, and all the unnecessary cleaning products I had that were tested on animals or used animal ingredients. So, in some respects it was overnight, but in others it was gradual. I had been a vegetarian, and a strict one (not a pescatarian or a "no red meat" vegetarian) for about a decade before that.

When I became vegetarian, there weren't a dozen brands of soy, hemp, or nut milk at my local grocery store, nor the few dozen vegan veggie burgers, hot dogs, and other products you can buy today. A lot has changed in the last two decades in terms of the availability of vegan products, and yet, remarkably little has changed for other animals. For the most part, the conditions of animal use have not changed. The number of animals being used is up. More and more vegetarians and vegans are turning back to eating meat, believing that humanely raised meat doesn't present us with a moral problem. I couldn't disagree more with this view, and it all relates to why I went vegan: a cat named Percy.

To be clear, Percy wasn't exactly my cat. He adopted me at the same time my first wife and my stepchildren did. He came with the family and with three other cats: Sam, an enormous dark grey tom; Butch, a white cat; and Five Fingered Lou, a grey tabby with five fingers. Percy was the smallest of all of them. He was also the most resilient. He had been hit by a car twice (don't let your cats out, people!) and had lost a good part of his tail in the process. The vets generally agreed that he had probably suffered some brain damage as a result of his near-death scrapes.

When I met him, Percy had a low, mono-tone meow. He sang in a bass voice that would have been perfect for "Stepping over Jordan" or "Swing Low, Sweet Chariot" if he had been a human being. Instead, his singing was more like something you'd expect in German electro music in the 1990s. But every time the kibble was poured out or the wet food was scooped out, Percy was there ready to eat. He made the best of the life that he had. The prospect that it would be in any way moral to take that life away when it suited me—no matter how well he was treated, no matter how much pleasure it might give me—seemed wrong. His life became a very important lesson to my own.

When we think of our own rights (what others owe us) and of our own well-being (what makes us happy and healthy), it's not that different from other animals. We're all unique. We're all individuals. We all have an interest in living our lives. We all have things that are objectively good for us (e.g., I go to the doctor and my cats go to the vet), even if they are sometimes uncomfortable or painful. It's not just a matter of whether or not other animals suffer when we use them, it's a question of whether it is right to use them at all. It was Percy who convinced me that it wasn't right to use other animals.

Over time, it dawned on me that if Percy had such an interest in his life (like I did), then surely other animals did as well. I started to do some research into animal ethology. Noninvasive ethology studies how animals behave themselves when they're left to themselves. It's an interesting field, and I still try to read up when I have the chance. The gist, how-ever, is that it was clear upon even very basic study that, to paraphrase Gary L. Francione, animals were sentient, they could feel pain, they had an interest in avoiding it, and they had an interest in continuing their lives, just like I did and just like Percy.

Everything I had done up until that point in my life with respect to nonhuman animals had been well-intended but misguided, except for caring for the animals in my personal immediate life. I realized that, in spite of my best intentions, being vegetarian for a decade had been mostly for naught. None of the other animals I wasn't eating had been given a get-out-of-jail-free card. They had just been sold to someone else.

The other animals I thought I was saving by only drinking their milk or eating their eggs were still being killed, as were many animals who were "unnecessary" to the profitability of animal agriculture. Male chicks who couldn't lay eggs were being killed. Male calves who couldn't produce milk were being raise for veal. I realized that I had been running up a debt my entire life taking from others what didn't belong to me. I had a subjective, arational, and passive relationship to nonhumans. I didn't want that. I wanted a relationship with animals that was objective, rational, and active—most of all, fair and compassionate, like my relationship with Percy. The first and most meaningful step I could take was to go vegan, so I did.

Cows, chickens, sheep, pigs, bees, and other animals have nerves, memories, fears, wants, and interests just like cats and dogs—just like you and I do. As individuals, as persons, they should have the right not to be used as someone else's property—just like you and I do. It didn't seem logical for me to have a relationship with Percy as though he were a member of the family while eating, wearing, being entertained by or otherwise using other animals. Animal use isn't necessary for human health or for the environment. In fact, when I sat down and measured all of the scientific evidence available to me, I found that there were no good reasons for me to be using other animals at all. And so I went vegan.

A lot of people have different ideas on what it means to be vegan. In my view, vegans are people who should take the rights of animals not to be used seriously and so they don't use animals, whether for food, clothing, or entertainment. I'm not a philosopher, but that sounded right to me. Since going vegan, I've read a number of books about veganism. By the time you will be reading this book, I will have been vegan for more than a dozen years (go me!). The most important books I read, however, were Gary Francione's *Rain Without Thunder* and *Introduction to Animal Rights: Your Child or Your Dog?* And most recently, Robert Torres's *Making a Killing*. It would be difficult to summarize the effect these books have had on the way I think about my relationship to nonhuman persons. If you want to learn more about the abolitionist approach to animal rights, I recommend visiting **www.abolitionistapproach.com.**

Nonhuman persons? Of course! I live with several cats now. They're all individuals. They all have different personalities, different quirks, different behaviors and different ways of being that make them each who he or she is. Julius, a Russian Blue, likes to run out into the hall every time I open my front door and then roll around on the hall carpet. Thor, a longhaired white cat, trills in an elegant sing-song when he meows. Fred, my black cat who lost the tips of his ears to frostbite (again, keep your cats indoors!), likes to head-butt me and is one the most loving cats I've ever lived with. Jasmine, Thor's sister, hides from everyone, but occasionally likes to poke me with her paw when I'm talking at length and not paying attention to her and to bite my toes when she's hungry. Zella, a gentle but formidable female Maine Coon mix, is the smallest, but nevertheless, she's the boss of them all. And my surly, fierce, and sour tortie, my sweet Harriet, growls, hisses, and swats at everyone else except for her adoptive mother and father.

In a legal sense, in the sense of how the world is, they belong to me like other property. But in the moral sense, in the meaningful sense of how the world should be, they obviously shouldn't belong *to me* the way my books and CDs do. They belong *with me* in the way my regular human children do, the way refugees would if I were caring for them, the way my parent might if they were still alive today and I were caring for them and so on. I believe unequivocally that all nonhuman animals deserve the same consideration for their interests, and I look forward and work toward the day when the human use of nonhuman animals is ended and their status as our property is abolished. Bigger cages and kinder treatment will never give them what we owe them: a recognition, embodied in a live daily practice, that they are ends in themselves and not a means to our ends. Veganism is the baseline to that practice.

So, why use animals if we don't have to? Change starts with us, individuals, not with donations to groups that propose more "humane" animal use, not with new regulations that keep the system in place and let us justify animal use to ourselves. By going vegan, we each have a unique opportunity to take a part in a struggle against injustice toward them, but also rewards us with opportunities for a more virtuous life for ourselves, a cleaner environment, better food distribution for other people, and most of all, food that's full of flavor! If you're not vegan, why not try it out? You could do it this Monday. Trade that milk in your cereal and coffee for soy milk (or rice milk or cashew cream or almond milk). Swap out that burger for the burger recipe in this book or any of the countless soy and nut burgers you can buy today. Tear up those tickets to the circus. Buy yourself some swank, nonleather shoes (go for co-op made!). Make a plan and phase out each animal product one by one if that's what it takes, but take animals seriously and go vegan. It's easier than you think.

But what about the food, yes? The food in this book represents what is mostly a ten-year journey toward building up recipes that I like. I know, always thinking of myself. But hopefully you'll like them as well. I wrote this book because I believe an increasing number of people are troubled by the way we use other animals and, at the same time, are interested in healthier, more environmentally friendly, vegetable-focused food. Still others are considering and adopting veganism and vegetarianism out of a deeply rooted concern for animals and a desire to be at peace with their consciences.

Some are interested in nonviolence and how other forms of social oppression—sexism, racism, ableism, and other forms of violence— relate to the harm we do to other animals. In short, a growing number of people are interested in veganism (often whether they know it or not), but one key hurdle to the adoption of veganism is knowing what to eat and, as important, how to cook it. Moreover, many vegan cookbooks don't address a range of skill levels and varying levels of knowledge about food chemistry and flavor theory, the availability of key ingredients and the palate of the average North American buyer. I wanted to write a book that would focus on building skills with and knowledge about food from a basic level on up, to achieve more complicated culinary work.

Further, as its title suggests, the book is also focused specifically on New American vegan cuisine: food that is relatively simple to prepare, relies where possible on local ingredients, food that is (mostly!) healthy, and tastes and looks great to the eye, while also challenging the palate to grow outside of the standard fast-food diet. New American cooking has enjoyed a resurgence in popularity in recent years, largely as fusion cooking has ebbed, in part because these styles of cooking, while they appeal to a cosmopolitan appetite (mine included!), do little to address what most nonvegans think of as eating well. There are obvious exceptions, of course. But because veganism has traditionally lent itself to fusion, and particularly Southeast Asian styles of cooking and dishes, cookbooks for vegans tend to be "special occasion" books today, providing a once-a-week,

maybe a once-a-month recipe. I want folks to use this book more regularly, and more important, to help them to become better cooks for themselves.

Of course, there is hardly a dearth of cookbooks for vegans available today, but in this book I've tried to focus on foods that are easy to prepare and provide a way for cooks to develop their skills over time. In part, that's what makes this book different from other books. People who like comfort food should like this book. People who aren't sure about veganism, but are curious about it or interested in eating healthy but are reluctant to use ingredients that are hard to find, hard to judge and hard to predict will also like this book. People should also feel encouraged to give this book as a gift to anyone they know who likes to fiddle in the kitchen (hint hint!), and I hope it will be very useful for families with vegan young adults and children.   •

What I also wanted to write was a book that would not only provide good recipes but foster a unique cuisine and a community around that cuisine that can innovate, improvise, and claim these dishes "as their own." For vegans, there are very few cooking shows and culinary schools. And not many cookbooks focus on educating would-be vegan chefs with respect to bringing out the best cuisine that a basis of roots, fruits, nuts, and shoots really has to offer. Some very good books include *The Mediterranean Vegan Kitchen*, *Vegan Vittles*, *Alternative Vegan*, *The Artful Vegan*, and *The Joy of Vegan Cookery*. Of course this is the short list, and there are many others. Even mainstream chefs—such as Charlie

Trotter, who wrote the appropriately titled *Vegetables*—are looking more and more to the flavor, texture, and color that plant-based foods provide to a dynamic and contemporary cuisine. There's still so much to be discovered with plant-based foods.

So, in the end, this book is different from most other cookbooks for vegans for a few reasons. First, it focuses on the American table from a vegan perspective. Many cookbooks for vegans draw on global fusion, and while that's fine, I wanted to do something a little closer to home. Second, the more sophisticated of these cookbooks tend to feature recipes that are complicated with hard to find ingredients. There's something to be said for just the right combination of ingredients and putting time into a plate. But I wanted a balance to my book of things that were simple and things that were more complicated, as well as some way for cooks to build skills. It shouldn't require a couple of years of experience as a celebrity chef to cook more than few recipes in a given book! I wanted to write something simpler.

Finally, I wanted to address what I really believe is at stake with veganism and what the real opportunities for it are. As we become more and more dissociated from our food as ingredients, and, worse perhaps, as we lose a refined understanding of how to prepare and share our meals, we lose the opportunity to build strong families and communities through a shared kitchen and a shared table. Veganism is a lived ethical practice focused on community and what we owe to others. A cuisine that is the natural corollary of this practice offers us a way to stem this growing depersonalization.

So, you'll notice that aside from one or two catchy titles, this book is mostly and modestly focused on recipes that build skill with, and knowledge of, food required to produce superior finished dishes, with room and encouragement to innovate and improvise. Be creative. I openly challenge everyone who uses this book to go past its recipes! Of course, theory and technique are unusual elements in many cookbooks, but these are really indispensable to building a cuisine. In fact, this growing divergence between how to prepare food (the mechanics) and why to prepare it in particular ways (the theory, and all the knowledge that theory embodies) is increasingly common.

This coincides with a general and growing divergence between us and our food over the last few decades especially in North America. Nowhere is this often more apparent than in the vegan community, where there are few long-standing traditions of food preparation, time-honored dishes or even culinary diplomas for chefs to drawn on as they reinvent standard American cuisine. Even with all of those challenges, we're going to be successful if we work thoughtfully, if we work diligently, and if we work together.

Chapter 1:
Terms, Techniques & Tools: A Brief Field Guide to What You Need & What You Need to Know

This book is organized mostly around building complete meals with a main dish and a couple of sides. The recipes will be useful for coursed dinners or when you just want some salad, a bowl of soup, or some breakfast, but the main focus is on building successful meals with a complete set of flavors. To that end, you'll notice that each of the recipes is coded for its level of difficulty, its time to prepare and the overall time it will take to complete, and what the major flavors are.

Flavor and texture

Theories of flavor vary a bit, but for the purposes of this book I've used eight terms to describe the flavors of the dishes: sweet, sour, salty, green, rich or fatty, savory, spicy, and fermented. You have taste buds that can distinguish the first four. There is reasonable debate about and scientific evidence to support the view that people can also distinguish the next two, fatty and savory, as they eat. The last two, spicy and fermented, are really just shorthands to help you understand what a dish will taste like before you cook it. Nevertheless, you may still be surprised by how some of the flavors of these dishes are described. And so I've provided a couple of explanatory notes.

What is a sweet flavor? Sweet is that delicious flavor that makes you feel relaxed and comforted. That's your blood sugar spiking! Carrots, other vegetables, and definitely fruits, are typically sweet, although some are both sweet and sour in combination. I could have split out starchy flavors separately, but I think eight flavors is enough. So, starchy flavors are listed as sweet in this book (e.g., potatoes, wheat bread, and other carbohydrates). In part, this is a matter more of chemistry than of flavor specifically. Mono- and disaccharides are simple sugars. They taste sweet immediately. But when you chew a complex sugar molecule (e.g., a polysaccharide or oligosaccharide) you break it up into mono- and disaccharides. You can establish this by chewing a cracker for a minute or two. It will become sweeter in your mouth. In short, polysaccharides and oligosaccharides don't necessarily taste sweet, but they are in terms of their chemistry.

What is a sour flavor? Sour is that wonderful flavor that makes your tongue contract and your face to pucker up! Pomegranate, lemon juice, vinegar, and other acidic ingredients are typically sour.

What is a salty flavor? Almost every dish in this book has a slightly salty flavor, in part because salt is added to most of the dishes. I doubt there will be very much debate about what is salty. As a flavor, salt is hard to describe, but you know it when you taste it. If you're interested in learning more about the food chemistry of salt, read the note on salt on page 10.

What is a green flavor? Green refers to the wonderful bitter taste of coffee and a number of green vegetables that you can taste toward the back of your tongue. Sometimes you'll see this flavor referred to as pungent. I've never liked the use of "pungent" to describe these flavors, since pungent is abstract. Green is pretty straightforward. Not everything green in color has a green flavor, of course, and some things that aren't green in color are bitter. No term is perfect, but to keep it simple, green refers to bitter flavors in this book.

What is a fatty flavor? There is some evidence that people can differentiate the amount of fat in a given dish, which has led some food scientists to argue that there is a fatty flavor. More commonly, what you'll read is that fat add to the "mouth feel" of a given dish. This seems pretty true. If you swallow a tablespoon of olive oil and then a half tablespoon of olive oil mixed with water, you can really tell the difference and it's not purely in the way that the tablespoon of liquid tastes. Sometimes you're in the mood for something rich and heavy and sometimes you're not, so I've identified fatty flavors.

What is a savory flavor? For the purposes of this book, savory specifically refers to umami, a Japanese term for the flavor of protein that is distinguishable from fatty and salty. It's actually not clear scientifically how well human beings can taste proteins. Certainly, they can't taste amino acids with the same expertise that the average household cat can. But savory has long a common concept in Asian theories of flavor, and an increasingly accepted concept in Western cooking. Moreover, I think it's a useful way to understand a lot of the flavors that are common to the American table.

What is a spicy flavor? Spicy describes a number of possibilities in terms of food chemistry. The most common kind of spicy flavor is when the sour element of a dish is really high (e.g., jalapeño peppers has an acidity that is similar in kind but different in degree to lemon juice and other sour flavors). But some spicy flavors (e.g., wasabi, horseradish, and to a certain degree, ginger) affect your mouth differently. This kind of spicy typically goes straight up through your nose. Some people like it hot, and others not so much, so I've identified spicy flavors.

What is a fermented flavor? For the purposes of this book, I've identified foods that specifically have a fermented flavor. Fermented is usually a combination of sweet, salty, and sour but it's also a flavor of bacteria. I've separated it out in part because, although almost all cultures have fermented foods, they're usually very much acquired tastes. It's usually not a big deal to eat adapt your palette to the sweet, sour, spicy, savory (umami), fatty, or green (bitter) flavors of another culture's cuisine, but if you grow up eating cheese and you try miso or natto (or vice versa), you'll probably experience some culinary culture shock.

Preparing your ingredients

Most of these recipes call for *mirepoix* (diced vegetables, typically carrot, celery, and onion), as well as garlic, ginger, peppers, other vegetables, rice, and legumes. If you're not familiar with how to prepare these vegetables, some simple instructions are below for common ingredients. Specific recipes may have specific instructions, however. Always remember to wash your fruits and vegetables (and your hands!) thoroughly first. Sensibilities about how to pick and prepare a given ingredient may vary quite a bit across locale and tradition. You may be accustomed to preparing a vegetable in a particular way, and that's fine. The points below are simplifications for people not used to working with the ingredients listed.

Two additional notes, however, are appropriate. First, always try to use fresh, whole food once you get the hang of and taste for a particular recipe. Go to your local health food store (HFS) and get your peanut butter fresh ground before your eyes. If you can, don't use a single dried herb. Buy fresh and do the conversions. Buy dried beans instead of canned. Why? Fresh foods typically have better nutritional value and, frankly, they taste better. Second, keep in mind that you may not like the taste of a given ingredient the first time around. In fact, new foods often take six or eight tries before we develop a taste for them. If you're a new vegan, it will take about six to eight weeks for your body and tastes to adjust. But broadening your palette is like any other kind of education. There may be a little culinary culture shock, but that's good for your palette. Having said that, don't force yourself to eat things you really don't like. What's most important about the dietary elements of veganism is that you eat foods you like that provide you with the right nutritional balance for you. Consult a physician or a nutritionist to find out what the right nutritional balance for you is.

But the great thing about veganism from a food perspective is that you have an incredible variety of foods from which to choose, all with different flavors, textures and colors, which also vary further by the style of preparation and in combinations with other foods. In fact, it's these plant-based ingredients and techniques of preparation that make most animal-focused foods taste good. But we already know this intuitively. Most meat (and most animal products in general) provides a basically a bland, often colorless palette and some texture (a dead body, after all), that is recreated into a "meal" by the skill of the cook, with the addition of many plant-based flavors.

It's the bun, catsup, pickles, salt, fat, fermentation, onions, mustard, sliced tomato, crisp lettuce, and all of the other plant-based foods, as well as the skill with and knowledge of preparation techniques (is it cooked over charcoal, propane, or wood, grilled, fried, or broiled?) that makes the burger great, not the animal who died to make it. Of course, some ingredients do taste better than others, but when we make the meal about individual ingredients and not the skills of the chef, we surfeit, if only unintentionally, the dedication of people who devote their lives to cooking.

A note on salt: Salt is both a flavoring and a catalyst in terms of food chemistry, and this note will cover both aspects of this ubiquitous condiment.

In terms of its chemistry, salt (as in sodium chloride) does a number of things. First, it helps preserve food by slowing the oxidization process. It also has antibacterial properties, and in part that's why salt is often used as part of a preservative process historically. Second, and more important to this book, salt also helps to cook food by chewing up the proteins in the cell walls of plants. What that means, in effect, is that the moment you add salt to anything, a cooking process of sorts has begun. The result is that cell walls burst, and typically that releases the ingredient's internal water. Almost all foods have some sort of water. Of course, that water isn't just plain water. It's water that has important chemical additive from the food itself. Frequently it's what ends up as juice if you juice a fruit or a vegetable, which means that it's water with a lot of flavor and often sugars. It's the release of those flavors and the sugars that bring the flavor out of the fruit or vegetable you're cooking out into the pan where it can mix with other flavors, while also allowing flavors to mix and penetrate the other ingredients of the pan. Imagine a number of floodgates to different reservoirs being opened all at once and all the resulting waters mingling. That's the chemical magic of salt. You will not be able to achieve similar results with equally salty but chemically different additives. As a process, cooking involves the heating and, frequently, the release of that water and the denaturation (the breaking apart) of protein chains, although that's not always the case. For example, you're typically adding water to grains. dried beans, etc. But in any case, salt is an important part of the cooking process. In part, this is why salt has been an important part of virtually all cuisines for a long, long time.

Having said all of that, salt is also an important flavor, one of the four basic flavors that you have taste buds built in to taste. Some people like their food saltier than others, and some foods taste fine without added salt. As a flavor, there are both a number of salts with distinct flavors (e.g., grey salt, fleur de sel, and so on), and there are number of salty foods that don't have sodium chloride (e.g., potassium chloride, Bragg's liquid aminos, herb blends sold as salt alternatives, and so on). You'll notice as you work through the recipes in this book that you start with a little salt (1/4 teaspoon) and then add salt at the end of the cooking process. In part, this is because I'm encouraging you to think about salt as both the chemical agent and the flavoring separately.

With that in mind, if you want to finish your dish with something other than fine-grained sea salt, go for it. In fact, I encourage you to experiment with other salty flavors. You can start by using coarse-grained sea salt as a finishing salt. Instead of adding another pinch of fine-grained sea salt to your dish, grind a pinch of coarse-grained salt between your fingers and sprinkle. You'll find coarse-grained salt increases the burst of salty flavor (something lots of people like) while also decreasing the overall amount that you need to use. In short, however, most cooking involves some kind of salt at some point. Use it sparingly. Unlike soups, where you can usually get away with adding a little water, if you add too much salt to sauces, salads and other dishes, especially dressings, they tend to be less forgiving. Start with 1/4 teaspoon of fine sea salt with these dishes and add more at the end. Going slow with salt is rarely a bad idea. Many dishes can be rescued if they're too sour, too sweet, or too spicy, but too salty is hard to salvage.

A quick note on oils: I've recommended vegetable oil in many cases in this book. You should use the vegetable oil you like. I use a blend of flax oil and extra virgin olive oil, or canola, for most of my sauté, often a little toasted sesame oil for flavor, and only very infrequently peanut oil (for high-temperature frying, which I almost never do). My preference, when I need to add fat, is to use a nut butter, olives, or avocados instead. The process by which oil is made subtracts most of the nutrition of the whole food. The nut butter, the mashed avocado, the minced olives, etc., retain a good portion of its taste and nutrition. However, like salt, oil is also a chemical agent in your dish. It functions in two ways. First, it creates a water barrier. A number of the recipes involving dough suggest that you brush your crusts with a little oil. In part, that's to keep the extra moisture of a sauce or even whole ingredients that produce a lot of moisture when heated from saturating your dough. Second, it conducts the heat, for lack of a better way to put it, that melts and caramelizes the sugars in certain foods when you sauté, most commonly, or when you roast or grill them. Unlike salt, it can be difficult to add fats at the end of the cooking process rather than at the beginning, but that shouldn't keep you from swapping out oils for whole foods where the former are not being used as a chemical agent as part of the cooking process.

A very quick note on sugars and agave nectar: There are increasing numbers of artificial sweeteners on the market, and stevia (an herbal sweetener) is becoming more popular in North America. Added sugars are typically a flavoring ingredient, but there are times when it is also a chemical agent, in which case it either caramelizes (as in crème brulée) or it is used as food for bacteria (in some slaws, in fermented foods, and in yeast dough, for example). In particular, the agave nectar in this book is often used to avoid cooking a simple syrup (which involves boiling water and sugar together), which is both a pain and because a lot of sugar is processed with animal bone char, I've kept it simple and built the recipes around agave. It's not difficult to find conversions, but not all of the recipes will work with regular granulated sugar.

Basil (and other green herbs): Fresh basil and other herbs come in various ways—and some health food sorts and organic farmers include the plant all the way down to the roots. If the stems of your herb are hard and inflexible (usually the case), remove the leaves and use the leaves only. If your stems are soft, a little stem is good for you. To tell if a stem is soft enough, it should be bendable like the leaf and very thin. If it's thicker than a coffee stirrer, no need to put that in your dish. Try to avoid using ground dried green herbs—rub the larger dried herbs between your thumb and forefinger when you add them to your dish.

Beans (and other legumes): Beans vary quite a bit in flavor, texture, color, taste, and their preparation. All the beans in this book call for dried legumes. You can use canned in a pinch or if you're just trying out a recipe, but working with dried beans is better because you have more control over the preparation and there will be less salt (virtually all canned foods have added salt that they don't tell you about on the ingredients label). You can also use jarred beans if you can find them. If you have a slow cooker, it's strongly recommended you use that to prepare your legumes (except for yellow split peas and red lentils, since these dissolve with cooking, at least in the recipes for this book). A slow cooker is a dead simple way to make the best, softest, and

nicest beans. Just adjust the cook times as appropriate depending on the type of legume involved.

When preparing legumes, carefully wash and pick through them looking for and removing anything that looks a stone (or anything that doesn't look like a legume for that matter). For the long cooking ones (chickpeas, red beans, etc.), if you can, soak the beans overnight in a covered bowl with enough water to cover them 1 inch or so. Drain the water the following day, about 1 1/2 hours before you'd like to serve. Bring 2 cups water and 2/3 cup beans (3:1 ratio) to a low simmer in a medium-sized pot on medium heat. Cover the pot with the appropriate, tight-fitting lid and reduce to low. Simmer for the appropriate amount of time depending on your legume. Cooking times will vary depending on if and how long you've soaked and the original conditions of the beans—if you didn't presoak, plan on 1 1/2 to 2 1/2 hours of cook time for the bigger legumes. The beans will be done when they are soft (but not like mashed potatoes). To test, pull one out, allow it to cool, and eat it. If it tastes done, it is done! If all the water is absorbed before the beans are done, just add more. Once the beans are done, remove from heat. Drain them in a colander when they're done.

Cantaloupe, honeydew, and other melons: Melons can be a little difficult to pick and prepare. Most groceries have them already cut and ready to eat. You can get your feet wet with melons by using precut. To pick a good melon, you're looking at a number of factors, typically including: is the color vibrant or it is discolored? When you thump it with a thumb, does it sound solid (usually still ripening) or does it sound a little hollow (usually ripe, but possibly overripe)? For the most part, you don't want the rind and you don't want the seeds. To prep your cantaloupe or honeydew, cut the melon in half and remove the seeds and any seriously discolored, overripe flesh. Cut into quarters (or eighths for larger melons) and carefully remove the rind with a sharp knife. The best way for you to do this (if you're not accustomed to this kind of knife work) is to lay the slice on your cutting board and slice the rind off this way.

Carrots: Remove the top and bottom inch or so of the carrot. Cut in half lengthwise. Place the flat part of the half-carrot onto the cutting board. Slice across the length of the carrot again. Cut across the width of the carrot in 1/4- to 1/2-inch chunks. For sliced carrots, cut in half length-wide and then slice the carrot width-wide at a 45-degree angle into slices about 1/8-inch wide. Once you have the 1/8-inch slices, you can go further and slice each slice into matchsticks instead of shredding. This takes some practice but it's a great way to practice precision work with your knife.

Celery: Remove the top and bottom inch of the celery stalk and any flowering parts of the stalk. If you have especially large stalks of celery, you may have to slice the stalk in half or even into quarters lengthwise to start. Then, chop the stalk into 1/4- to 1/2-inch chunks width-wise.

Chard: Chard is a wonderful leafy green that comes in a number of varieties. Wash thoroughly and trim the stems about 1 inch above where the leaves start to flower out. Chard tends to cook like spinach and arugula although it holds its texture slightly better.

Chipotle: Chipotle is basically smoked jalapeño pepper. The smoking process turns it a bright red. Chipotle doesn't really taste as citrusy, but it is just as spicy. You'll probably find either jarred or dried chipotle peppers. For dried, rehydrate as appropriate. Most of the recipes assume jarred, which is much easier to work with.

Garlic: Place the clove of garlic on the cutting board. Place the flat of your knife on top of the cutting board, holding the handle carefully. Smash the clove of garlic with the flat of your knife by pressing down firmly with the palm of your free hand (being careful to avoid your knife edge). Remove the skin of the garlic. Mince the garlic finely, until it approaches a mush of garlic. Sprinkle a pinch of sea salt into the garlic and mince to the desired consistency. One clove typically yields 1 teaspoon, while 2 to 3 yield a tablespoon, but it varies depending on the size of the cloves.

Ginger: Cut a piece of ginger from the root for an appropriate amount: about the size of your thumb to the first joint for 1 teaspoon. Peel the skin of the root thoroughly but carefully with a knife. Mince the peeled ginger until it approaches a mush of ginger.

Guar gum: Some of the recipes in this book suggest guar gum as an optional ingredient. Guar gum's nothing to be afraid of. It's in a lot of the foods you already eat. It's an emulsifier (it helps things to hold together) and a stabilizer (it helps things to hold together over time). You only need a little. You won't get a lot of additional hold by adding more guar gum.

Legumes (lentils, yellow split peas, etc.): Carefully wash your dried legumes and pick through them, removing anything that looks a stone (and anything that doesn't look like a legume, for that matter).

Kale: Like chard, kale comes in a lot of varieties. In this book, "kale" generally refers to green curly kale. But there are other varieties, including Russian and black kale. Russian tends to be curly like regular green kale, but black kale (also called dinosaur or lacinato kale) tends to have a texture more like collards. In general, kale is a wonderful green vegetable full of flavor, nutrition, and texture.

Miso: Miso comes in various flavors with varying degrees of fermented flavor. Generally, the darker it is, the stronger the flavor. Because it has a strong fermented flavor, it may take a few tries to develop a taste. Start with white and go darker for richer flavor, but be sure to keep it all refrigerated after opening.

Mangoes: Mangoes are a bright yellow fruit. Pick mangoes that yield to gentle pressure but without soft spots. Mangoes can be a little difficult to pare and stone (they have a big pit referred to as the stone) and there are a couple of ways to do it depending on how you're using the mango. Since you'll be shredding or finely chopping your mangoes in this book, begin by carefully removing the skin with a sharp knife. Then slice the mango around the stone the like you're carving wood. Remove any pieces of the mango stone you accidentally cut off with your mango slices. Shred and chop the slices as necessary.

Mushrooms: Carefully wipe fresh mushrooms clean with a damp, clean cloth, and then prepare as the recipe requires. For button and cremini mushrooms, that usually means removing about 1/4 to 1/2 inch of the stem and then slicing across the mushroom in 1/4-inch slices or smaller.

Nut butters: In a sauce or dressing a nut butter typically plays a few roles. It provides some emulsification (it helps hold things together), it adds some body (it makes things thicker), and it adds some fatty flavor (which gives the dish a nice mouth feel). This book generally assumes unsalted and unsweetened (which is always preferable, since you can then control the amount of sweetness and saltiness). Salted and sweetened nut butters aren't a serious problem (most brand-name peanut butters are both), but when using salted or sweetened nut butters, reduce the amount of salt or sweeteners as appropriate.

Nut butters also represent the whole, if somewhat processed, food. Oils, in contrast, are not whole foods and much of the flavor, texture, and nutrition are lost when a food is processed into oil. Unfortunately, you can't really sauté with nut butter. Nevertheless, this book tries to use nut butters instead of oil where possible. Nut butters vary quite a bit in terms of their flavor and consistency. Although you can often substitute one for another, you should be aware of how that will change the flavor. Be sure to store your nut butters in a refrigerator once opened.

Onions: Cut the onion in half width-wise. Peel off the outer layer so that the husk is removed. Turn one half of the onion onto its flat side. Slice through the onion width-wise in 1/4 to 1/2-inch slices. Slice through the onion lengthwise in 1/4 to 1/2-inch slices. Repeat with the other half. Chop any greens coarsely.

Peppers: Cut the pepper in half length-wise. Be careful if you're chopping jalapeño peppers, using gloves if you have sensitive skin. Open the pepper by pulling on both of the opened sides. Remove all of the seeds, pith and stem (all of the stuff that isn't bright green). Mince the pepper until it approaches a mush of pepper.

Potatoes: Potatoes come in literally dozens of varieties each with slightly different textures, tastes, and colors. Blue potatoes make for a fabulous and colorful addition to the plate. I'm partial to fingerlings (little mini potatoes) because they're easy to prepare: just two slices into quarters and the fingerling is pretty much ready for anything. There are no baked potato recipes in this book, but baked potatoes also make for a good, relatively simple side dish and you can serve them with many of the sauces in Chapter 3. With this book, you'll probably be working with larger potatoes and you'll want to cube them (either for steaming or roasting). Begin by slicing

the potato in half lengthwise. Place the flat edge down on the board and slice about half way between the board and your hand (be careful!). Slice the potato in half lengthwise, and slice each half in half lengthwise. Now, cut the slices width-wise in 1/2-inch segments. What you want are 1/2-inch cubes of potatoes, but what's important is that the pieces of potatoes are about the same size. Washing your potatoes is very important. Also, while potatoes keep for a while, they're past due if they're soft and yielding to the touch.

Rhubarb: Don't use aluminum or copper pots (with copper cooking surfaces). Look for fresh, firm stalks and trim the ends like you're trimming celery. You may have to peel the rhubarb slightly if it's particularly woody.

Rice: Give your rice a good wash and pick through looking for and removing anything that doesn't look like a grain of rice. Rice varies quite a bit in terms of their cooking times, and there are a lot of specialized rice out on the market today (e.g., brown and wild rice mixes, brown and mahogany rice mixes). For regular long-grain brown rice, 45 minutes cook time should be sufficient, but if you buy packaged, follow the instructions as appropriate.

Scallions: Typically in this book, you're mincing scallions and using both the white and the green. To do this, wash your scallions and remove any discolored strands (peel them off), and cut off the bulb about 1 inch from the bottom, and then proceed to mince, or follow the directions specific to the recipe if you're using a different cut.

Squashes: It saddens me tremendously that this book only has one squash recipe. But the truth is, most squashes can be difficult to pick and prepare, often make a very large dish, or require a fair amount of knife work to prepare, sometimes requiring a cleaver. Squashes are a fabulous set of vegetables with a number of very different varieties: spaghetti squash, acorn squash, butternut squash, and so on. You may be able to find fresh or frozen butternut squash already cut, in which case you can substitute it for most of the sweet potato and pumpkin dishes in this book (butternut squash usually takes a little less cooking time than sweet potatoes). Or, if you want to get fancy, make some spaghetti squash and toss it with any of the pasta-friendly sauces in this book.

Sweet potatoes: Sweet potatoes have long been a staple of American cooking and yet you hardly see them except on the holidays. That's a shame. Sweet potatoes are not only really good for you, they also taste great. Peel them like a regular potato, slice into 1/2-inch rounds (follow the instructions for potatoes as above) and steam them, or roast them whole for a low-effort, quick, sweet, and colorful side dish.

Sun-dried tomatoes: Sun-dried tomatoes are a great way to add a little red color and flavor to a dish. Typically, you'll find these dried or jarred in oil. Dried is probably better for the recipes in this cookbook. They'll be less expensive, and most of the recipes assume you'll be rehydrating them anyhow. To rehydrate,

you want about twice as much boiling water as you have tomatoes (so, 1/2 cup boiling water to 1/4 cup sun-dried tomatoes). Steep in the water for about 20 minutes, or until the tomatoes are soft.

Tomatoes: Typically, for the purposes of this book, you'll be preparing tomatoes cored, seeded and chopped. In that case, cut the tomatoes in half and remove the seeds and pith and anything that isn't tomato-colored. Chop as directed.

Being a better cook & being a better eater

Unfortunately, teaching you what you would learn in one cooking class is well beyond the scope of this book. If you have time, take a course (or go for a diploma). It will be well worth it. Nevertheless, this book does try to teach you something, but the goal of this book is to help you cultivate a habit of eating well. You deserve it. To that end, I've provided some brief notes on how to make the most use out of this book, and I hope you'll find them helpful. Where you find them lacking, this book will have piqued your curiosity enough to learn more from other sources.

Cooking in particular and hospitality in general are arts that have lost their prominence in American life, and we should all lament that process—more than lament it, take the steps we can to forestall it and return the table to the center of American life that it once was, and to bring to the forefront of our priorities the shared dialogue and the acknowledgment of others in our families and communities and what we owe them, which the table embodies. Your table calls you to be present in your own life and the lives of others who are important to you. If it achieves nothing else, I hope this book helps you to be a better host and a better guest in the broadest meanings of those words.

Understanding the basics of technique. As I've said, this book is no replace-ment for a cooking class. But I can provide you with a few notes on technique. What follows are a few points of guidance for you, combining practical tips and existential wisdom.

Don't overload your pan. This is both a literal and a metaphorical piece of advice. Overloading the sauté pan is a common mistake for inexperienced cooks when they sauté. But in a broader sense, improvisational cooks often make too much and then try to work it all together, and the recipe ends up all out of proportion and things don't come together. Relax. Enjoy your work. If a dish doesn't come together, it's not the end of the world, but you can often rescue a dish, or not have to rescue a dish, with some good up-front planning.

Use the right knife. Again, both a literal and a metaphorical piece of advice. A good cook has two to three knives to use with frequency to achieve specific tasks. Most knives sold in a block will spend virtually all of their lives in the block. More important, cooking is often a matter of using the best tool for the job, but it sometimes calls on us to use tools in ways we didn't expect. What's important for both your safety and the success of

your dishes, though, is that you avoid using the wrong tool, whether it's the wrong knife (a dull knife is almost always the wrong knife), the wrong emulsifier, or the wrong flavor combination. Good planning and thinking about the big picture of the work you're creating will help you get a sense of what tool is appropriate when.

Combine the flavors that you like. Don't let other people tell you what tastes good to you. Don't make yourself miserable eating foods you don't like. Chances are very good there's another food out there with similar nutritional value that you do like (e.g., figs and collards both provide important nutrition, but they have very different tastes and textures). Eat that instead. Mix it in with other foods you do like. Develop your palate. Create a personal cuisine. Be receptive to the tastes of others, but don't forget that your own is important.

Treat the plate like a work of art. Your work is an expression of your skill, commitment and effort. When you plate and present your food, consider that it is the denouement of your work. At this point, the mouths are watering at the smell, but lots of people also eat with their eyes. You've probably spent a couple of hours making it. Take an extra 10 minutes to really make your work shine by thinking about how you can present it best. It's fun, and a good expression of creativity. Paint the sauce onto the bottom of the plate, or tower your food up with microgreens. What's important is that you have fun and make something that's beautiful to you.

Seek balance in your dishes. Balance is actually a very important part of cooking. A dish that's too sour, too sweet, too spicy, or, worst of all, too salty, is a crime against the palate. Although the flavor of your dishes can and probably should tilt toward one particular flavor, the plate functions best and most fully with a balance and hint of all of the major flavors, or at least most of them.

Be creative — and this means innovating more than inventing. With one or two exceptions, most of these recipes have at least three flavors. Most of them have four or five. But very few of them make use of all the flavors this book addresses, but provide you with suggestions on how you could add additional flavor. This is for two reasons. First, it's to keep the dishes simple. Second, it's to provide you with an opportunity to be creative and to expand on simple dishes to create something more complicated. Improvising is a serious skill that takes creativity and practice to master. This book encourages you to be creative and go further, not just with lip service but with every recipe, and at your own pace.

Don't be afraid of diversity. New things often taste weird. That's just the way your palate works. Imagine Cro-Magnon humans roaming the wilderness putting whatever in their mouths because everything tasted good. How long would the species have lasted? Instead, some things taste pretty good the first time we try them (e.g., lots of fruits), but other things often take several tries before we develop the taste. Developing and cultivating your palate is a matter of trying new things, often a few times,

including stuff that tastes absolutely terrible the first time. Try to distinguish between something that tastes bad and something that simply has a strong taste that you're not sure about. These are different things. Sometimes it's hard to tell the difference, but that doesn't mean that there isn't any difference at all. Also, some ingredients taste great when prepared a particular way but just plain awful prepared another. You won't know until you try.

Remember that everyone starts somewhere. Even with an educated palate, people's tastes vary (or we'd all want the same dish all the time), and they vary with the amount of time they want to put into an individual meal, what the weather's like, what you've been eating lately, whether or not you smoke, whether or not you're on medication, etc. Lots of factors influence how we taste. Most New American dishes are reinterpretations of basic comfort foods, which become comfort foods because they provide a sophisticated but not overly difficult to produce set of flavors. Just as there's nothing wrong with liking cheap beer, there's nothing wrong with liking cheap food. But you may as well do yourself a favor and try them all. Developing your palate (at least when it comes to beer) is a shorthand expression for developing a full sense of what Pabst Blue Ribbon and Chimay each taste like, why they taste differently in an objective sense, as well as which you prefer and why. I'm afraid your only recourse in this kind of situation is to buy the beer and wine made without animal products available and to taste them all (responsibly, of course!). More important, once you're on your

Vincent Guihan | New American Vegan

way to developing your palate, don't go off and act like an annoying food snob. Enthusiasm is terrific. But no one likes annoying food snobs who think they know more than they do about food, and there's always something more to learn. Food is for preparing, eating, and enjoying in gratitude and in good company.

Plan, plan, and then plan some more. I can't stress planning enough. I believe so firmly in good planning that I've already mentioned it a couple of times in this section, and now I'm writing a whole paragraph about it. That may seem odd coming from someone who's cooking philosophy sounds a lot like "make it up as you go," but improvisational cooking is like improvisational jazz. When you solo as a jazz artist, you're improvising within the context of an established rhythm, cadence, and sound. You are hearing the pattern and meaningfully, playfully improvising based on that. The same is true of improvisational cooking. You must understand the rules and patterns of foods, food chemistry, technique, flavor, and texture (even color and layering on the plate), and have a sense of how your improvisation will unfold with respect to all of those factors in order to create a beautiful, delicious and interesting dish. Planning is the first step.

A brief glossary •

I've tried to avoid technical cooking terms in this book, except where the words themselves are amusing (e.g., *amuse bouche*) or where they will probably be useful to understanding technique. I've provided a brief glossary in this section to further explain some of the terms used in this book. This is by no means complete.

Amuse bouche: An amuse bouche is an amusement for your mouth! It is a very small dish, served in preparation for the meal. It can be served with the aperitif or as an alternative to it.

Aperitif: An aperitif is an opening drink for a meal. Common aperitifs include Dubonnet, red vermouth, and other dry spirits.

Appetizer: An appetizer is an opening course, served before the entrée (the entrée is typically the main course of a meal).

Blanching: Blanching is a technique for lightly boiling food for a short period of time (typically only several minutes) in lightly salted water. Blanching is often used to loosen the skin of fruits and vegetables or to reduce the bitterness of certain vegetables.

Braising: Braising usually involves searing and then cooking in a pan with a suitable amount of moisture to soften the sear. Technically, you're braising the Cutlets Cacciatore in Chapter 5, but otherwise you won't braise very much at all in this book. Typically, with seitan and other savory ingredients it's the other way around: you're adding moisture and then searing the food.

Coddling: Coddling refers to heating a liquid to just below a specific temperature point (usually boiling, but not always). When you make the white sauce in the Tofu Florentine recipe, you'll be coddling the tarragon aioli.

Chiffonade: To chiffonade is to cut into long thing strips, like julienning. Unlike julienne, however, chiffonade typically refers specifically to herbs and involves the rolling up the herb leaves lengthwise, like a newspaper, and then slicing through in small strips.

Chopping: Chopping is the most basic kind of knife work. For the purposes of this book, instructions include rough chopping and fine chopping. For rough chopping, you're chopping to the point that your pieces are in the 1/2 to 1-inch range. For fine chopping, your pieces should be 1/4 to 1/2 inch. To chop smaller than 1/4 inch, you're typically mincing.

Deglazing: Deglazing is the process of scraping caramelized bits from the cooking surface of the pan (be sure to use stainless steel or other types of pans). Usually, this involves the addition of wine to the pan and scraping with a wooden spoon. You can also use lemon juice and vodka, or lemon juice and tamari. In terms of food chemistry, what's important to the deglazing process is the combination of cooling the pan, adding liquid that can be quickly boiled off, and a light acidity. Don't deglaze nonstick pans.

Dicing: Dicing is a slightly more complicated knife technique, usually grouped into small (1/4-inch dice), medium (1/2-inch dice) and large (3/4-inch dice). What dicing involves is trying to cut the ingredients into small, evenly sized cubes. This takes practice and it can be more or less difficult depending on the vegetable. Some vegetables are hard to work with because of their texture, and some are hard to work with because of their shape. Do your best to cut evenly, and for heaven's sake be careful!

If you want to practice your dicing, start with carrots. Trim the ends. Cut it in half lengthwise. Place the flat side down and do your best to trim off the edges in a straight line, leaving as much of the carrot as possible intact. Next, turn the carrot onto a flat side so that the remaining rounded edges can be trimmed in the same way you trimmed the previous edges, so that you have a mostly rectangular carrot wedge now. Slice it in half lengthwise (and then into quarters if it's a large carrot). Then slice width-wise until you have a little pile of cubed carrots. You may find that you need to slice the carrot in half height-wise. This is a great way to accidentally cut yourself, but if you're serious about practicing, carefully hold the carrot vertically against the board. Pick a spot halfway between the board and your palm and carefully slice through the carrot. Better to give this a try with tofu first.

Digestif: A digestif is a finishing drink for a meal. Common digestifs include cognac, sweeter liqueurs, and other spirits.

Double boiler: A double boiler is a particular cooking gadget for melting chocolate. Double boiling can also accomplished the old-fashioned way, with two pans.

Dressing: Dressing, as a verb, refers to the addition of a dressing or other ingredients. This is typically at the end of preparation.

Emulsification / stabilization: Emulsification is a chemical process in which polar and nonpolar ingredients are combined homogeneously in a single solution, for example, combining oil (nonpolar) and vinegar (polar) using an emulsifier, like mustard. Stabilization is a chemical process in which an additional ingredient helps to maintain the emulsification. Some ingredients are just emulsifiers (e.g., minced garlic), but some both emulsify and stabilize an ingredient (e.g., guar gum).

Flavor layers: Flavor layers refer to discernible layers of flavors in a given dish. For example, a breast of seitan that is glazed, breaded, and then sauced has several flavor layers.

Grilling: Grilling is a technique in which food cooked using a medium-high, direct, and dry heat (a lot like roasting). In North America, it usually refers to using a grill in order to create grill marks. This seasons the food while allowing moisture and, in some cases, fat to drip free from the food.

Hors d'oeuvres: An hors d'oeuvre is typically a tray of light foods that are served before dinner. These are typically finger foods, often with drinks. Canapés, crudités, bruschetta, etc. are hors d'oeuvres. If you do serve your hors d'oeuvres with drinks, think about the match of the flavors. Most aperitifs are lightly bitter, lightly sour, with a hint of sweet. Complement the drinks with hors d'oeuvres that are slightly salty, lightly spicy, or lightly sweet.

Julienne: To julienne is to cut into long thin strips, typically vegetables and meats.

Cut the ends of whatever you're julienning so that you have a nice rectangular shape, and then carefully slice in 1/8-inch strips. If you really want to be fancy, turn your julienned strips 90 degrees clockwise and then cut those pieces into 1/8-inch strips. This is a common technique for garnishes, where you want very small dice.

Mincing: Mincing is to chop very, very fine. Mincing achieves a few things. First, you may want to add a small amount of an ingredient with a strong taste (or an expensive ingredient), evenly throughout a dish, and mincing will achieve that. Second, and for the most part in this book, what you're really doing with mincing is chopping it so finely that the moisture and the natural oils of the food are coming out onto the board, so that when you add the ingredient to the dish, the flavors are already on the surface and don't require a lot of additional cooking, if any. Your pieces should be smaller than 1/8 inch, often achieving a paste with garlic and ginger, but with kale and other greens they should just be relatively small.

Plating and presentation: Plating refers to the arrangement of food on the plate itself. Presentation refers to the arrangement of the meal as a whole.

Poaching: Poaching is to cook a food in boiling water (typically eggs, meats, etc., but also pears). You poach the tofu in a solution of water and white vinegar in the Tofu Florentine recipe, for example.

Puréeing: For the purposes of this book, puréeing refers to blending several ingredients until smooth.

Pastry: Pastry typically refers to both the product of and the skills required to producing pastries, widely defined to include both desserts and savory dishes, particularly those that involve work with flour and baking.

Roasting: Roasting is a technique in which food is cooked using medium-high and direct dry heat (usually involving a roasting pan, but not always). Oven roasting applies this technique in the oven (usually heated to broil, but not always). Roasting over open coals, on spits, and other ways of roasting are common. What's important is the dryness of the heat. Ingredients should form a single layer on the pan, not be stacked up if possible.

Roulade: Roulade is largely a presentation but also a cooking technique. For the purposes of this book, roulade refers to wrapping stuffs with seitan so that a roll is formed. Roulade is typically tied with string and then prepared.

Sautéing: Sautéing is the cooking technique you'll use most in this book. It involves a number of things: heat, fat, sugar, and moisture. Basically, it's pan-frying food in a particular way so that foods lose a little moisture (but not all), brighten their colors (overcooking dulls the colors), slightly softening their textures (overcooking turns them to mush), while also browning their sugars. All of this helps the foods to retain some measure of their discrete flavors and textures while also sharing them with the rest of the pan. In terms of food chemistry, it involves heating the fatty acids of the oils and caramelizing the sugars of the

foods. One of the most common mistakes that new cooks make is to overload the pan. This involves adding too much to the sauté pan so that the combination of heat, fat, and food sugars is not great enough to produce caramelization and instead, the food basically steams. So, you have to strike a balance when it comes to stirring: you don't want to stir the food until it has browned lightly, but you don't want it to burn. Some recipes (not in this book) call for sautéing using water. This is really more of a light steaming.

Slicing: For the purposes of this book, slicing typically refers to slicing lengthwise, usually in small strips.

Simmering: Simmering is similar to coddling, except that you want the foods to be just below the boiling point or just above it. In essence, it's a very soft boil.

Steaming: Steaming is a technique in which food is cooked in a steamer (typically a pan with an insert that has a tight-fitting lid) rather than boiled or fried.

Tools you'll need & tools that are nice to have

This list isn't exhaustive, but provides some starting points. Some of them are nice-to-haves and some of them are must-haves (I've started with the latter).

Knives: Knives are a very important part of this book, since preparing vegetable food involves a great deal of knife work (mostly repetitive chopping). So, a cook should have a good set of knives. Some indications of a good set include three rivets in the handle, a good handle weight, and a stainless steel or high-carbon stainless steel edge (not the same as a carbon steel edge). The sharpness of a knife is very important, and dull knives should be avoided. Also, you should understand which knives are for what type of cutting. A serrated knife should be used when a clean cut is needed for food like tomatoes or bread, which pressure can easily deform, or for when you're doing intricate cutting. A regular chopping knife (e.g., a chef knife, a santoku, a cleaver) should be used for most regular chopping tasks (e.g., carrots, tofu, celery, and kale). Basically, if you feel the knife work you're doing is like using a pencil, use a utility knife. A paring knife should be used for paring, and a bread knife for bread, assuming you have these. For the most part, many cooks rely on two or three knifes. Focus on building familiarity with two knives to start. I recommend that you use a proper chef knife or a santoku for most of your chopping and that you use a serrated utility knife for most of your other work. Use a paring knife, a bread knife, a carving knife, and so on, if you have these when you need to, but definitely try to avoid using the wrong knife for the wrong kind of work. For example, don't use a serrated utility knife, a bread knife, or a carving knife for chopping vegetables. I use a santoku, but not to slice bread. The santoku is an excellent knife for repetitive chopping tasks but a chef knife is also a good knife. You could always buy both and see which you like or use, depending on the specific task.

Pots and pans: Pots and pans are an important part of a cook's kitchen, and unlike knives, you'll probably use a full set. I've tried to keep it simple, describing the size of the pan required for recipes. You don't need to rush out and buy a proper sauté pan or a proper saucepan to use this book, but if you have them, use them. If you buy a set of pots and pans, you'll be buying a full set, but if you have a choice, get one with a steamer. Pots and pans are an investment, but typically, you get what you pay for. Also, this book largely assumes that you're using stainless steel pans of some sort or another. My own set is stainless steel with copper bases. Pans vary widely both in how they distribute, absorb, and release heat. You may find that the cook times vary depending both on your stove (gas and electric stoves vary) and your pans. Having a clear idea of how your pans conduct heat will help you prepare this book's recipes (and most recipes) more successfully. Copper, stainless steel, and aluminum should all work in roughly the same way. Steel pans may not distribute heat as evenly as other types of metal. Cast iron pans typically take longer to heat but they also hold their heat longer. What is important for the purposes of this book is that you allow your pan as a whole to warm before adding your oil for sauté, and that you then let the oil heat thoroughly before adding ingredients.

A hand blender: These are relatively cheap now and extremely useful. If you want to make do with a potato masher, a whisk, or a mortar and pestle, by all means, but a hand blender will save you a lot of kitchen time and aggravation. If you can afford it, get yourself a good one.

I went through about four hand blenders (some of them relatively pricey) in a year. I finally found one that I liked and that had enough power (400 watts) to do what I needed it to do.

Bowls: I typically use glass unless I have to use plastic. You should have a few small ones, a few big ones, and a few in the middle.

Nice-to-haves: Some things, although not absolutely necessary, are nice to have. With this list, I'm assuming that you have the most basic kitchen utensils (e.g., a spatula, a ladle, a can opener, etc.).

- A ravioli cutter (good for pasta & crusts)
- A melon baller (nice for small scoops of sorbet, gelato, etc.)
- A pastry/grill brush (good for vegetables and pastry work)
- A roasting pan (good for roasting vegetables)
- A pie wedge (it's just useful when you need it, and a fork or spatula won't do).
- A cleaver (if you want to do a lot of squash work, get yourself a cleaver and save yourself a lot of aggravation).

A brief grocery list

Again, this list doesn't cover every ingredient you'll need for this book, just the ones you'll probably need to get from your local health food store (HFS), including when the foods are out of season, or otherwise have to order online.

- Amaranth
- Arugula (also referred to as rocket—you should be able to find this at your grocery, but if not, your HFS may carry it)
- Agave nectar (you can use organic sugar in most of these recipes, but I prefer and recommend the use of agave)
- Arrowroot powder (you can use cornstarch if you can't get arrowroot)
- Black currants
- Collard greens
- Couscous (your grocery may have it, and it may not)
- Cranberries (dried)
- Dates (dried)
- Dulse (none of the recipes call for it, but dulse is another sea vegetable you can use to season your dishes, plus it's purple)
- Earth Balance (or other vegan margarine—make sure you buy a margarine that doesn't have whey and is fortified with vitamin D2, not vitamin D3, which is sourced from animal ingredients)
- Figs (dried)
- Guar gum
- Gluten flour (also called vital wheat gluten)
- Kale (green, Russian, black)
- Lentils (black beluga, red)
- Liquid smoke (again, your grocery should carry this, but you may have to go to an HFS)
- Maple syrup
- Miso (white, or red if you want a little more flavor)
- Nut butters (other than peanut, including macadamia, cashew, and pepita)

- **Nori** (green flakes, toasted sheets)
- **Nutritional yeast**
- **Quinoa** (white is fine, but you might also want red)
- **Rhubarb** (you may have to buy frozen from your HFS if it's not in season)
- **Stevia** (a sweetener that doesn't use sugar, but with a slight aftertaste—none of the recipes call for stevia, but you might want to experiment with replacing some of the agave nectar in strongly flavored dishes)
- **Soy/nut/hemp milk** (may as well try a few and see what you like)
- **Tamari** (many groceries carry tamari, but you never know)
- **Teff** (flour, not whole, unless you have experience grinding flours from whole grains)
- **Tofu** (both silken and regular)
- **TVP** (crumbles, not slices)
- **Vegenaise** (or other vegan-appropriate mayonnaise)
- **Wakame** (dried is fine)
- **Worcestershire sauce** (get one that's made without animal products; most are not).

Some final notes before you get started:

In these recipes, salt is always fine-ground sea salt unless specified otherwise. However, you can finish almost any dish in this book with coarse-grained sea salt if you prefer (see the note on salt, page 10).

Kosher salt can be substituted for coarse sea salt.

Soy sauce is always Japanese soy sauce unless noted otherwise, and tamari is always Japanese tamari.

In this book, I don't use fancy salt (e.g., fleur de sel, grey salt, etc.). I'm not opposed to them, but if you have to go to the HFS just to get the salt...but seriously, if you have them and know how to use them, by all means!

Sugar should always be fine-ground, organic, sugar cane sugar. Many processed can sugars are bleached with bone char, but this varies widely by geography. Beet sugar is not processed with bone char, and neither is fructose. But for the most part, this book sticks to agave nectar as a sweetener. You can use other sweeteners, but not everything will be a 1:1 swap, depending on how the sweetener is being used.

Flour should always be all-purpose whole wheat unless otherwise specified. You can substitute all-purpose for pastry, but it's really not recommended. Soft flour and hard flour are slightly different. Soft flour tends to be more like pastry flour, while hard flour tends to be more like all-purpose. Also, be prepared for the grinds of these to change if you buy them in bulk, and even across different brands. This will all affect in modest ways the amount of water required to form a dough.

Garlic, ginger, jalapeño, and cilantro are always fresh in these recipes, never dried.

The rest of the spices are for dry amounts. Obviously, it's normal to prefer fresh spices, but a lot of people want to use what's in their kitchen. You can certainly substitute fresh. The typical conversion is 1 tablespoon fresh to 1 teaspoon dried. Using dried, give the spices a good rub between your fingers when you add them to the pan. Also, try to avoid ground dried green spices. Their flavor dissipates very quickly. For cumin, coriander, etc., use ground unless you have a spice grinder or are familiar with popping seeds with heated oil.

Brown mustard refers to brown mustard the condiment, rather than the spice.

If you smoke, you may want to add additional spices to improve the taste. Smoking dulls your palate.

If you are on any specific medications, you may also find that your sense of taste is also affected by the medication. This is especially the case with mood-altering medications, with new studies suggesting that folks with depression and other mood disorders may actually taste foods fairly differently.

I do all of my cooking on an electric induction cooktop and in an electronic oven. Times and temperatures are based around that. With gas ovens, baking may take longer. With a gas stovetop, it will probably take less time and you will probably want to lower the heat recommendations.

Finally, you may also want to increase the amount of certain spices in winter or summer (e.g., spicier food in summer will give you some nice gustatory sweating).

Now we have come to the end of the beginning. You're ready to start cooking!

Deciphering the time/difficulty glyphs:

| 5min | 10 | 15 | 20 | 25 | 30 | 35 | 40 | 45 | 50 | 55 | 1hr | 2 |

DIFFICULTY
EASY

DIFFICULTY
MOSTLY EASY

DIFFICULTY
MODERATE

DIFFICULTY
COMPLICATED

Chapter 2:
Soup Is Good Food (for Vegans!)

Soup is the original comfort food. It is easy to improvise, makes great use of leftover ingredients, and few dishes present as beautifully as soup does. Of all dishes you're likely to prepare, soup tends to be the most forgiving and the most salvageable if you make a mistake. So, it's a good place for beginning cooks to start. This chapter addresses soups in all their splendor from the simple borscht to the fulfilling and hearty vegetable and legume stew. Recipes begin with creating basic stocks, on to simple purée soups, finishing with more complicated stews, with a little bisque and gumbo tossed in for good measure. If you want to learn how to use your hand blender for more than smoothies or what to do with half a dozen half portions of leftover vegetables, this is the chapter.

Basic Vegetable Stock

Basic vegetable stock is a building block for a number of recipes. This is just a recipe for a jarred stock that you might use for risotto or pilaf for example, where you want the vegetable flavors but not the vegetables themselves. If you want a quick vegetable soup, though, you can always just add the vegetables back in with some dried herbs, a little black pepper, and some sea salt.

 **DIFFICULTY**

Flavors: Sweet, green, salty

Equipment: A medium bowl, a wide-bottomed pan capable of holding 6 cups water (do not use a pan with nonstick coating to make stock), and a jar with a tight-fitting lid capable of holding at least 8 cups liquid (sterilized if you will be keeping the stock for more than 1 day)

Ingredients

- ▶ 1 tablespoon vegetable oil
- ▶ 1 medium onion (red, white, or yellow are fine), finely chopped
- ▶ 2 medium carrots, finely chopped
- ▶ 2 medium stalks celery, finely chopped
- ▶ 1/4 cup white wine
- ▶ 4 cups water
- ▶ 1/4 teaspoon sea salt (more to taste or depending on how you plan to use stock)

Optional: Dry herbs of your choice, considering the dish you plan to make with the stock

Instructions

Begin by chopping the ingredients (see the introductory notes on preparing vegetables if you're not sure how to get started). When you're ready, you're going to sauté your vegetables. Stir regularly but not continuously (see the note on sautéing, page 22). You want to ensure your vegetables brown but do not burn.

First, heat the pan on high. Wait a minute until the pan is warm and add the oil on high until it is ready (a drop of water will sizzle). Add 1/4 teaspoon sea salt to the pan. First, add the onion and sauté for 3 minutes. Add the carrot and sauté for 3 minutes. Add the celery and sauté for 2 minutes. Sauté on medium-high heat until the vegetables start to wilt and brown. Sauté for 2 to 3 minutes more once the vegetables are browning, and then remove from heat. Remove the vegetables from the pan. Put them into a medium bowl and repurpose for another recipe if you like, or discard.

To finish the stock, return the pan to heat and deglaze (see the notes on deglazing, page 20) by adding the wine and scraping the bottom of your pan with a wooden spoon. Reduce the wine by 1/2. Remove from heat. Add 4 cups water. Taste and add salt as necessary. Stock shouldn't be too salty (so, not as salty as a prepared soup, for example), since you'll add additional salt when you prepare a meal with it. Stir thoroughly and then carefully pour your stock into the jar.

If you will be keeping your stock for more than a day, make sure your jar is thoroughly sterilized.

Going further

It's hard to describe the basic flavor of vegetable stock, but its constituents are primarily sweet with a little green. Sometimes, you'll hear it described as a "brown" flavor, in large part because of the sugars that are caramelized as a part of the cooking process. When you are done with this recipe, you'll have a lot of wonderful sautéed vegetables. Don't waste them! Many cooks pitch the vegetables after preparing the stock. Instead, I recommend reserving and using the vegetables if you can in another dish. You can do what you like with them. Toss them into chili. Add them as a quick side dish to a meal. Add them to another soup. Or, if you want to use your stock right away, add the vegetables back in, add some sea salt, black pepper, and dried herbs, and you're ready to go!

But you'll probably want to use this as a jarred stock. Basic vegetable stock is something you can use in a number of recipes, not just for soup! Stock is typically used to prepare risotto and pilaf in order to add more flavor during the cooking process. For a light stock cook the vegetables for the recommended amount. For a darker stock, cook the vegetables slightly longer and use red wine. Add herbs and spices to customize your stick how you like. This recipe based largely on common European vegetables (sometimes referred to as *mirepoix* in French and *sofritto/sofrito* in continental Italian and Spanish). Other American cooking styles build stocks from different flavors.

For example, it's not uncommon to find carrot replaced with green bell pepper in the American South or other peppers in the American Southwest. Other cuisines, like Japanese for example, start with fish and mushrooms as their basic stock flavors. But generally the important things for a good vegetable stock are: the natural sugars of the ingredients (the browning of the sugars provide a fair amount of the stock's flavor); the water content (stock vegetables release a lot of their water when they cook, helping mix their flavors, and vegetables without a lot of water content typically don't make for good stock); and the sturdiness of the vegetables (they have to hold their shape a bit while cooking). They should be edible and tasty raw (potatoes don't make for good stock) and they should smell good (vegetables with good aromatics make for good stock). Don't be afraid to experiment!

Quick, Rich Borscht

Borscht is a simple, beautiful, and sweet soup that's good cold or hot, with soy sour cream, arugula and walnuts, or baked potato and dill. It's an Eastern European favorite common to New England and Chicago. Borscht is often a broth soup or a pulp soup. In this recipe it's a purée. I hate to waste vegetables! Add one of the optional garnishes to turn a simple comfort soup into something fancy!

 **DIFFICULTY**

Flavors: Sweet, salty (with sour, green, fatty garnishes)

Equipment: A large bowl, a wide-bottomed pan capable of holding 4 cups water, and a hand blender (or a potato masher)

Ingredients

- ▶ 4 cups water
- ▶ 3 large beets, peeled and finely chopped (about 2 1/2 cups)
- ▶ Sea salt (start with 1/2 teaspoon and add more to taste)

Optional: Add a dollop of soy Sour Cream (page 65); Artichoke, Caper, and Black Pepper Butter (page 59); or the Avocado Creton (page 57) if you have extras of these. Or add 1/4 cup packed baby arugula, minced, and 1 tablespoon chopped walnuts in a small mound in the center. Or add 1/2 boiled potato and a sprig of fresh dill if you want something a little more traditional.

Instructions

Begin by preparing ingredients. Peel and chop beets. Cut the tops (the leafy greens) off the beets (you can keep these and use them for salads or for side dishes, but you won't need them for this dish). Remove the tough outer skin of the beets carefully with a knife and discard. Chop the peeled beat into 1/4 to 1/2-inch chunks the way you chop an onion.

Next, add 4 cups water to your pan. Bring the water to a boil on high heat and add the sea salt. Add the beets. Boil the beets until soft (approximately 10 to 15 minutes). Remove from heat and let stand for 10 minutes to cool. Purée the ingredients with a hand blender or mash thoroughly with the potato masher and a wooden spoon. Taste and add salt as necessary. Ladle into soup bowls and garnish. This makes 2 large bowls or 4 regular-sized servings of soup.

Going further

Borscht is a wonderful winter soup when served hot and a great summer soup when served cold. If you serve it cold, the sour cream makes a great garnish!

Luxurious Carrot & Cashew Soup
with Agave & Chipotle Ribbon

Simple, rich, and bright orange, this is a great, light, and flavorful soup for fall.

 **DIFFICULTY**

Flavors: Sweet, sour, salty, rich, spicy, green

Note: You'll need to get the agave nectar and possibly the chipotle at your local HFS.

Equipment: A large bowl, a wide-bottomed pan capable of holding 8 cups water, a hand blender, a whisk (a fork will do), and a small bowl

Ingredients

Soup

▶ 4 medium carrots, chopped (about 3 cups)

▶ 3 cups water (or 1 cup water and 2 cups stock)

▶ 1 teaspoon minced fresh ginger

▶ 1 tablespoon cashew butter

▶ Sea salt (start with 1/2 tsp & add more to taste)

Ribbon

▶ 2 tablespoons agave nectar

▶ 1 teaspoon lemon juice

▶ 1/2 teaspoon minced chipotle

▶ 1 tablespoon fresh cilantro, minced

Optional: If you have trouble getting your agave to pour, add a teaspoon water (temperature has a serious effect, and if you keep your agave in the fridge, it will be difficult to pour). Not everyone has fresh chipotle lying around. Use a pinch of cayenne pepper and a dash of liquid smoke for those who only like it a little spicy, and 1/8 to 1/4 teaspoon for those who like it a little hotter. The chipotle adds a little red contrast for this soup, which will be lost with the cayenne, but it will add the flavor.

Instructions

Begin by preparing ingredients. Bring the water to a boil on high and add your chopped carrots. Reduce to medium-low and simmer for 15 minutes, or until the carrots are soft. Add the ginger and cashew butter, and then blend with the hand blender until creamy and smooth. Taste and add salt as necessary. Ladle the soup into bowls. Whisk the agave nectar, chipotle, and lemon juice together to form a simple syrup. Drizzle in zigzags or a spiral over the surface of the soup. Sprinkle the minced cilantro in the center. This soup yields 4 small bowls or 2 bigger ones.

Going further

This is a simple soup that introduces the basics of flavor layers. The soup is sweet, salty, and rich. The ribbon adds an additional layer of sweet, sour, and spicy. The cilantro adds the green. If you don't like the chipotle, agave, and cilantro, you can always garnish this soup with some Mango Chipotle Salsa (page 62) and Sour Cream (page 65) or with a tablespoon or two of Tarragon Aioli (page 64) for something with a little more herb flavor.

Cream of Broccoli Latte with Soy Foam

Cream of broccoli soup was a comfort food for me as a child and was one of the few ways I'd eat broccoli. This soup adds a little fancy presentation to the traditional bowl-ful of green and comforting goodness.

 **DIFFICULTY**

Flavors: Sweet, green, rich, salty

Equipment: A large bowl, a wide-bottomed pan capable of holding at least 6 cups liquid, a hand blender, and a milk frother/espresso machine

Ingredients

▶ 2 large heads broccoli, stemmed and coarsely chopped (about 4 cups florets)
▶ 3 cups water (or 1 cup water and 2 cups stock)
▶ 1 cup unsweetened soy milk
▶ 4 tablespoons nutritional yeast
▶ 1 tablespoon minced fresh garlic
▶ 1 teaspoon tamari
▶ 1 teaspoon lemon juice
▶ 1 tablespoon macadamia nut butter
▶ Sea salt (start with 1/2 teaspoon and add more to taste)

Optional: Double the garlic for a richer soup.

Instructions

Begin by preparing ingredients. Mince the garlic. Remove the bottoms of the broccoli stems by cutting about 1 inch off the bottom of the stem. Cut the broccoli into 1/2 to 1/4-inch chunks, removing any leafy stems. Add broccoli to the boiling water. Bring 3 cups water to a boil in a medium-sized pan. Add all the remaining ingredients except for the soy milk and the nutritional yeast to the pan. Return to a boil, and reduce to medium-low heat. Simmer the broccoli 10 minutes until thoroughly cooked. Remove from heat. Add the nutritional yeast. Purée the ingredients with a hand blender (or mash thoroughly with the potato masher, but this will leave you with a lumpier soup).

If you are using an espresso machine, froth the milk until warm and frothy. If you have a thermometer, 100° F will do. Otherwise, it should be warm to the touch but not scalding—if you're not sure, be careful! Spoon the resulting foam (the bubbly part of the milk) into a separate cup or bowl.

If you are using a blender or cold-temperature frother, warm the milk in a saucepan until it's about 100° F. It should only be lightly hot to your touch. You don't want to scald yourself! Froth as best as you can. Spoon the resulting foam into a separate cup or bowl.

If you're not at all interested in this frothing business, just warm the 1 cup soy milk in a separate pan and add to the soup.

Add the warm soy milk to the soup (you're cooling the soup this way) and stir until blended. Taste and add salt as necessary. Ladle into soup bowls. Spoon the foam on top of the soup and serve. This makes 2 large bowls or 4 regular-sized servings of soup.

Going further

Not everyone has an espresso machine, but you can pick up a hand-powered milk frother at most outdoor equipment stores. A blender may work if you're lucky! But even if you don't want to go fancy with this soup, it still looks and tastes great. The foam is really just for presentation. For a thicker texture, reserve 1/4 cup soy milk and whisk with 1 tablespoon arrowroot starch and whisk into the soup after it is off-heat, but before adding the soy milk. For a colorful garnish, throw a little thinly sliced scallion on top, or some minced sun-dried tomato.

Tangy Pumpkin, Tomato & Jalapeño Soup

Very common ingredients in the American Southwest, sweet pumpkin, tangy tomato, and spicy jalapeño are combined in this soup for late fall when just about everyone has some spare pumpkin and a jalapeño takes the chill off the wind.

Flavors: Sweet, salty, sour, spicy

Equipment: A hand blender, latex gloves for sensitive skin, and a pan with a tight-fitting lid capable of holding 6 cups water

Ingredients

- ▶ 2 cups water or vegetable stock
- ▶ 2 cups pumpkin purée (canned saves time, but if you want to work from scratch, go for it!)
- ▶ 1 small jalapeño pepper, seeded and minced (about 1 tablespoon, or less if you don't like it spicy)
- ▶ 4 medium tomatoes, cored, seeded, and chopped (about 2 cups)
- ▶ 1 tablespoon vegetable oil or the nut butter of your choice
- ▶ 1 tablespoon minced fresh garlic
- ▶ 1 teaspoon minced fresh ginger
- ▶ 1 teaspoon ground cumin
- ▶ 1/4 teaspoon cloves, ground
- ▶ 1/2 teaspoon coriander, ground
- ▶ 1/4 teaspoon sea salt

Optional: This is a spicy soup. You can always add 1/4 teaspoon black pepper instead of the jalapeño pepper if you prefer something quite a bit milder. Swapping the oil for a tablespoon of macadamia or cashew butter will add some richness to this soup. Tahini is also good, but it will provide a nuttier taste. If you really want to taste the pumpkin, macadamia is preferred. Add 1 tablespoon minced cilantro for a little green flavor and extra color for garnish.

Instructions

Begin by preparing ingredients. Bring 2 cups water to a boil. Prepare your vegetables and spices. Once the water has come to a boil, add the chopped tomatoes and spices. Decrease the heat to medium and simmer uncovered. Reduce by 1/3. This shouldn't take more than 15 minutes. Remove from heat. Add the pumpkin and oil or nut butter. Stir to combine, then blend with the hand blender until smooth. Decrease the heat to medium-low. Cover the pan and return the soup and cook for another 3 minutes. Remove from heat and let stand for 5 minutes. Taste and add salt as necessary. Ladle into bowls.

Going further

This is a very rich and full-flavored soup with good body. A little minced cilantro for garnish will give it some extra color and add a bright green flavor.

Stick-to-Your-Ribs
Yellow Split Pea & Greens Soup

This is a rich and flavorful soup with a beautiful combination of gold and green colors. It's also a wonderful warming and filling soup for those winter months in colder climates.

Flavors: Sweet, salty, green, savory

Equipment: A large bowl, a small pan with a tight-fitting lid capable of holding 4 cups liquid, a wide-bottomed pan capable of holding 8 cups water, and a hand blender

Ingredients

- ▶ 5 cups water (or 3 cups water and 2 cups stock)
- ▶ 1 cup dry yellow split peas
- ▶ 1 tablespoon vegetable oil
- ▶ 1 cup packed kale, finely chopped
- ▶ 1 tablespoon minced fresh garlic
- ▶ 1 teaspoon minced fresh ginger
- ▶ 1/2 teaspoon ground cumin
- ▶ 1/4 teaspoon black pepper, ground
- ▶ Dash of liquid smoke
- ▶ 1/2 teaspoon sea salt

Optional: A little sprinkled paprika makes a brightly colored garnish, and a little sprinkled cayenne pepper makes a brightly flavored one.

Instructions

Begin by preparing your ingredients. Bring 5 cups water to a bowl on a high heat. Thoroughly wash yellow split peas. Add the split peas to the water, reduce to low, and cover. Simmer the split peas for 2 hours or until they start to disintegrate. When the peas are ready, blend with a hand blender until smooth, cover, and simmer on low while you prepare your other vegetables and spices.

First, stem your kale about 1 inch above where the leaves start to flower out, discard the stems, and finely chop the leaves. Next, bring the oil to heat on medium-high in the larger pan. Add 1/4 teaspoon sea salt. Add the spices and liquid smoke to the pan and sauté for 2 minutes. Add the kale to the pan and sauté for 3 to 5 minutes, until the kale is bright green and slight wilted. Remove the kale from heat. When the split peas are dissolved, remove them from heat. Add the kale to the split peas and stir until thoroughly combined. Let stand 10 minutes. Taste and add salt as necessary. Ladle into soup bowls. Garnish with a little paprika to add a little red or with cayenne pepper to add a little spice.

Going further

If you want a quicker cook, replace the yellow split peas with red lentils. If you want a more peppery soup, replace the kale with arugula (no need to sauté, just chop and toss).

Zesty Sweet Potato, Black Currant & Jalapeño Soup

Sweet potato is an American favorite. Beautifully orange, sweet, easy to prepare, and full of beta carotene and other nutritional factors—what's not to like? The black currants and jalapeño add wonderful, slightly sour and spicy tones.

 **DIFFICULTY**

Flavors: Sweet, spicy, slightly sour

Equipment: A medium-sized pan able to hold 8 cups liquid, and a hand blender (optional but recommended)

Ingredients

▶ 1 large sweet potato, peeled and chopped (about 2 1/2 cups)
▶ 4 cups water (or 2 cups water and 2 cups stock)
▶ 1/4 cup dried black currants
▶ 1 tablespoon jalapeño pepper (more if you like it spicy)
▶ 1 teaspoon minced fresh ginger
▶ 1 teaspoon lime juice
▶ 1 teaspoon ground cumin
▶ 1/2 teaspoon coriander, ground
▶ 1 heaping tablespoon peanut butter
▶ 1/2 teaspoon sea salt
▶ 2 teaspoons packed fresh cilantro, minced

Optional: Add 2 tablespoons red lentils at the beginning with the sweet potatoes to give it a heartier taste and texture.

Instructions

Begin by preparing ingredients. Add the water to a medium-sized pot and bring to a boil. In the meantime, peel the sweet potato, just like peeling a regular potato. When peeled, cut the sweet potato into cubes about 1 inch by 1 inch.

Chop the jalapeño before adding, making sure to mince it thoroughly if you don't have a hand blender. Add the jalapeño and all of the other ingredients except the cilantro to the pot once the water is boiling. Decrease the heat to medium-low (on an electric stove, 3 to 4 will do) and simmer the ingredients until the sweet potato is soft (about 20 minutes, but this depends on the size of the chunks—smaller chunks means shorter cooking time if you're in a rush). Remove from heat and let stand for 5 minutes. Purée the soup with a hand blender until smooth. Retaste and, if necessary, add salt in 1/4 teaspoon amounts until it's salted to your taste.

If you don't have a hand blender, mince the jalapeño pepper thoroughly before adding it to the pan. Use a potato masher with some aggressive stirring with a wooden spoon to purée the soup when the sweet potato is done.

Let the soup stand another 5 minutes to cool. In the meantime, mince the cilantro. Chances are good you'll use your hand to guess this measure, and that's fine. You want something about the size of 2 marbles. Ladle the soup into bowls and garnish with the chopped cilantro by sprinkling equal portions in the middle of each bowl. This makes 2 large bowls or 4 regular-sized servings of soup.

Going further

This soup already has a lot of flavor, but you can still add more. Add a little extra peanut, tahini, macadamia, or cashew butter if desired to give it a creamier texture (better mouth feel) and richer taste. Or, add 2 tablespoons red lentils and cook for 30 minutes to add a nice savory flavor and a more rustic texture. If you want a sweeter soup, roast your sweet potatoes whole for approximately 40 minutes, let cool, peel, and chop.

Exotic Mushroom & Sea Vegetable Bisque

This soup is simple and delicious, and an easy way to add sea vegetables and mushrooms to your diet.

 **DIFFICULTY**

Flavors: Sweet, salty, savory

Equipment: A wide-bottomed pan capable of holding 4 cups water and a hand blender

Ingredients

- ▶ 3 cups water (or 1 cup water and 2 cups stock)
- ▶ 1/2 cup dried mushrooms (maitake, shiitake, or porcini preferred; no need to stem, just toss them in)
- ▶ 1/4 cup dried wakame, crumbled
- ▶ 1 cup unsweetened soy milk
- ▶ 1 tablespoon arrowroot powder
- ▶ 1 tablespoon minced fresh garlic
- ▶ 2 tablespoons green nori flakes
- ▶ Dash of liquid smoke
- ▶ 1/4 teaspoon black pepper
- ▶ Sea salt (start with 1/4 teaspoon and add more to taste; this should be a slightly salty soup)

Optional: Alaria is wakame that's grown in the Atlantic Ocean. You can use that instead of wakame for this recipe.

Instructions

Put the water, dried mushrooms, and wakame into your pan and bring them to a boil. Reduce to medium-low and simmer the ingredients for 15 minutes. In the meantime, prepare your other vegetables and spices. Whisk the arrowroot, garlic, and soy milk until thoroughly blended. Remove the soup from heat and thoroughly blend with your hand blender. Return to heat and add the soy milk mixture to the soup and stir thoroughly until it thickens. Add the remaining ingredients. Remove from heat and let stand 10 minutes. Ladle into soup bowls. Sprinkle equal parts of nori flakes into each bowl for garnish. This makes 2 large bowls or 4 regular-sized servings of soup.

Going further

This soup is a great and simple way to add a variety of different mushrooms and sea vegetables to your diet. Sea vegetables taste great and are very nutritious. If you like mushrooms, this soup is a great way to experiment with their different and unique flavors.

Grandpa Vince's Homemade
Chickenless Soup

Okay, so I'm not a grandfather, but this is a classic comfort soup in the remaking. Chicken soup was another of my favorites as a child. This version replaces the minced chicken with TVP (texturized vegetable protein). Just what the doctor ordered!

 **DIFFICULTY**

Flavors: Sweet, salty, savory

Equipment: A large bowl and a wide-bottomed pan capable of holding 4 cups water

Ingredients

- 1 tablespoon vegetable oil
- 1 tablespoon tarragon
- 1/2 tablespoon savory
- 1/2 teaspoon marjoram
- 1/4 teaspoon black pepper
- 1 medium white or yellow onion, finely chopped
- 2 medium carrots, coarsely chopped
- 2 medium stalks celery, coarsely chopped
- 2 tablespoons minced fresh garlic
- 1 tablespoon tamari
- 1 teaspoon lemon juice
- 4 cups water (or 2 cups water and 2 cups stock)
- 1/2 cup TVP crumbles (not chunks)
- 1 cup packed greens (spinach, black kale, or arugula preferred), finely chopped
- 2 tablespoons nutritional yeast
- 1/2 teaspoon sea salt

Optional: 1/4 teaspoon cayenne pepper if you like a little spice to your soup. Add a dash of liquid smoke to add a little extra savory flavor.

Instructions

Begin by preparing ingredients. Add the oil to the warmed sauté pan and heat it on high until warm. Add 1/4 teaspoon sea salt and all the dry herbs. Sauté for 1 minute. Add the onion and sauté for 3 minutes. Decrease the heat to medium-high. Add the carrot and sauté for 3 minutes. Add the celery and sauté for 2 minutes. And then add the garlic. Sauté on medium-high heat until the vegetables start to brown. Once they are browning, sauté for 2 to 3 minutes more. Add the tamari and lemon juice to deglaze the pan and sauté for 1 minute. Add 4 cups water. Taste and add salt as necessary (you'll probably need more).

Return the soup to a boil and decrease the heat to medium-low. Add the TVP. Simmer ingredients for 10 minutes. Remove from heat. Add the greens and the nutritional yeast. Let stand for 5 minutes. Taste and add salt as necessary, although you should probably be fine at this point. Ladle into soup bowls.

Going further

This soup is a well-balanced classic, but a little chipotle or some additional black pepper will give it some additional kick, and a little minced fresh dill never killed anybody.

Fresh Pineapple, Red Pepper
& Arugula Gazpacho

Aside from being a colorful, flavorful, and light soup, it's a great way to practice your knife work! Great for winter months when you miss the sun, and great for summer months when you want something light. The arugula gives this soup a really great fresh, green flavor, and the walnuts that extra notch of texture and flavor. The pineapple and cantaloupe should be nice and ripe to give this soup the best flavor and color.

Flavors: Rich, salty, sour, sweet, green

Equipment: A large bowl, a sharp knife, and a hand blender

Ingredients

- ▶ 1 red pepper, cored, seeded, and finely diced
- ▶ 1 cup tightly packed baby arugula, minced
- ▶ 1 small red onion, peeled and minced (about 1/2 cup)
- ▶ 4 cups ripe pineapple (about 1 whole cored pineapple), 1 cup minced and 3 cups reserved and liquefied
- ▶ 1 cup ripe cantaloupe, finely diced
- ▶ 1/2 cup chopped walnuts
- ▶ 1/2 teaspoon sea salt (more to taste)

Optional: Add 1 teaspoon fresh, minced jalapeño for a little spice. Swap the cantaloupe for honeydew for a slightly sweeter soup. For a more traditional gazpacho flavor, replace one of the liquefied cups pineapple with a cup of liquefied cantaloupe.

Instructions

Begin by preparing ingredients. When ready, add everything but the reserved 3 cups pineapple to the large bowl. Blend 3 cups pineapple separately with the hand blender, and then pour the liquefied pineapple over the remaining ingredients. Let stand for about 1 hour, then ladle into bowls. This makes 2 large bowls, or 4 regular-sized.

Going further

This is a relatively easy soup, and full flavored. Add the jalapeño in those hot summer months for a little gustatory sweating. Add 2 tablespoons nutritional yeast for a little extra flavor and nutrition.

Old-Fashioned Hearty Lentil
& Vegetable Soup

This is a simple and hearty soup, with great nutritional balance, a lot of flavor, and beautiful color.

 **DIFFICULTY**

Flavors: **Sweet, salty, sour, savory**

Equipment: A large bowl, a small pot with a tight-fitting lid, a wide-bottomed pan capable of holding 4 cups water, and a hand blender

Ingredients

Lentils
▶ 3 cups water
▶ 1 cup green lentils (black or brown will also work, but red will tend to dissolve in this soup)

The rest of the soup
▶ 3 cups water (or 1 cup water and 2 cups stock)
▶ 1 tablespoon vegetable oil
▶ 1 medium onion (red, white, or yellow will be fine), finely chopped
▶ 1 tablespoon minced fresh garlic
▶ 2 medium carrots, coarsely chopped
▶ 2 medium stalks celery, coarsely chopped
▶ 8 medium-sized cremini or button mushrooms, thinly sliced
▶ 3 ripe, medium tomatoes, cored, seeded, and chopped
▶ 1 cup packed baby spinach, stemmed and coarsely chopped

▶ 2 tablespoons baby spinach, minced, for garnish
▶ 1/2 teaspoon dried basil, rubbed
▶ 1/2 teaspoon dried oregano, rubbed
▶ 1/2 teaspoon dried marjoram, rubbed
▶ 1/4 teaspoon ground black pepper
▶ 1/2 teaspoon sea salt

Optional: 1/4 teaspoon cayenne pepper or more black pepper if you prefer your soup with a little extra spice.

Instructions

Bring 3 cups water to a boil on a high heat. Add the lentils to the water, reduce to low, and cover. Simmer lentils until done, 30 to 40 minutes (this varies by lentil type and by the specific temperature of the pan—so check at 30 minutes, but anticipate that it may take as long as 45).

About 20 minutes in, prepare your vegetables and spices. Heat the oil on medium-high heat until is it ready. Add 1/2 teaspoon sea salt to the pan. First add the onion and sauté for 3 minutes. Add the carrot and sauté for 3 minutes. Add the celery and sauté for 2 minutes. And then add the garlic. Sauté for 2 minutes, and then add the mushrooms. Sauté for another 5 to 8 minutes. The vegetables will start to brown the pan lightly. Sauté for 2 to 3 minutes. Once the vegetables are browning add the tomatoes and deglaze

the pan. Sauté for another 2 minutes. Add 3 cups water. Bring the soup to a boil and decrease the heat to medium-low.

When the lentils are ready, drain and add them to the soup. Add the remaining herbs and spices. Simmer for another 5 minutes. Roughly chop the greens, add them to the pan and stir to combine. Remove from heat and let stand for 10 minutes. Taste and add more salt as necessary. Ladle into soup bowls and garnish with chopped spinach (or flat-leaf parsley, basil, or the herbs of your choice) in the center.

Going further

As you become more and more familiar with different legumes, you can always branch out. There are several different kinds of lentils (black, green, brown, puy, and more), all with slightly different flavors and textures, but they all have slightly different cook times.

Fiery Illinois Corn Chowder

My father would roll over in his grave if I wrote an American cookbook and didn't include Illinois corn chowder. But if you've never been to Illinois, it tends to be corn and alfalfa as far as the eye can see (once you're outside of the Chicago area) and corn in all its variety is a common side dish. Frankly, I've always found corn chowder a bit bland and never had the heart to tell my dad. I've added some chipotle to spice things up, but you can always leave it out for something more traditional. This is a wonderful soup, full of vegetable flavor and color, but also sweet and mellow. It's more of a comfort soup, like the potato and broccoli soups in this chapter, but you can easily add spicy or green flavors to bring out some contrast. This version uses roasted corn for a slightly richer flavor. It's one mean soup!

 **DIFFICULTY**

Flavors: Sweet, salty, savory, and lightly spicy

Equipment: A large bowl, a medium-sized bowl, a wide-bottomed pan capable of holding 4 cups water, a hand blender, and a baking sheet big enough for 4 ears of corn

Ingredients

Corn

- ▶ 4 ears unhusked corn on the cob (about 3 cups, with 1/2 cup or 1 ear's worth reserved)
- ▶ 1 tablespoon vegetable oil for roasting
- ▶ 2 cups unsweetened soy milk
- ▶ 2 tablespoons cornstarch

The rest of the chowder

- ▶ 1 tablespoon vegetable oil
- ▶ 2 dashes liquid smoke
- ▶ 1 teaspoon ground cumin
- ▶ 1 teaspoon minced chipotle
- ▶ 1/4 teaspoon black pepper, ground
- ▶ 1 medium red, white, or yellow onion, peeled and finely chopped
- ▶ 2 medium carrots, trimmed and finely chopped (about 1 cup)
- ▶ 3 medium stalks celery, trimmed and finely chopped (about 1 cup)

- ▶ 2 tablespoons minced fresh garlic (use half if you're not overly fond of garlic)
- ▶ 1 teaspoon lemon juice
- ▶ 2 cups water or stock
- ▶ Sea salt (start with 1/2 teaspoon and add more to taste)

Note: Fresh corn is easy to get in the Midwest, but if you're stuck using frozen corn, you want about 3 cups. Try to avoid canned corn for this recipe. Canned corn has a lot of added salt, and you may have a harder time producing the creamy texture of this soup.

Optional: Add an extra 1/4 teaspoon black pepper or 1/4 teaspoon cayenne pepper or more chipotle for more spice. If you want a smoother, creamier chowder (for folks who don't like chunks of vegetables), purée about half of the soup when it is done. If you like your chowder sweeter, add 1 to 2 tablespoons agave nectar into the corn and soy milk mixture. Leave out the chipotle for a milder soup. Sprinkle with a little cayenne or a little paprika or garnish with some minced fresh cilantro at the end for a little extra color.

Instructions

Begin by preparing your ingredients.

If you're using fresh corn, preheat your oven to 350° F. Pull the husks down to the end of the corn (but don't remove). Carefully remove the silk. Give your ears

of corn a good wash. Brush or rub the kernels with vegetable oil. Wrap each ear back up in its husk. Ensure that the ear is well wrapped with the husk. Once the oven is heated, put the husked corn in on an oiled baking sheet. Roast for 30 minutes, or until the corn is done (varies by oven). When the corn is done, pare off the kernels with a knife into a medium-sized bowl.

If you're using frozen corn, let it thaw and rinse thoroughly. If you don't let it thaw, it will affect the moisture balance of the soup. Add it to the medium-sized bowl (less the 1/2 cup reserved). Add 2 cups unsweetened soy milk and blend with the hand blender. Blend until the corn is fairly well blended. It should be smooth and chowder-like. Add the reserved whole kernels. Add your cornstarch and mix until it is thoroughly dissolved. Now prepare your vegetables and spices.

When your corn and your vegetables are ready, heat oil on high heat until is it ready. Add 1/2 teaspoon sea salt, cumin, liquid smoke, black pepper, and chipotle and leave it for 1 minute. Add the onion and sauté for 3 minutes. Then add the chipotle and decrease the heat to medium-high and add the carrot and sauté for 3 minutes. Add the celery and sauté for 2 minutes. Then add the minced garlic. Sauté

on medium-high heat until the vegetables start to wilt and brown. Sauté for 2 to 3 minutes. Add 2 tablespoons of the 2 cups water and the lemon juice to the pan and deglaze. Add the remaining water.

Return the soup to a light boil and then add your corn and soy milk mixture, as well as the remaining ingredients. Stir thoroughly until your soup returns to a simmer and your cornstarch thickens (this will take several minutes). Cover, reduce the heat to low, and simmer for 10 minutes. Remove from heat and let stand for 10 minutes to cool. Taste and add salt as necessary. Ladle into soup bowls. This makes 2 large bowls or 4 regular-sized servings.

Going further

If you're from the Corn Belt, the wonderful flavor of corn completes you. But if you want a little more flavor, dust a little chili powder on top to add a little heat. Toss on some minced cilantro or arugula for a bright green garnish. When I make this soup, I add a diced red pepper and about 2 cups collard greens, stemmed coarsely chopped. I also double the red and black pepper and garnish with cayenne.

Deep South Gumbo Z'Herbes

This is a great Deep South soup and a great way to add more greens to your diet. If you don't have all of the greens below, don't worry about it. Use the greens you have. This soup is also a great way to use up small amounts of greens when you have a little more than you expected. Traditionally, there's a lot of knife work to this soup. You may want to use a food processor to chop your greens to save time. You should be able to acquire enough fresh greens and herbs to make a reasonable version of this soup from a local grocery, but you may have to go to your HFS if you want to use all fresh herbs or to get all of the greens if they're not in season.

⏰

Flavors: Sweet, salty, green, rich, savory

Equipment: A large bowl, a whisk (a fork will do), a wide-bottomed pan capable of holding at least 12 cups liquid, a small pan with a tight-fitting lid capable of holding at least 4 cups liquid, and a food processor is a nice-to-have with all this chopping!

Ingredients

Rice
- ▶ 2 cups water
- ▶ 1 cup long-grain brown rice
- ▶ 1/4 teaspoon sea salt

Roux
- ▶ 3 cups unsweetened soy milk
- ▶ 1/4 cup vegetable oil
- ▶ 3 tablespoons whole wheat flour

Soup
- ▶ 3 cups water (or 3 cups stock)
- ▶ 2 tablespoons vegetables oil
- ▶ 1 cup fresh spinach, finely chopped
- ▶ 1 cup fresh arugula, finely chopped
- ▶ 1 cup fresh chard, finely chopped
- ▶ 1/2 cup fresh collard greens, finely chopped
- ▶ 1/2 cup fresh kale, finely chopped
- ▶ 1/2 cup fresh carrot tops, finely chopped
- ▶ 1/2 cup fresh mustard greens, finely chopped
- ▶ 1/2 cup fresh beet greens, finely chopped
- ▶ 1/2 cup fresh Italian parsley
- ▶ 3 tablespoons minced fresh garlic
- ▶ 1 large green bell pepper, finely chopped
- ▶ 2 stalks celery, finely chopped
- ▶ 1 medium-sized onion, finely chopped
- ▶ 1 tablespoon dried thyme
- ▶ 1 tablespoon dried savory
- ▶ 1 tablespoon dried sorrel
- ▶ 1 tablespoon dried tarragon
- ▶ 1 teaspoon dried marjoram
- ▶ 2 dashes liquid smoke (more if you like it really smoky)
- ▶ 1 teaspoon sea salt

Optional: If you can find fresh replacements for the dried herbs, use those instead. Reserve 1 teaspoon, minced (assuming you're serving multiple people) of your favorite green for garnish for each bowl. Red chard makes for nice color contrasts. The 3 tablespoons of wheat flour or arrowroot will produce a somewhat thick soup. If you prefer your soup a little thinner, just add 2 tablespoons.

Vincent Guihan | New American Vegan

Instructions

Begin by preparing your ingredients. Start with chopping your vegetables and preparing spices. Heat 2 tablespoons oil on medium-high heat until warm. Add 1/4 teaspoon sea salt to the pan. First add the onion and sauté for 3 minutes. Add the green pepper and sauté for 3 minutes. Add the celery and sauté for 2 minutes. And then add the garlic. Sauté on medium-high heat until the vegetables start to brown. Sauté for 2 to 3 minutes once the vegetables are browning. Add the spinach and sauté for 5 minutes, or until wilted. Add the arugula and sauté for 5 minutes until wilted. Add the remaining greens and stir fry until wilted. Slowly and carefully add 8 cups water and bring to a boil. In the meantime, wash and mince all of your greens. Add 1 teaspoon sea salt.

Next, prepare your rice. Put your rice on separately in a small pan. Bring the 2 cups water and sea salt to a boil. Add the rice, reduce to low, cover, and simmer for about 30 minutes (or until all the water has been absorbed, depending on the type of rice you use).

Next, prepare your roux. Add 3 table-spoons oil to the small pan and warm it on high heat. Bring the oil to heat. Add 2 tablespoons flour and stir to mix thoroughly mashing any lumps. Continue to stir as the flour begins to brown (this will take 2 to 3 minutes). When the flour has browned, slowly pour in the unsweetened soy milk, stirring thoroughly as you pour to avoid lumps. Return to a light simmer and stir until the whole wheat flour thickens (should take 2 to 3 minutes). Remove from heat and add all dried spices to the white sauce.

When your soup has come to a simmer, whisk in your browned roux, pouring slowly and stirring constantly to avoid clumping. Cover and cook at least an-other 10 minutes. Remove from heat and let stand for 10 minutes to cool. Taste and add salt as necessary. You'll almost cer-tainly want to add salt at this point, but add it in 1/2-teaspoon-sized pinches, stir, taste, and repeat as necessary.

To plate, add 4 spoonfuls of rice to each bowl and then ladle the soup on top. Garnish with fresh minced greens if you'd like. This soup serves 4 with big bowls of gumbo or 8 smaller ones.

Going further

This is a big soup (a holiday soup, actually, served for Lent). You can always experi-ment with smaller proportions, making creamed spinach soup, creamed arugula soup, a nice broth of carrot greens. When you have made this soup, you will have found, picked, and prepared about a dozen greens. There are a lot more not included in this soup, but probably about thirty greens are available in most big city markets these days. Virtually all of them are good for you, taste good when properly prepared, and represent a low-calorie, high-nutrition part of a sound plant-based diet.

Getting Past the Recipes:
What Makes a Good Soup?

Virtually all cuisines have soup in some form or another. There are probably a lot of reasons for this. First, boiling is a good way to ensure that foods are thoroughly cooked and bacteria are killed. Second, most cuisines would have been developed at times of relative scarcity. Reusing items that were hard to come by but were getting long in the tooth and making the most creative use of common vegetables provides most of the earliest ways of thinking of cooking as a system. So, historically, soups provided a simple way to use leftover ingredients that were more difficult to come by or to change the flavor of ingredients that, while all over the place, maybe didn't taste so great all by themselves. In part, that's why so many classic soups involve vegetables (e.g., greens, celery, carrots, onions) and bread. Fresh bread becomes stale quickly but can easily be repurposed to thicken up a soup.

Why do so many of us still like soup? Well, soups look good. They often rely on either a brightly colored vegetable, or simple off white creamy look, or a variety of vegetables, and vegetables just look great. They also smell good. Like baking bread, hot soups release a lot of moisture into the air, and with that moisture, wonderful aromatics. Finally, because the ingredients are boiled and softened as part of the boiling process, that typically makes them easy to digest and convert into blood sugar. Soup relaxes people partly because it's easy on the stomach and partly because of the sugar high. It also tends to replenish the body's electrolytes (particularly with salt), but that varies a bit depending on the soup in question. Unlike salad, soup can go toward a single ingredient (e.g., borscht) or towards a variety (vegetable soup). What makes a good soup is that it looks, smells, and tastes good to you. Experiment!

Chapter 3:
Get Saucy!

In virtually every vegan-owned refrigerator I have ever witnessed, the most common items are condiments. It's true. Conduct your own informal survey and you'll find that vegans love sauces, dressings, gravies, dips, and spreads. If you can put it on a vegetable, toast, or tofu, chances are good that a vegan will have tried it or tried to make a plant-based version. It's telling that this chapter has the most recipes in the book, and to be honest I really had to whittle this list down. The chapter addresses sauce, from the simple salad dressing to the more complicated creations of the would-be vegan saucier. Recipes begin with simple oil-and-vinegar dressings, and move on to gravies and coulis, to more complicated traditional *haute cuisine* sauces (e.g., roux, béchamel, etc.), to *nouvelle cuisine*, and to the simpler, lighter, and healthier fruit- and vegetable-focused sauces. If you want to learn how to make your own salsa, astound friends and family with your gourmet saucing skills, or learn how mustard acts as an emulsifier, this is the chapter for you!

Simple Vinaigrette Salad Dressing

Salad dressing is very easy to make, and once you're used to preparing your own you'll have more control over both the nutrition and the flavor of your salads. You'll wonder why you ever bought bottled. Vinaigrette is salty, sour, and rich, which means it accentuates salads rich with sweet (e.g., carrots, onions, tomatoes) and green ingredients (e.g., various lettuces, cucumbers, endive). What's important about this recipe is the proportions (3:1 oil and vinegar, or oil and lemon). You could use 1 cup oil, 1/3 cup vinegar, 2 to 3 tablespoons mustard, 1 teaspoon black pepper and sea salt to taste if you wanted a larger quantity. The advantage to a larger quantity is that you have dressing on hand when you want it and you can experiment more easily with extra ingredients. If you plan to keep it in the fridge, be sure to put it in a jar with a lid after sterilizing the jar and the lid.

 **DIFFICULTY**

Flavors: Rich, sour, salty

Equipment: A small bowl and a whisk (a fork will do in a pinch)

Ingredients

- ▶ 3 tablespoons olive oil
- ▶ 1 tablespoon apple cider vinegar (or lemon juice if you prefer)
- ▶ 1/2 teaspoon brown mustard
- ▶ 1/4 teaspoon black pepper
- ▶ Sea salt (1/4 teaspoon should do, but add more to taste if needed)

Instructions

Whisk all of the ingredients together in a small bowl until well-combined. Taste and add salt as required. Pour over your salad. Gloat about how easy it is to make your own salad dressing.

Going further

Now you know the basic recipe for vinaigrette. You can make all kinds of wonderful salad dressings now. Add a tablespoon of nutritional yeast for a little body and flavor. To notch up the savory flavor, add a 1 teaspoon dry savory, tarragon or other herbs, or 1 tablespoon fresh herbs: savory, or a dash of liquid smoke. Add puréed fruit for something sweeter. Add 1 teaspoon nori flakes for a little green and a little sea flavor. Swap out the apple cider for balsamic or pomegranate juice in equal proportions for something a little ritzier. Swap out the olive oil with flax or walnut oil for a higher percentage of omega-3s. It's entirely up to you. What's important is that if you want your dressing to hold together, you'll need an emulsifier. Garlic will emulsify a little, but mustard, nut butters, guar gum, and other emulsifying agents are just fine for a dressing

Simple Slaw Dressing

One of the simplest, easiest, and quickest ways to enjoy your vegetables is to pickle them. You don't need jars and a lot of apparatus and experience to do light pickling. Some salt, sugar, and vinegar will get you started.

 **DIFFICULTY**

Flavors: Salty, sour, sweet

Equipment: A small bowl and a whisk (a fork will do)

Ingredients

- 1/4 cup apple cider vinegar
- 1 teaspoon agave nectar
- Sea salt (start with a pinch and add more to taste, the dressing should be slightly salty)

Optional: This is enough for 2 cups of sliced vegetables, but the recipe easily doubles if you want to make a larger batch. To keep this recipe simple, you may want to swap the agave nectar for a teaspoon of organic sugar or other sweetener. But this is not a recipe with which you can use stevia or artificial sweeteners.

Instructions

Whisk everything together in a small bowl. Pour over your vegetables and let stand covered on a counter for 1 to 2 hours, mixing every 30 minutes or so. If you want a more pickled flavor, refrigerate overnight.

Going further

There are a few things that need to be noted about this recipe. First, it's not a substitute for jarred pickling, which is an involved process that ensures you don't accidentally give yourself food poisoning. Don't leave your vegetables out on the counter for an extended period of time. If you want to leave them overnight, refrigerate them. Second, not all vegetables are equally good for this recipe. Choose vegetables with a lot of their own moisture (onions, carrots, cabbage, kale, collards, daikon, etc.) and a lot of their own flavor. Ideally, you should pick vegetables that have a lot of scent. Also, don't be afraid to use fruits for a slaw. Mangoes, papayas, and other sturdier fruits will work great, while adding some of their own natural sugars and some vibrant color and flavor. Finally, the sugar (whether it's actual granulated sugar, agave nectar, maple syrup, etc.) plays a very important role in this dish. Let's just say it helps the fermentation process along. You can't easily substitute artificial sweeteners with this dish successfully.

Having said all of that, this is a great, low-fat, and simple dressing for all sorts of wonderful vegetables. It's a great way to add flavor if plain raw vegetables aren't your thing. This recipe is simple and delicious all by itself, but there are also all kinds of ways to add flavor. Add some dill. Add some black pepper. Add a little aioli for a creamier slaw. Add some tarragon, savory, and thyme, a little brown mustard, or some caraway seeds. Switch the vinegars: try some balsamic, ume vinegar, malted vinegar, wine vinegar, or brown rice vinegar. The basic combination of sweet, salty, and sour is what counts in this recipe.

Raspberry Coulis

Great with pancakes, coffee cakes, or just toast, raspberries are full of flavor, are a beautiful deep red, and are full of antioxidants. My grandmother had raspberry bushes growing up, and now my in-laws do, as well. Although nothing beats fresh raspberries, frozen will do in a pinch. This recipe is a simple sauce based on the mostly unadulterated flavor of the fruit, with no cooking at all.

 **DIFFICULTY**

Flavors: Sweet, sour

Equipment: A small bowl and a hand blender, or a mortar and pestle if you prefer to go old-school

Ingredients

- ▶ 1 cup fresh or frozen raspberries
- ▶ 1 tablespoon agave nectar
- ▶ 1 teaspoon lime juice or lemon juice
- ▶ Pinch of sea salt

Instructions

If you're using frozen fruit, allow the raspberries to come close to room temperature. Give the fruit a good rinse and shake off any water. Add the fruit to the bowl. Add the agave nectar. Blend with your hand blender until smooth. Taste and add salt as required.

Going further

As far as sauces go, there's nothing simpler than coulis. And yet the approach affords a lot of creativity and complexity, both in terms of flavors and presentation. You can make coulis with lots of fruits and vegetables: mangoes, blueberries, tomatoes, red peppers. If you like fresh, raw food, this is a simple way to add it to your diet. For more savory coulis, add a little garlic or other herbs and sea salt to taste. For example, I like the Kiwi Jalapeño Coulis (page 53) with seitan. It's beautiful, spicy, sour, and green. Add a little nut butter to the mix for a richer mouth feel and a creamier taste. It's not just easy to eat blended fruit, it's also seriously gourmet.

Nori Tahini Spread

This is a simple combination of great-tasting ingredients as a simple spread. It's not particularly cream-cheese-like, but that's probably the closest nonvegan reference. The nori adds a little sea flavor and some nice green color. To ensure a nice, thick consistency, refrigerate the tahini and tamari and use cold water. Add the extra nutritional yeast to firm up the consistency. You'll probably have to go to your HFS to find nutritional yeast, white miso, nori flakes, and possibly even the tahini.

 **DIFFICULTY**

Flavors: Rich, salty, sour, fermented

Equipment: A small bowl, a whisk (a fork will do in a pinch)

Note: Usually referred to as tahini, sesame seed butter varies quite a bit in terms of its thickness. You want the thicker kind that resembles nut butter rather than the thinner kind that pours easily. If you can swish it a little in the jar, it's the thin kind. If you can't get thicker sesame seed butter, reduce the amount of water and tamari, only adding a little of each until you have the thickness you like (it should be about the consistency of room-temperature margarine). Or, you can always use cashew butter. Otherwise, start with 1 tablespoon tamari and 1 tablespoon water and add more of one or both to control the texture and the saltiness of your spread. Miso also varies in terms of its saltiness, so be sure to add the tamari and water last. If you find this is the right consistency for you (it should spread easily), then just add a pinch of salt if you don't find it salty enough rather than adding additional tamari.

Ingredients

▶ 4 tablespoons sesame seed butter (or macadamia or cashew butter if you want something creamier)
▶ 2 to 3 tablespoons nutritional yeast
▶ 1 to 2 tablespoons tamari
▶ 1 to 2 tablespoons water
▶ 1 tablespoon green nori flakes
▶ 1 teaspoon lemon juice
▶ 1 teaspoon white miso
▶ Pinch of sea salt (if the miso and the tamari aren't salty enough)

Instructions

Put everything in the small bowl except the tamari and water, and mix until well combined. Add the tamari or water until you have the right consistency and saltiness to your taste. If you find that it's getting too thin, add salt instead of tamari (you probably won't need any). You're done. Double or triple this recipe if you want leftovers.

Going further

This is a very simple spread with a lot of flavor and a dotted green color. It goes great on a bagel or with a baguette. Use it with crackers. If you don't like the flavor of tahini, swap in some macadamia, cashew, or almond butter instead. If you're not sure about the nori, skip it (or add a pinch of powdered kelp, wakame, or dulse instead). Add a little garlic if you want some additional flavor.

Spinach, Arugula & Walnut Pesto

This recipes takes pesto in a slightly different direction. In spite of its almost celebrity status in small, rustic jars on grocery shelves, pesto was originally a basic sauce for leftovers and garden-variety herbs—delicious, but humble and, in fact, very practical. Variations on "pesto" are common in Europe wherever regular people like a quick sauce with a lot of flavor (e.g., Spanish pesto, the French pistou, which uses bread as a thickener rather than nuts, similar to English bread sauce, and so on). My variation turns what is a traditionally a smoother sauce into one that's slightly thicker so that it's a little more flexible. Great for those omega-3 fatty acids, walnuts add a slight bitter flavor and a firmer body to this classic sauce compared to pine nuts, which are great in their own right. Arugula greens add a nice peppery flavor and a considerable amount of nutrition. The spinach adds some sweet. This sauce is one big beautiful creamy green, and an excellent way to start adding greens (remarkable in their flavor varieties) to your diet.

 **DIFFICULTY**

Flavors: Rich, green, salty, sour

Note: You'll need to go to the HFS for the nutritional yeast and possibly some of the optional ingredients. You can make this dish without the nutritional yeast, but it adds flavor and body.

Equipment: Either a hand blender with a chopping attachment, a food processor (optional but recommended), or a mortar and pestle (very traditional)

Ingredients

- ▶ 1 cup packed baby spinach
- ▶ 1/4 cup packed baby arugula
- ▶ 1/4 cup packed fresh basil leaves
- ▶ 3 tablespoons chopped walnuts
- ▶ 1 tablespoon minced fresh garlic
- ▶ 1 tablespoon extra virgin olive oil
- ▶ 1 tablespoon lemon juice
- ▶ 1/2 teaspoon sea salt
- ▶ 2 tablespoons nutritional yeast

Optional: An extra tablespoon of olive oil will make this sauce slightly smoother for pastas. Lemon zest brightens up the lemony flavor. Add 1/4 cup rehydrated sun-dried tomatoes, 1/4 cup roasted red pepper, olives, capers, white miso, red miso—there are a lot of ways to add flavor to your pesto.

Instructions

Begin by preparing your ingredients. Wash the greens. Stem the basil if necessary. Put everything into the chopper or food processor (or mince very finely with your knife, or grind all together in your mortar and pestle). Blend until smooth. Taste and add salt if necessary.

To serve, spoon this sauce over pasta and mix, spread it on a bagel, or just eat it straight! It's delicious and the fats are good for you.

Going further

This is a great basic sauce. Pesto is delicious and very flexible. Olives or capers add a wonderful sour flavor. Adding some reconstituted and minced sun-dried tomatoes will add some wonderful sour and sweet flavors while adding a warm, rich red color. Roasted red peppers accent the sweet and slightly bitter flavor, a hint of fire, and also give this sauce a wonderful bright red. Adding a little lemon zest will also greatly enhance the lemony taste and smell of your pesto, so if you really like lemons, add about 1/4 to 1/2 teaspoon zest. If you like the arugula, switch out the spinach altogether. Don't like walnuts? Toasted almonds or the traditional pine nuts will also work. Or add a little white miso to add flavor and creamy texture. The flavor profile is rich, sour, green and salty. Add it to pasta (sweet) or to mushrooms (savory) or a little of both for a highly flavorful plate of food or use it as a sauce for gourmet pizza. Don't be afraid to make it the way you like it and never pay $5 for a tiny jar of pesto again!

Kiwi Jalapeño Coulis

This takes the coulis concept in a slightly different, more savory and spicy direction. It's still dead simple, bright green, and delicious! This is a great sauce for more flavorful dishes. It goes well with seitan and roasted/grilled tofu, but would also work with chickpea cutlets and similar dishes—anything with strong savory or fatty flavors.

 **DIFFICULTY**

Flavors: Sweet, sour, spicy

Equipment: A small bowl, a sharp knife or a paring knife, latex gloves for sensitive hands, and a hand blender

Ingredients

- ▶ 3 large kiwis or 4 smaller
- ▶ 1 teaspoon agave nectar
- ▶ 1 tablespoon minced jalapeño pepper (1 smallish pepper should do, or half of a larger one) or more if you like it really spicy
- ▶ 1/4 teaspoon sea salt

Instructions

Carefully pare the kiwi with the knife and add to a bowl. It's like peeling any other fruit, except that kiwis have no core. You can also eat the skin, although it's up to you with this sauce. Carefully mince the pepper and add to the kiwi. Add the agave nectar. Blend with your hand blender until smooth. Taste and add salt as required.

Carefully drip your coulis over the entrée in a nice zig-zag or paint it onto the plate or do something that looks creative and engaging to you.

Going further

A little minced cilantro or mint would complete the flavor profile.

Kalamata Olive
& Dill Pickle Tapenade

Tapenade is delicious and simple. Again, not a traditional American dish, but it's all over the place nowadays. It's also a great way to add fatty acids to your diet in a flavorful way. Tapenade makes for a good sandwich spread, a good starter on crackers or thin slices of French bread, and a good garnish for seitan—wherever you want to add a lot of concentrated flavor to a small space. Although this recipe suggests you can swap pickles for the capers, that would provoke cries of heresy among people who really like tapenade. The capers give it a unique flavor, but capers and kalamata olives are relatively pricey. You can use regular black olives, but the flavor won't be as rich.

 **DIFFICULTY**

Flavors: Rich, salty, sour, sweet

Equipment: A small bowl, and a hand blender (a whisk or a fork will do, but it's a lot of mincing)

Ingredients

- ▶ 1 cup kalamata olives, pitted and minced
- ▶ 1/4 cup jarred garlic pickles (not dill), minced (or 1/4 cup capers if you want something more traditional)
- ▶ 1 tablespoon minced fresh garlic
- ▶ 1 teaspoon lemon juice
- ▶ Pinch of coarse sea salt (if the olives aren't salty enough)

Optional: 1/4 cup rehydrated sun-dried tomatoes, minced, and/or 1 tablespoon sweet whiskey.

Instructions

Begin by preparing your ingredients. Add everything to the small bowl and blend with your hand blender. Or, you can mince everything by hand, if you prefer a more textured and rustic tapenade. Taste and add salt as necessary.

Going further

Tapenade is very flavorful as it is, but traditionally, it's a flexible dish with lots of regional variations. You can always add some hot pepper or other herbs, or even a little agave nectar, a little rehydrated wakame, mirin, or sweet whiskey to your tapenade for extra flavor.

Rosemary Fig Sauce

This is traditionally an Italian flavor combination, but it goes nicely with tofu or seitan.

 **DIFFICULTY**

Flavors: Sweet, sour, rich, green

Equipment: A hand blender and a pan capable of holding at least 4 cups liquid

Ingredients

- 1 cup water
- 6 calimyrna figs, stemmed and chopped
- 1/2 teaspoon fresh rosemary, minced
- 1/4 teaspoon ground black pepper
- 1 teaspoon minced fresh garlic
- 1 teaspoon lemon juice
- Dash of liquid smoke

Instructions

Begin by preparing your ingredients. Bring the water to a boil on a high heat. Add the ingredients to the pan and reduce to medium-low heat. Let the figs hydrate on a low simmer for about 10 minutes and for the sauce to reduce slightly. Remove from heat. Blend with your hand blender. Taste and add salt as required. This sauce is best plated by dripping spoonfuls onto the main dish.

Going further

Rosemary is not for everyone, but it goes nicely with figs. Replace the rosemary with 1/2 teaspoon minced fresh cilantro (add the cilantro at the end) if you really don't like rosemary. Again, because of the flavors in this sauce, it goes well with a savory main dish.

Roux, Velouté & Béchamel

Roux is the basis for many traditional French and Italian sauces, and velouté and béchamel are the two most common building blocks between roux (flour and fat) and a finished sauce. Roux continues to be prominent in a great deal of American cooking, particularly in the South and of course everywhere French and Italian cooking have influence. It's remarkably simple to make, but difficult to master. Fine restaurants often have a chef whose sole job is to manage the sauces (the saucier). But within the last few decades, saucing has changed (more on this at the end of the chapter) from heavier, fattier sauces toward healthier and more colorful alternatives. This recipe focuses on how to build a traditional roux but also how to use arrowroot powder as an alternative.

 **DIFFICULTY**

Flavors: Rich, salty, sweet

Equipment: A small bowl, a larger bowl, and a pan capable of holding 2 cups liquid

Ingredients

- ▶ 1 tablespoon vegetable oil
- ▶ 1 tablespoon whole wheat flour or arrow-root powder
- ▶ 1 cup vegetable stock or unsweetened soy milk
- ▶ Sea salt (start with 1/4 teaspoon and add more to taste)

Instructions

To build a traditional roux, heat your oil until nice and warm on high heat. Add the flour slowly and stir until the flour is well coated and all signs of clumps have been dissolved. Sauté lightly for 2 minutes, longer if you're making a brown roux. Gently and slowly whisk in the vegetable stock for a velouté sauce or the soy milk for a béchamel. Keep stirring until the flour begins to thicken, remove from heat and add ingredients as appropriate or enjoy your white sauce.

To make an arrowroot-based sauce, add a tablespoon of cold stock, cold water, or cold soy milk to a small bowl and whisk with until dissolved. Bring the rest of your stock or soy milk to a simmer on high in the saucepan. Remove the pan from heat and stir until the sauce thickens.

Going further

You have the basic constituents now for many great sauces. Add lemon, or a tablespoon of catsup, or some fresh tarragon and vinegar to accent your simple white sauces. Or blend some dried mushrooms and broth. Or reduce some orange juice, bourbon, or anything else that you think tastes good and thicken it up with a little arrowroot. Use greens, herbs, vegetables, or fruits in your sauces. Experimentation is the only way to progress. As a way to add color and flavor to a plate, sauces are simply unparalleled (which is why they tend to be so significant in most developed cuisines).

But why should you use arrowroot or flour? It will be a little harder to find arrowroot and you may have to go to your HFS. However, arrowroot is easier, more flexible and more forgiving than a traditional roux. For example, you can hand blend your ingredients as you like and then add your thickener. Adding your thickening agent last will allow you to control the sauce as a whole until you have the flavor and body the way you want it. With a roux, you may very well have to make it several times before you get the pan temperature and the pour of the stock/soy milk slow enough, your whisk fast enough, etc., to avoid clumping, and that can be a little frustrating.

Also, the chemistry is slightly different. Wheat is a glutenous flour, and hand blending it to remove lumps after the fact seriously limits its potential as a thickening agent. On the other hand, arrowroot will "unthicken" if you try to add some ingredients after you've added your arrowroot. You can also do nice translucent sauces with arrowroot, which you can't do with a traditional roux. But having said that, you can't create a nice, rich, brown roux with arrowroot the way you can by cooking your flour a little. So, there are positives and negatives to both. That's why I've provided both techniques. Choose the one that best fits your cooking style and learn its ins and outs.

Avocado Creton

Creton is a French-American spread that's historically made from pig fat. Featuring avocados, I should say that this dip is a very metaphorical reinterpretation, but it's healthier, more beautiful, and of course more virtuous. It's almost a moral imperative to try this spread!

Flavors: Salty, sour, rich, savory

Equipment: A small bowl, and a whisk (a fork will do)

Ingredients

▶ 2 avocados, pitted, peeled, and mashed
▶ 1 teaspoon lime juice
▶ 2 dashes liquid smoke

▶ 1/4 teaspoon coarse sea salt

Instructions

Add everything together in a small bowl and mash with the whisk or fork until well combined and creamy. Add coarse sea salt to taste. This spread should be lightly salty. You can use fine salt, but it won't be quite the same.

Going further

This is a simple spread for bread, toast, rolls, biscuits, crackers, and other largely sweet flavors. Or add a dollop to seitan for a very simple, rich, and colorful main dish.

White Bean & Parsley Dip

This is a simple dish like hummus and other bean dips. It's a beautiful white with flecks of green, relatively low fat, and great with vegetables, on bagels, or with pita bread. The parsley may seem a little strange, but parsley's not just a garnish. It's really good for you and it adds a lot of texture and fresh green flavor to this dish.

You may have to go your HFS to get dry cannellini beans, but this dip works with other white beans.

 **DIFFICULTY**

Flavors: Sweet, savory, rich, green, salty, sour

Equipment: A pan with tight-fitting lid capable of holding 4 cups water, a medium-sized bowl, and a hand blender or food processor

Ingredients

- 1 cup dry cannellini beans
- 3 cups water
- 1 tablespoon lemon juice
- 2 tablespoons minced fresh garlic
- 1 tablespoon extra virgin olive oil
- 1 cup packed curly parsley, finely chopped
- 1/2 teaspoon coarse sea salt

Optional: 1 tablespoon oil or 1 to 2 tablespoons tahini, some paprika

Instructions

Begin by preparing your beans. Add your water and your beans to the pot. Bring to a simmer on medium-low heat and then reduce to low. Cook the beans until soft (this should take about 2 hours, but it depends on your soak time, see the section on beans in Preparing Your Ingredients, page 9).

When the beans are ready, drain and rinse them in a colander. Add the beans to the bowl, add the garlic, lemon juice, parsley, and olive oil. Add the sea salt and blend the ingredients thoroughly with a hand blender. Taste and add salt as necessary.

Going further

A lot of legumes taste good with garlic, lemon, and parsley. Try this dish with chickpeas or lentils but add the optional tablespoon of oil or, even better, a tablespoon or two of tahini, since these beans aren't as creamy by themselves. Garnish with a sprinkle of paprika to add a nice warm red color. If you find the curly parsley is not to your liking, try flat-leaf parsley. This is a full-flavored dish already, but add some hot pepper or some nutritional yeast to round it out. Serve it with pita, fresh crackers, or fresh bread.

Artichoke, Caper
& Black Pepper Butter

Like the Avocado Creton (page 57), this is a simple and flavorful spread. If you don't want the capers, you can always leave them out. This is a great spread for bread, toast, rolls, biscuits, crackers, and other largely sweet flavors and works well as a flavorful garnish for seitan. But it also makes a good dip for veggies.

Flavors: Salty, sour, rich, savory, spicy

Equipment: A small bowl, a hand blender, and a whisk

Ingredients

- ▶ 1 cup artichoke hearts (buy bottled, not canned, and be sure to drain and rinse)
- ▶ 1 teaspoon lemon juice
- ▶ 2 tablespoons macadamia butter (you can substitute cashew or almond, but this will affect the flavor)
- ▶ 1 tablespoon minced fresh garlic
- ▶ 1/2 teaspoon dry black pepper, ground
- ▶ 1 tablespoon whole jarred capers, minced
- ▶ 1/4 teaspoon coarse sea salt

Optional: You may have to go to your HFS to get the macadamia butter, and you can also substitute tahini for it to get a stronger but different taste. You can substitute fine sea salt, but coarse is preferred. For a lighter butter, hand whip with a whisk for 100 strokes.

Instructions

Begin by preparing your ingredients. Drain and thoroughly rinse your artichokes (although if you know how to prepare artichokes from scratch, go for it!). Purée everything in a small bowl with your hand blender until well combined. Add coarse sea salt to taste.

Going further

Ever try a dip that you just couldn't get a vegetable to stick to if it meant saving your life? Cling is an important part of a successful crudités plate. It's the nut butter, as well as the garlic and the artichokes themselves, that give this recipe more cling. On the other hand, you'll really need a hand blender for this butter in order to get the just right texture.

Caesar Salad Dressing

No American cookbook would be really complete without a recipe for Caesar salad dressing, but virtually all Caesars are made with animal ingredients (they often have eggs, dairy, pork, and anchovies). This recipe gives you all the flavors of a traditional Caesar.

Flavors: Rich, salty, sour, savory, fermented

Equipment: A small bowl and a whisk, fork, or hand blender

Ingredients

- ▶ 1/2 cup boiling water
- ▶ 2 tablespoons whole dried wakame (or alaria), crumbled
- ▶ 2 tablespoons tahini
- ▶ 1/4 cup nutritional yeast
- ▶ 1 tablespoon minced fresh garlic
- ▶ 1 teaspoon lemon juice
- ▶ 1/4 teaspoon ground black pepper
- ▶ Dash of liquid smoke
- ▶ Sea salt (start with 1/4 teaspoon and add more to taste)

Optional: Coarse sea salt works well in this dressing. Add 1/2 teaspoon capers for a little something extra in terms of the flavors, or a little extra black pepper for a little more spice.

Instructions

Begin by preparing your ingredients. Bring the water to a boil, add it to the bowl and add your wakame. Let the wakame reconstitute for about 20 minutes. Reserve the water (don't drain!). If you don't have a hand blender, mince the wakame as finely as you can and then add to the bowl and whisk with the other ingredients. Otherwise, add everything to the small bowl and blend with your hand blender until smooth.

Going further

This is a traditional Caesar and is relatively full-flavored, assuming you'll use it with sweet and green vegetables (e.g., romaine lettuce, tomatoes, red onions). You can substitute the wakame for kelp flakes if that's easier for you, but you won't get quite the same flavor from nori. There's also no rule that says you can't add a little hot pepper. Cut the water in half for a great dip for vegetables.

Ginger, Garlic & Tahini Dressing

This is a simple dressing great with greens, noodles and as a dip for other vegetables.

Equipment: A small bowl and a whisk (a fork will do)

Flavors: Rich, salty, sour, fermented

Ingredients

- ► 1/2 teaspoon minced fresh ginger
- ► 1 teaspoon minced fresh garlic
- ► 1 tablespoon lemon juice
- ► 2 tablespoons tahini
- ► 2 tablespoons nutritional yeast
- ► 1 tablespoon water (or more if you're dressing a green salad)
- ► Sea salt (start with 1/4 teaspoon and add more to taste if required)

Optional: Add liquid smoke and 1 tablespoon olive oil; Tabasco or other hot sauce.

Instructions

Begin by preparing your ingredients. Add everything to a small bowl and whisk until well combined. Taste and add salt as necessary.

Going further

This is a simple dressing with a lot of strong flavor. It goes well with green and sweet flavors. You can substitute other nut butters (peanut, cashew, almond, macadamia, etc.), but this will change the flavor. In this dish, the nut butter acts as the basic emulsifier and stabilizer.

Peanut, Chipotle & Lime Dressing

This is a great and simple dressing for all kinds of rice, noodles, and vegetables, but particularly starchy root vegetables and greens with a strong flavor like collards or mustard greens.

 **DIFFICULTY**

Flavors: Sour, spicy, rich, salty, savory

Equipment: A small bowl, a sharp knife, and a whisk (a fork will do in a pinch)

Ingredients

- ► 2 tablespoons peanut butter
- ► 2 tablespoons tamari
- ► 2 tablespoons lime juice
- ► 1 tablespoon agave nectar
- ► 1/2 teaspoon minced chipotle
- ► Sea salt

Optional: Add a tablespoon of water to the dressing if you're having it with pasta or other grain-focused salads—with stuff that tends to absorb moisture. With cooked vegetables and crudités, it should be fine as is. Reduce the nut butter by 1/2 and add 1 tablespoon water for a green salad. Add a little sea salt to taste if you find the tamari's not salty enough. If you don't have chipotle lying around add 1/4 teaspoon cayenne pepper or, for something less spicy, 1/4 teaspoon black pepper.

Instructions

Begin by preparing your ingredients. Add everything to the small bowl and whisk. Taste and add sea salt as necessary.

Going further

This is a fairly simple peanut sauce, but you can easily use it as a base to expand both the flavor and the texture. Peanut goes well with a number of flavors, noodles, veggies, your pick!

Mango Chipotle Salsa

Replacing the tomatoes, mango adds a sweet and sour component to traditional salsa. The bright yellow of ripe mango with the deep red of bell pepper and the bright green of the cilantro create a sauce that is simple, full of flavor, and beautiful on the plate.

 **DIFFICULTY**

Flavors: Sweet, sour, green, spicy

Equipment: A large bowl, and a hand blender with a chopping attachment, or a food processor (optional but recommended)

Ingredients

- ▶ 2 large, ripe mangoes
- ▶ 1 red bell pepper
- ▶ 3 small limes
- ▶ 1 green bell pepper
- ▶ Half a Spanish onion
- ▶ 1/2 teaspoon minced chipotle
- ▶ 1 teaspoon minced fresh garlic
- ▶ 1/4 teaspoon sea salt (or to taste, but it should taste as though it needs a little bit of salt)
- ▶ 1/4 cup packed fresh cilantro

Optional: 1 tomato—for the traditionalists.

Instructions

Begin by preparing your ingredients. Coarsely chop your pepper and put the pieces of the pepper into your food processor/chopper and mince (should only take 30 seconds). Start on a low setting so that you're not liquefying the pepper. If you don't have a food processor or a hand blender, mince the pepper until you have a lot of red liquid and the pieces of pepper are quite small—about half the size of rice grains. Add the red pepper to the large bowl. Repeat the same process with the green pepper. Then repeat the same process with the onion.

Next, carefully pare the mango like you're paring an apple. The skin will be slightly thicker, and the core larger. Once you have pared the mango, slice off pieces until you have hit the core (don't include the core). Mince your sliced mangoes in the food processor or hand blender, or with a knife, then add the mango to the large bowl. Peel, mince, and add the garlic.

Next, add the chipotle (use 1 whole teaspoon chipotle if you want something spicier). Cut the limes in half and squeeze their juice directly into the bowl, watching out for seeds. Stir until well mixed (should be 25 stirs). Let stand 10 minutes. Add the sea salt, taste and add more sea salt as needed. Mince approximately 1/4 cup packed cilantro with the food processor or with a knife. Add to the bowl. Stir again and serve.

Plating: A nice white ramekin makes for a great plating option if you want to do chips and salsa. Otherwise, spooning it over the food on a white plate will bring out the color.

Going further

Mango provides a wonderful alternative to tomato and it frequently adds more flavor. Try mango as a substitute in chili or make your own catsup with it. No mangoes? Not a problem. Use pineapple instead, but chop it coarsely instead of mincing it for a chunkier salsa. If you want something a little more traditional with this recipe, cut, seed and chop a tomato and toss it in with everything else. The flavors for this salsa also goes well with mushrooms, beans, tofu, or seitan, which provide rich, salty and savory flavors. Add it to some lentils and salad greens with a little extra virgin olive oil for a quick and delicious salad. Serve with tortilla chips, or spoon over burritos.

White Miso & Hazelnut Butter Dressing

Miso is both a flavor and a nutritional powerhouse. This dressing pairs it with hazelnut butter and lime for a rich, creamy dressing. You'll probably have to go to your HFS to find white miso, and possibly even the hazelnut butter, although both are relatively common in larger cities.

 **DIFFICULTY**

Flavors:
Rich, salty, sour, fermented

Equipment:
A small bowl and a whisk (a fork will do in a pinch)

Ingredients:

- ▶ 1 heaping tablespoon white miso
- ▶ 2 tablespoons extra-virgin olive oil
- ▶ 1 heaping teaspoon hazelnut butter (peanut butter will also do in a pinch)
- ▶ Juice from three small limes (golf-ball-sized)
- ▶ 1 scant teaspoon minced fresh ginger
- ▶ 1 tablespoon minced fresh garlic
- ▶ 1/4 teaspoon black pepper
- ▶ 1/4 teaspoon sea salt

Optional: Add 1/4 teaspoon lime zest for a little extra flavor. For grain salads and cooked vegetables, it should be fine as is. For green salads, add 1 tablespoon water and reduce the olive oil by half (and you'll probably need a little more salt).

Instructions

Begin by preparing your ingredients. Peel and mince your garlic and ginger and add to the small bowl. Cut the limes in half and squeeze the juice from each lime half directly into a small bowl, watching out for seeds. Add the remaining ingredients. Mix with a fork or a whisk until thoroughly blended. Taste and add salt as necessary.

Going further

This dressing is a good flavor pairing for green and grain salads. Add a little horse-radish, wasabi, or chile to add a little heat.

Tarragon Aioli

In a nutshell, aioli is basically mayo with a little garlic. This sauce adds a little tarragon to the mix for a savory, béarnaise-like dip and spread. It's great on sandwiches, for mock meat salads, and as a dip for veggies.

Flavors: Sour, sweet, salty

Equipment: A small bowl, a medium bowl, and a whisk (a fork will do, although a hand blender is also nice for this recipe)

Ingredients

- ▶ 12-ounce package silken tofu (firm, aseptically packed is preferred)
- ▶ 1 tablespoon lemon juice
- ▶ 1/2 teaspoon white vinegar (you can use apple cider vinegar or ume vinegar if you prefer)
- ▶ 2 tablespoons extra virgin olive oil (or macadamia nut butter for a thicker sauce)
- ▶ 2 tablespoons minced fresh garlic
- ▶ 1/8 cup packed fresh tarragon, stemmed and minced, or 1 tablespoon dried tarragon, rubbed
- ▶ Sea salt (start with 1/4 teaspoon and add more to taste)

Optional: 1 teaspoon chervil, 1/4 teaspoon guar gum.

Instructions

Begin by preparing your ingredients. Add the oil, tarragon, lemon juice, and vinegar to the small bowl and let stand for 10 minutes (or longer). Put everything else in the medium bowl and blend with a hand blender until well combined. Add the tarragon mixture to the medium bowl and stir to combine. Taste and add sea salt as desired.

Going further

Aioli is fairly flexible sauce. In terms of its chemistry, aioli is a way to add a number of ingredients whose chemistry doesn't necessarily hold together well (e.g., oil and lemon juice). The mayo (in this case, the silken tofu) is basically an emulsifier (it holds everything together). Guar gum is also an emulsifier, and for this recipe it just adds a little extra hold. You can pick it up in most health food stores and in some groceries that have a lot of baking supplies. Feel free to experiment with a lot of different flavors. Begin by flavoring the other liquid ingredients, particularly the vinegar, and then add the silk tofu to hold everything together.

Sour Cream

This is a simple sour cream recipe, great with pierogies, mashed potatoes, tacos, black bean soup, and all the other wonderful dishes that benefit from sour cream.

 **DIFFICULTY**

Flavors: Sour, sweet, salty

Note: You'll probably have to go to the HFS to get the agave nectar. You can substitute organic sugar but the consistency won't be identical

Equipment: A small bowl and a whisk (a fork will do, although a hand blender is also nice for this recipe)

Ingredients

▶ 12-ounce package silken tofu (firm is best, aseptically packed)
▶ 2 tablespoons lemon juice (or more to taste)
▶ 1 teaspoon white vinegar, or apple cider vinegar or ume vinegar
▶ 1 tablespoons extra virgin olive oil or macadamia nut butter
▶ 1 tablespoon agave nectar
▶ Sea salt (start with 1/4 teaspoon and add more to taste)

Optional: 1 tablespoon minced garlic, 2 tablespoons nutritional yeast, 1 teaspoon white miso

Instructions

Put everything in the bowl and blend with a hand blender until well combined. Taste and add sea salt as desired.

Going further

This is a very simple and straightforward sauce. It goes well with a variety of dishes, but particular starchy flavors, savory foods, and greens. It also makes a great dip for those who are fans of sour cream and crudités. Sour cream is also great with cooked, finely chopped collard greens. Add garlic, nutritional yeast, miso—whatever combination of flavors you like.

Basic Tomato Herb Sauce

Of course, it would be impossible to publish an American cookbook without some sort of tomato sauce. Americans eat a lot of tomatoes: on pizza, spaghetti, in catsup—the tomato is ubiquitous. You'll find fresh tomatoes in just about every grocery in the United States, but what you won't find are tomatoes that really taste like tomatoes. I remember when I was a boy and tomatoes tasted like something. Today, a lot of them taste like water, and that's a serious shame. But even the ones without that strong tomato flavor tend to be rich in lycopene. If you can, check out your local farmer's market for fresh tomatoes that really taste the way they're supposed to taste. This sauce hinges on good-tasting tomatoes, so use ripe, flavorful ones. If they are not good and ripe (they should yield to light pressure but still be slightly firm), then you will end up with a sauce that is not quite the right color of red, that has a slightly more acidic taste, that doesn't have that wonderful flavor of tomatoes, and is probably thicker than it should be. Smaller tomatoes (nectarine-sized) are generally better than larger ones. They have a higher tomato flesh to seed/core ratio, which is what makes plum/Italian tomatoes even better for these kinds of sauces. If you can't find fresh, ripe, good tasting tomatoes, substitute 2 cups canned or jarred crushed tomatoes, preferably organic.

DIFFICULTY

Flavors: Sweet, sour, salty, green

Equipment: A small bowl and a hand blender (or a mortar and pestle if you prefer to go old-school)

Optional: Use half of the herbs if you're making a bloody mary, smoothie, etc. Add 2 tablespoons nutritional yeast to any application for a little more flavor and nutrition. For a spicier red sauce, prepare the pasta sauce and add 1/4 teaspoon cayenne pepper. Add a pinch of rubbed sage, thyme, and rosemary for something more traditional.

Ingredients

- 6 small, ripe tomatoes, 3 large, cored and seeded, or use 12 plum tomatoes (should yield about 2 cups crushed tomatoes)
- 1 teaspoon lemon juice
- 1 tablespoon minced fresh garlic
- 1 tablespoon dried basil, rubbed
- 1 teaspoon dried oregano, rubbed
- 1/2 teaspoon dried marjoram, rubbed
- 1/4 teaspoon black pepper, ground
- Sea salt (start with 1/4 teaspoon and add more to taste)

For a cooked red sauce

- 2 tablespoons extra virgin olive oil
- 1/2 small red onion, peeled and minced
- 1/4 cup red wine

Instructions

Prepare your tomatoes, onions, and herbs. Add everything to a bowl and blend with a hand blender. Store in the fridge and use as you like for coulis or a spicy bloody mary.

If you want a cooked sauce for pasta (lots of people do!), blend the tomatoes separately until crushed. Bring 2 tablespoons extra virgin olive oil to heat on high in a saucepan. Add the dry herbs and sauté for 1 minute. Add the onion, peeled and finely chopped, and sauté for 2 minutes. Decrease the heat to medium-high, Add the garlic and sauté for 2 minutes. Add the wine and deglaze the pan. Add the tomatoes, the lemon juice, and any other remaining and optional ingredients to the pan and bring the sauce to a boil gently in a pan on medium-high heat.

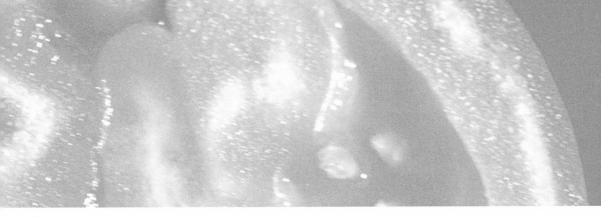

When your sauce is simmering, cover the pan loosely with the lid, so that steam can escape and so you don't end up with tomatoes all over your stove. Reduce by about 1/4 to 1/2 depending on how thick you like your sauce and the kind of pasta you have (thinner sauce for shells, bow-ties, and other pastas that catch sauce; thicker for penne, noodles, and baked pastas). If your tomatoes are not perfectly ripe and flavorful, reducing a little more often helps, as does additional simmering.

The reduction should take about 15 minutes for a thicker sauce. When reduced, cover tightly with the lid and simmer on low stirring occasionally for as long as you like (simmering for an hour or so will really help the flavors blend). If you have time, this is recommended. Always wait and taste at the end to determine whether or not to add salt, and if so, how much. Add a couple of tablespoons nutritional yeast for additional flavor.

For a good pizza sauce, you only need about half of a batch. Prepare the sauce like the pasta variation above and add 1 teaspoon agave nectar, 1/4 teaspoon dried thyme, rubbed.

If you want to make your own catsup, leave out the dried herbs, reduce by 2/3 (it should be a little thicker than catsup normally is). Add agave nectar and white vinegar to taste, and then jar. Really, you can make your own. Add a little mango or a little hot pepper for extra taste. If you're going to keep it a while, just make sure you sterilize your jar first.

Going further

This is a very basic sauce to get you started. I'm not even going to assume whether or not you plan to cook it. Maybe you want a little pizza sauce. Maybe you want something you can toss onto pasta (if you do, double the recipe and then reduce by about 1/4 to 1/2 when you cook it depending on how thick you like your sauce). Maybe you want a little tomato coulis for a breast of seitan. Maybe you want an herbed glass of tomato juice or maybe you have plans for a wonderful, fresh bloody mary. You have the main constituent of all of these concoctions now. Do with it as you will!

Part of what makes tomatoes so versatile is their middle-of-the-road flavor. They're not overly sour, not overly sweet, but they do have a great taste, good body, bright color, and a flavor that goes well with lots of others. They're also beautiful, whether they're red, yellow, orange or green, and increasing numbers of heirloom tomatoes are becoming available.

Jalapeño Cheeze Sauce

When I was growing up, the neon yellow of macaroni and cheese, chili-cheese hot dogs, and nacho cheese was ubiquitous in Chicago. This recipe reproduces that rather than a real cheese sauce, but it's a good way to add a little nutrition, flavor, and rich mouth feel to your dishes.

 **DIFFICULTY**

Flavors: Rich, salty, sour, fermented, spicy

Equipment: A small bowl, a whisk (a fork will do in a pinch), and a pan capable of holding at least 1 cup liquid

Ingredients

- ▶ 1 cup unsweetened soy milk
- ▶ 1/4 cup nutritional yeast
- ▶ 1 tablespoon lemon juice
- ▶ 1 tablespoon tahini
- ▶ 1 teaspoon minced fresh garlic
- ▶ 1/2 teaspoon minced fresh ginger
- ▶ 1/2 teaspoon agave nectar
- ▶ 1 teaspoon fresh jalapeño pepper, seeded, cored, and minced, reserving 2 rings of pepper for garnish if you like
- ▶ 1/2 teaspoon turmeric
- ▶ 1 teaspoon paprika (Hungarian preferred), ground
- ▶ 1 teaspoon dried onion powder
- ▶ Dash of liquid smoke
- ▶ Sea salt (start with 1/4 teaspoon and add more to taste)

Thickener
- ▶ 1/4 cup unsweetened soy milk
- ▶ 2 teaspoons arrowroot powder

Optional: 1 tablespoon cilantro to add some green flavor and color. If you can't find fresh jalapeño, add 1/2 teaspoon of lemon juice and 1/4 teaspoon of cayenne pepper. Leave out the pep-

per altogether for a nice simple soy cheese sauce. Halve the soy milk for a spread that does well on toast or for grilled cheeses.

Instructions

Begin by preparing your ingredients. Assemble in a small pot all the ingredients, except the soy milk and arrowroot powder for thickening. Mix until well-combined. Bring to a boil and gently simmer 10 minutes, or until reduced by 1/4. Be careful to avoid letting your soy milk boil over. In the meantime, whisk the arrowroot powder and the reserved soy milk in a small bowl until the arrowroot is dissolved. Remove the sauce from heat and add the arrowroot mixture and stir vigorously until the whole sauce thickens (should only take a minute). Use as desired!

Going further

This is a simple, flexible cheese-like sauce. If you don't like jalapeño, you can leave it out. If you want a simple white cheeze sauce, leave out the turmeric and the paprika. You can leave the nutritional yeast out, but you'll lose a lot of the sauce's flavor and you should use slightly more than 1 tablespoon arrowroot (a heaping tablespoon should do). If you want to give it a slightly stronger fermented flavor, add 1 teaspoon miso when removing the soy milk from heat, but before whisking the arrowroot in. Use white miso for a milder flavor, or red for something more full-bodied. As this sauce cools, it thickens. Add it to toast and then broil it for a few minutes in your oven to make rarebit or spread it between two pieces of bread to make yourself a simple grilled cheeze. Play around with the proportions until you get it just the way you like it.

Pomegranate Jalapeño Sauce

This is a simple barbecue-style sauce. Its origins are Iranian, but pomegranate is showing up all over in American cooking. It goes well with tofu and seitan. This is a spicy sauce! It's also a very nice shade of purple.

 **DIFFICULTY**

Flavors: Sweet, sour, rich, spicy

Equipment: A pan capable of holding at least 4 cups liquid and a hand blender

Ingredients

- ▶ 2 cups pomegranate juice
- ▶ 1 to 2 tablespoons minced fresh jalapeño pepper (add more for a spicier sauce)
- ▶ 1 tablespoon minced fresh garlic
- ▶ 3 tablespoons walnuts, ground to butter (or 2 tablespoons walnut butter if you have it)
- ▶ 1 tablespoon agave nectar (more to taste)
- ▶ Sea salt (start with 1/4 teaspoon but you may need 1/2 teaspoon)

Optional: Instead of jalapeño pepper, you can substitute 1/4 to 1/2 teaspoon cayenne pepper and 1/2 teaspoon lemon juice. This won't bring quite the same citrus taste that fresh jalapeño does, but it's a little more convenient. If you don't want it as spicy, add less jalapeño or, for a really mild sauce use 1/4 teaspoon black pepper. If you don't have walnuts or walnut butter, you can always use a little tahini if you like. This will change the flavor and color, but it will still be good.

Instructions

Begin by preparing your ingredients. Grind your walnuts, separately if you can, then whisk with the rest of the ingredients. If you grind your walnuts at the end, the sauce will still work but it will be slightly more textured than if you grind your walnuts to butter first. Add all of the ingredients to the pan, bring to a simmer on high heat. Reduce to medium heat and reduce by 1/2. This should take about 15 minutes. Blend the sauce with a hand blender. Taste and add salt as necessary.

Going further

Sour, sweet, rich, salty, and spicy all go well together with a savory flavor. Although this sauce works well with seitan and tofu, it would also work well with chickpeas, portobello mushrooms, and other foods. It also makes a very flavorful dip for raw vegetables.

Orange Sauce

Orange sauce is common in both Eastern and Western cuisines. Citrus flavors go well with salty and savory flavors and this sauce provides a beautiful orange accent to any dish. In American cooking, this dish made it big in the late '70s/early '80s. Everyone was jogging, quitting smoking, and eating *à l'orange* (and, in general, experimenting with French sauces like this one). Even my parents made it a couple of times. The key to this recipe is good orange juice. Organic, pulpy, not-from-concentrate orange juice is preferred. The better the orange juice, the better the sauce.

 **DIFFICULTY**

Flavors: Sweet, sour, salty, rich, green

Equipment: A small bowl, a whisk (a fork will do in a pinch), a zester (a serrated knife will do), and a pan capable of holding at least 4 cups liquid

Thickener

▶ 2 teaspoons arrowroot powder
▶ 1/4 cup orange juice

Optional: 1/2 teaspoon orange flower water. Add a little chipotle and cilantro to add some spice and green flavor to the sweet and sour of this sauce.

Ingredients

▶ 2 cups orange juice (1/4 cup reserved for the thickener below)
▶ 1 tablespoon vegetable oil
▶ 1 teaspoon dried onion powder, ground, or 1/4 cup minced fresh shallots
▶ 1 tablespoon fresh orange zest, minced (organic preferred)
▶ 1 tablespoon agave nectar
▶ 1/2 teaspoon minced fresh ginger
▶ 1/2 teaspoon coriander
▶ 1/4 teaspoon toasted dark sesame oil
▶ 1/4 teaspoon ground black pepper
▶ 1/4 teaspoon ground nutmeg
▶ 1/4 teaspoon ground cloves
▶ Sea salt (start with a good pinch, but you'll need to add more to taste)

Instructions

Begin by preparing your ingredients. Add the oil to the pan and heat on medium-high. When ready, add your herbs and sauté for 2 minutes. If you're using fresh shallots, add them after about 2 minutes and sauté for another 2 minutes. Add all of the remaining ingredients to the pan except for the reserved orange juice and arrowroot powder for the thickener. Lower the heat to medium and simmer. Reduce by about 3/4 (this should take about 15 to 20 minutes). Whisk the reserved orange juice and the arrowroot powder and set aside. Bring the orange juice and other ingredients to a simmer. Remove from heat and whisk in the arrowroot mixture until the sauce thickens. If the sauce doesn't thicken immediately, you may need to return the pan to heat and simmer a little before the arrowroot thickens. Taste and add salt as necessary.

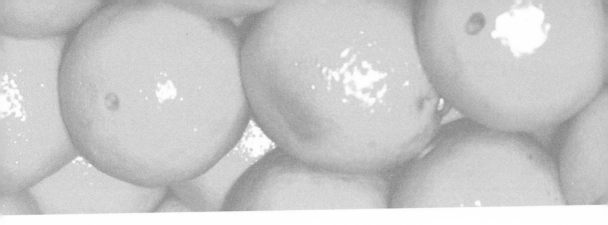

Plate this sauce by drizzling it over the entrée with a tablespoon. Take a tablespoon of sauce and then pour it over the entrée and let it run out over the sides. Typically 3 to 4 tablespoons of sauce will suffice for each serving (this makes 2 heaping servings of sauce or 4 more sparing ones).

Going further

You'll probably want to use this sauce primarily for accenting a cooked plate—typically seitan or tofu, but it also goes well with sturdy green vegetables like broccoli. Add a little hot pepper to increase the flavor. Where does the "green" flavor come from in this dish? From the orange zest. The zest of citrus fruits tends to add a slightly bitter flavor to any dish. In part, that's why zest is a common ingredient in many sauces. It adds a green flavor without adding a green color.

Simple Caramel Sauce

This is a sweet sauce. It goes well with desserts when you want a quick sauce to accent bread pudding, coffee cake, or ice cream, but it also provides the basis for the Three-Pepper Whiskey Sauce (page 76).

 **DIFFICULTY**

Flavors: Sweet, rich

Equipment: Two small bowls, a saucepan capable of holding at least 4 cups liquid, and a whisk (a fork will do)

Ingredients

▶ 1 cup good, sweet whiskey or cognac
▶ 1 teaspoon agave nectar
▶ 1 tablespoon nut butter (macadamia, cashew, and almond are fine, as is peanut butter but that will really influence the taste)
▶ Pinch of sea salt

Thickener

▶ 1 tablespoon arrowroot powder
▶ 1/4 cup vanilla soy milk

Optional: For a thicker, sweeter sauce, start with 1 1/2 cups whiskey, reduce by 2/3 (should take another few minutes) and increase the soy milk to 1/2 cup.

Instructions

Whisk together the whiskey, the agave nectar, nut butter, and the sea salt in a small bowl. Bring to a simmer on medium heat in a saucepan and reduce by 1/2 (this should take about 15 minutes). Whisk together the unsweetened soy milk and the arrowroot powder. Remove the sauce from heat, and whisk in the arrowroot mixture and stir until the sauce thickens. Let stand for 5 minutes to cool. Serve hot by drizzling over your dessert or plate in a ramekin if you want the sauce on the side.

Going further

Whiskey and cognac both do well in this sauce. You could also add a little cocoa to add a little bitter flavor, 1/2 teaspoon of white miso instead of the sea salt to add a little fermented flavor, or even 1/4 cup of berries or a tablespoon of lemon to bring a sour accent to this dish. But it's wonderful and simple all by itself.

Spicy, Sweet & Sour
Pineapple Peanut Sauce

This is a simple and rich sauce, good with pancakes, sweets, rice, pizza—just about anything with peanut butter or pineapple is good.

 **DIFFICULTY**

Flavors: Sweet, sour, rich, salty

Equipment: A small bowl and a hand blender

Note: You may have to go to your HFS for the agave nectar, or you can substitute a tablespoon of sugar if that's more available.

Ingredients

- 1 cup chopped pineapple
- 1 tablespoon unsweetened peanut butter (skip the agave if you use sweetened)
- 1 tablespoon white vinegar
- 1 teaspoon agave nectar
- 1/2 teaspoon cayenne pepper
- Sea salt (start with 1/4 teaspoon and add more to taste, this sauce should be lightly salty)

Instructions

Add all ingredients to a small bowl. Purée with your hand blender until smooth.

Going further

This sauce goes well with a number of dishes, primarily as an accent. You can add additional flavor depth by grilling the pineapple to draw out its natural sugars or swap the red chile flakes with sriracha, jalapeño, or other spices of your choice.

Strawberry Chipotle Sauce

Fiery, sweet, sour, but most of all red, this is a simple but elegant sauce with a lot of layered flavors. It's not for everyone, but it's a fine sauce nevertheless, probably the most sophisticated in this book. Not that long ago in American cooking, it wasn't uncommon to mix fruits, herbs, and other ingredients into more complicated and nuanced sauces. This sauce goes best with tofu and seitan, but it could also double as a veggie dip for adventurous souls.

 **DIFFICULTY**

Flavors: Sweet, sour, salty, rich, spicy, savory

Equipment: A small bowl, a whisk (a fork will do), and a pan capable of holding 4 cups liquid

Ingredients

- 1 1/2 cup strawberries, tops trimmed (use fresh or freshly frozen)
- 1 tablespoon tahini
- 1 teaspoon minced chipotle
- 2 tablespoons tamari
- 1 teaspoon lemon juice
- 1/4 teaspoon black pepper

Optional: This is a spicy sauce, but you can always cut back on the chipotle if you need to. If you can't lay hands on chipotle, you can use 1/4 teaspoon cayenne pepper and a dash of liquid smoke, but it won't be quite the same. If you leave the peppers out entirely, it's not a bad sauce, but it will lose some complexity.

Instructions

Begin by preparing your ingredients. Add all of the ingredients to a medium-sized bowl. Blend with the hand blender until smooth. Add the mixture to the pan and simmer on low until reduced by about 1/2.

Going further

This sauce is mainly for seitan and tofu, but you could twiddle the flavors by replacing the strawberries with raspberries or even blueberries. Don't be afraid to experiment!

Red Lentil, Red Onion
& Red Wine Gravy

This is a very simple gravy, sweet, savory, and very nutritious. It's very low-maintenance and great for meals that need a quick gravy or for when you're preparing more elaborate meals and a complicated gravy is the last thing you need. It's the figs that make it shine. Figs and other dried fruits are a good way to add visual shine to your dishes without adding a lot of calories.

 **DIFFICULTY**

Flavors: Rich, salty, savory, sweet

Equipment: A small bowl, a larger bowl, and a pan capable of holding 3 cups liquid

Optional: Add a tablespoon of nut butter or white miso for extra body and flavor. Use black lentils and black raisins for a darker, more textured gravy. Add a couple tablespoons of nutritional yeast for extra flavor and nutrition, or add 1 teaspoon red miso for a stronger, more flavorful gravy.

Ingredients

- ▶ 1 tablespoon vegetable oil (or nut butter)
- ▶ 1/2 cup dry red lentils
- ▶ 3 dried calimyrna figs, stemmed and finely chopped
- ▶ 1/4 cup red wine
- ▶ 1/2 medium red onion, finely chopped (about 1/2 cup)
- ▶ 1 1/2 cups water
- ▶ 2 tablespoons minced fresh garlic
- ▶ 2 tablespoons tamari
- ▶ 1 tablespoon lemon juice
- ▶ 1 teaspoon dried tarragon, rubbed
- ▶ 1 teaspoon ground cumin
- ▶ 1/2 teaspoon dried savory, rubbed
- ▶ 1/2 teaspoon ground black pepper
- ▶ Dash of liquid smoke
- ▶ 1/4 teaspoon sea salt

Instructions

Begin by preparing your ingredients. Add your vegetable oil to the pan and bring to heat on high. Add the onions and sauté for 5 minutes. Add the remaining herbs and sauté for 2 minutes. Add the lentils and the figs to the pan and sauté for another 3 minutes. Add the red wine to deglaze the pan and sauté 2 to 3 minutes, or until the wine has reduced by about 1/2. Add the water and bring the gravy to a boil, reduce to low, cover and simmer for 30 minutes or until the lentils have lost their shape. Blend with a hand blender until smooth. Taste and add salt as necessary.

Going further

Red lentils make this gravy simple and straightforward, but you could also use mung beans or black, brown, or green lentils to generate various shades of color. This gravy goes well with savory, sour, and green flavors.

Black Currant & Horseradish Sauce

This is a simple glaze, wonderful for tofu and seitan. It also works well as a glaze for potatoes and sweet potatoes. Alternatively, you can simmer it on the stove for about 5 minutes and then use as a plated sauce.

DIFFICULTY

Flavors: Rich, salty, savory, sweet, spicy

Equipment: A small bowl and a hand blender

Ingredients

- ▶ 1/4 cup water
- ▶ 1/2 cup dried black currants
- ▶ 2 tablespoons horseradish mustard, prepared
- ▶ 1 tablespoon minced fresh garlic
- ▶ 2 tablespoons vegetable oil (preferably olive oil)
- ▶ 1 tablespoon tamari
- ▶ 1/4 teaspoon dried rosemary, rubbed
- ▶ 1/2 teaspoon dried savory, rubbed
- ▶ 1/2 teaspoon dried tarragon, rubbed
- ▶ 1 teaspoon onion powder
- ▶ 1 tablespoon white vinegar
- ▶ 1 tablespoon agave nectar
- ▶ 1/2 teaspoon ground cumin
- ▶ Pinch of sea salt

Optional: If you don't have or don't like horseradish mustard, you can always use brown mustard, but it won't have the same kick. You can also substitute red wine vinegar or apple cider vinegar for the white vinegar for a less sharp taste.

Instructions

Begin by preparing your ingredients. Bring the water to a boil, and add it to the currants in the small bowl. Let the currants rehydrate for 10 minutes. Add all of the ingredients to a small bowl and blend with a hand blender until smooth. Depending on how dry the currants are, you may need to add up to 1/4 cup more water. Taste and add salt as necessary.

Going further

Black currants aren't the easiest thing to find, but what you really want is the wonderful combination of sour and sweet that the black currant provides.

Three-Pepper Whiskey Sauce

I'm an Irish American. I consider whiskey to go well with just about anything. This is a simple, spicy, sweet, and sour sauce that brings the flavor of whiskey to a rich gravy. It picks up on a bourbon sauce, a common, modern sauce in the American South.

 **DIFFICULTY**

Flavors: Sweet, sour, salty, rich, green, spicy

Equipment: A small bowl, a whisk (a fork will do in a pinch), a zester (you can also use a serrated knife), and a small pan

Ingredients

- 1 tablespoon vegetable oil
- 1/4 teaspoon ground black pepper
- 1/4 teaspoon ground dried cayenne pepper
- 1 teaspoon ground cumin
- 1/2 small red onion, peeled and minced
- 1 tablespoon minced fresh jalapeño pepper, or chipotle if you want something smokier
- 1 tablespoon minced fresh garlic
- 1 teaspoon minced fresh ginger
- 2 tablespoons lemon juice
- 1 tablespoon tamari
- 1/2 to 1 teaspoon lemon, lime or orange zest, minced (more if you like zest)
- 1 cup good whiskey (Jameson's, Jack Daniels bourbon—what matters is the sweetness of the whiskey)
- Sea salt (start with 1/4 teaspoon and add to taste)

Thickener
- 1/4 cup unsweetened soy milk
- 1 to 2 teaspoons arrowroot powder (more for a thicker, gravy-like sauce, less for something thinner)

Optional: You can also go hotter with this dish with habañero peppers if that's your thing!

Instructions

Begin by preparing your ingredients. Add the oil to the pan and heat. Add your dry herbs and sauté for 1 minute. Add the onion and sauté for 3 minutes. Decrease the heat to medium-high and add the garlic and ginger and sauté for 2 minutes. Add the lemon juice, tamari, and zest and deglaze the pan for 2 minutes. Add the whiskey. Bring the whiskey and the rest to a light boil. Lower the heat and boil lightly, and reduce by 1/2 (this should take about 15 minutes).

In the meantime, whisk the soy milk and the arrowroot powder until the arrowroot is dissolved and set aside. When the sauce has reduced, remove from heat and whisk in the arrowroot mixture. Stir until the sauce thickens. Taste and add salt as necessary.

Plate this sauce by drizzling it over the entrée with a tablespoon. Take a tablespoon of sauce, hold it over the entrée, and let the sauce drip out. A few tablespoons of

sauce will suffice for each serving (this makes 2 heaping servings of sauce or 4 more sparing ones).

Going further

This recipe easily doubles for dinner parties. You'll probably want to use this sauce primarily for accenting a cooked plate (typically seitan or tofu, but it also goes well with sturdy green vegetables like broccoli). Add a little hot pepper to increase the flavor. Where does the "green" flavor come from in this dish? From the citrus zest. The zest of citrus fruits tends to add a slightly bitter flavor to any dish. In part, that's why zest is a common ingredient in many sauces. It adds a green flavor without adding a green color.

The horseradish really brings out the contrast. You could always use a little pomegranate juice and some raisins instead. You could use cranberries and a little extra agave nectar. Add a little minced cilantro to the finished dish for a complete set of flavors.

Porcini Mushroom
& Red Wine Gravy

This is a wonderful, rich gravy with a lot deep flavors. It goes well with other rich-tasting dishes, and it's a beautiful, shiny scarlet-brown on the plate.

 **DIFFICULTY**

Flavors: Rich, salty, sour, savory, sweet

Equipment: A small bowl, a larger bowl, a sharp knife, and a sauté pan capable of holding 4 cups liquid

Note: You will probably have to get the porcinis from your HFS.

Ingredients

- ▶ 1 tablespoon vegetable oil for sautéing, plus an additional 1 tablespoon for roux
- ▶ 1 tablespoon whole wheat flour
- ▶ 1 1/2 cups vegetable stock (or, if you don't have stock, use the soaking water for the porcinis)
- ▶ 1/4 cup dried porcini mushrooms
- ▶ 1/2 cup minced shallots (use vidalia onion if you can't find shallots)
- ▶ 1/4 cup red wine
- ▶ Sea salt (start with 1/4 teaspoon and add more to taste, your gravy should be slightly salty)

Optional: If you want to add garlic or other dry herbs, add them as part of the sauté process. For lighter, herbier gravies, add 1/2 teaspoon tarragon and savory; 1/4 teaspoon cumin and black pepper are better for darker, bolder gravies. For a stronger wine taste, increase the red wine to 1/2 cup.

Instructions

Begin by preparing your ingredients. Reconstitute the mushrooms as per the directions on the package. In the absence of directions, add 1 cup boiling water to the porcinis in a small bowl and soak for 20 minutes. Drain the porcinis when they are reconstituted. If you have stock, you can discard the soaking water. If you don't have it, use the soaking water from the porcinis and 1/2 cup water.

Once the mushrooms and shallots are ready, bring a tablespoon of oil to heat on high in your pan. Add 1/4 teaspoon sea salt to the pan. Add the shallots and sauté for 2 minutes. Decrease the heat to medium-high and add the mushrooms and sauté for another 2 minutes, until the bottom of the pan starts to brown lightly, and then sauté for another 2 minutes. Remove the pan from heat. Add the shallots and mushrooms to a small bowl. Return the pan to heat and deglaze the pan with the red wine. When the wine has reduced by at least half (this should take 2 to 3 minutes and the pan will be getting dry again), pour the remaining wine (the reduction) into the bowl and remove your pan from heat. Add the stock to the bowl, and blend thoroughly with your hand blender.

Next, return your pan to heat, add the second tablespoon of oil, let it warm for a minute, and then slowly add the flour, carefully whisking it in to the oil to avoid clumps. Prepare a basic roux (see the instructions, page 56) and cook the oil for 2 minutes. If you want a darker gravy, brown the roux by cooking it longer in the oil.

When your roux has formed, slowly pour in your blended stock (stirring constantly) until the flour has thickened and you have a nice, rich gravy. Simmer for another 10 minutes on medium-low or until the gravy is the thickness you like. Pour into a warmed gravy boat if you have one (a larger warmed ramekin will do if that's what you have) and serve promptly. No one likes cold gravy!

Going further

I've recommended porcini, but you could always use other mushrooms for this dish. If you use fresh mushrooms, sauté them thoroughly. Other dried mushrooms—morels, chanterelles, black trumpets, etc.—also do well in gravies, but not every mushroom does. If you want to use an exotic mushroom you've never heard of, be sure to check the recommended preparation for that mushroom. But what if I don't like mushrooms? Well, this recipe isn't for you: try the Red Lentil, Red Onion, and Red Wine Gravy (page 74) instead!

Maple Mustard Sauce

A New England–inspired sauce, this goes well with tofu and seitan. This sauce is really intended to be more of a glaze, but it also makes a good dip for raw veggies.

 **DIFFICULTY**

Flavors: Sweet, sour, salty, savory

Equipment: A small bowl and a whisk

Ingredients

- 2 tablespoons tamari
- 4 tablespoons prepared brown mustard
- 2 tablespoons maple syrup
- 1/4 teaspoon ground cumin
- Dash of liquid smoke
- Sea salt
- Small pinch of ground black pepper

Optional: Double the recipe to use as a sauce, glaze for seitan. Quadruple the recipe and add 4 tablespoons water to cut the thickness a little to use as a raw vegetable dip. Add 1/4 teaspoon rubbed dill if you like.

Instructions

Add your ingredients to the small bowl and whisk. Taste and add more salt or pepper as required. You're done.

Going further

This is a simple sauce that's good for a variety of uses. Build on the simple flavors with garlic, or onions, cilantro, horseradish, or any number of ingredients to round out the flavor set.

Simple Mornay Sauce

This is a simple and quick sauce that doubles as a quick gravy for those times when you want something creamy and yummy. Miso gravy really doesn't do this sauce justice. It's also not really a mornay sauce, except insofar as both miso and nutritional yeast add a fermented flavor that's provided by dairy cheese in a traditional mornay. But, then again, this sauce really isn't a velouté or an alfredo, either, and not even really a "white sauce" insofar as it's not particularly white (it's a nice light tan). Whatever you want to call it, it tastes great, is really simple and it goes well with savory flavors, green vegetables, broccoli, pasta and a number of other foods. You can add black pepper, capers (for a simple picatta), and any other flavors you like!

 **DIFFICULTY**

Flavors: Sweet, sour, salty, rich, fermented

Equipment: A small bowl, a whisk (a fork will do), and a pan capable of holding 2 cups liquid

Ingredients

- ▶ 1 tablespoon white miso
- ▶ 1 cup water
- ▶ 2 tablespoons nutritional yeast
- ▶ 1 teaspoon lemon juice
- ▶ 1 tablespoon cold water
- ▶ 2 to 3 teaspoons arrowroot powder (Use 2 teaspoons for a thinner sauce, 3 for more of a gravy consistency)
- ▶ Sea salt (add to taste if the miso isn't salty enough for you)

Instructions

Bring the water to a boil on high heat. Reduce to low. Add the miso, nutritional yeast, and lemon juice and stir until dissolved. Whisk the arrowroot and cold water together until dissolved and add the mixture to the pan. Stir until thick (should be less than a minute). Taste and add salt as necessary.

Going further

This is a simple and light sauce for those moments when you want something quick. There are more complicated white sauce recipes later in this chapter, but there will always be times when you want something nice that only takes a few minutes and doesn't involve a lot of chopping.

Getting Past the Recipes:
Dressings, Sauces & Gravies

Sauces and dressings are prominent in many cuisines. They both add high points of flavor and color to a dish. Pasta is pretty bland-looking by itself, but a little tomato sauce makes it a beautiful and flavorful red, while pesto makes it lively, rich, and green. Dressings and sauces both rely on multiple flavors, both require body, etc. But what's the real difference here? There are some things that are important about dressings and sauces in terms of food chemistry, and those basic differences in chemistry inform what makes a good dressing and what makes a good sauce—not that these things are mutually exclusive.

Traditionally, dressings tended to be a cold preservative addition to a dish. In terms of their presentation, they tend to be muted, a visual undertone to otherwise brightly colored main ingredients—think salad greens, tomatoes, etc. In terms of their flavor, they vary from mild to pronounced, but they typically complement sweet and green flavors with sour, fatty, and salty flavors (although this varies quite a bit). In terms of its chemistry, a dressing needs a reasonable amount of body and cling (hence the oil) so that it will cling to the ingredients. Finally, a dressing typically includes ingredients like lemon juice, garlic, salt, and other antibacterial, anti-oxidizing ingredients to help the food stay fresh for a few days (refrigeration still isn't worldwide and is only a few decades old even in North America).

In contrast, sauces tended to be a colorful or flavorful addition to a canvas that lacks color and flavor (ever wonder why chicken dishes almost always have sauces?). In terms of their presentation, they tend to be brightly colorful, and the best sauces have a visual texture (e.g., white sauces are typically creamy, and coulis tend to be rougher, while the best sauces all tend to be shiny and inviting). Although, again, it varies, sauces tend to be more immediate in their use. Sauces, such as béchamel, are precise in how they are prepared and used traditionally because sauces don't hold together as easily or as long as dressings do. They also tend to be more precise in their ingredients and in the measurements. Flavor-wise, a sauce tends to add a couple of strong high notes (a strong sweet flavor, a strong sour flavor, a strong spicy flavor, etc.) to a blank, savory-flavored canvas on a cooked plate. Because sauces are typically heated (although this also varies greatly), you have to be slightly more careful about the emulsifiers (the ingredients that hold the other ingredients together). So, a little mustard is typically fine as an emulsifier for a vinaigrette, but many sauces need flour, arrowroot, or stronger emulsifiers in order to hold their body and provide the right mouth feel when they're cooked.

Looked at properly, it's not entirely clear where pesto fits into this continuum (sauce or dressing?), but I don't make the rules. Having said that, it's worth noting that many of the condiments that cultures outside of the United States, France and other highly "refined" cuisines defy easy categorization. In any case, there has also been a serious revolution in saucing in the last thirty years of cooking or so. The old, heavy white sauces of French cuisine (easily distinguished from vinaigrette and other dressings) have been replaced by fresher, more dynamic and more flavorful sauces that cut out the dairy and flour in favor of fruits, vegetables, and herbs that can provide lighter, brighter, and healthier alternatives. So, although it's an increasingly minor semantic distinction between what's a sauce and what's a dressing—and what's a foam, what's a mousse, what's a glaze, what's a coulis, etc. Nevertheless, some important considerations remain in terms of chemistry. If you plan to keep food for a couple of days with primarily cold ingredients, make sure there's a combination of oil, salt, acid (e.g., lemon juice) and antibacterial agents (e.g., garlic, onions) in your sauce or dressing. If you plan to serve the sauce right away, a bold and beautiful addition to a cooked plate, make sure that you have the right emulsifiers in your dressing or sauce.

Chapter 4:
Side Dishes or Plate Partners?

This chapter addresses what everyone (vegan or otherwise) loves deep down in their herbivorous souls: complex carbohydrates, flavorful greens, and all the other vegetables that make a meal complete by building your plate with simple side dishes.

When I was a kid, we ate "side dishes." They came out of a can or out of the package and were usually corn or green beans or rolls and sliced bread. The nonhuman animal that lost its life to be my "dinner" sat in the center of the plate in a tragic, hierarchical, and unnecessary ritual. It was also pretty flavorless. No offense to my brothers and sisters who believe boiling is the best way to prepare all foods, but Irish-American culture isn't really well known for its culinary achievements.

As a vegan, I feel it's my duty to speak up: it's wrong to call them side dishes. Can kale help it if it's wonderful all by itself with a little sea salt and garlic? And what about roasted potatoes and onions? Enough said. Furthermore, The Simpsons has lied to you; salad is an awesome way to win friends and influence people. In fact, salad is often a critical component of what many people consider to be a full meal. And yet, many mainstream restaurants insist on serving you iceberg lettuce with some gross wilted stuff that looks like it crawled out of the back of the crisper. Is it a conspiracy? And of course, everyone is entitled to enjoy a cornucopia of starchy goodness that includes rices, quinoas, wheats, squashes, and delightful dough pockets that include calzones, runzas, burekas, strombolis, and more.

Recipes begin with simple overviews of how to prepare basic salads, beans, cooked vegetables, grains, and doughs, going on to show how to use them in slightly more complicated side dishes. If you want to learn how to get that wonderful healthy and satisfied feeling that comes from low-glycemic-index carbs, or if you're not sure how to add more vegetables to your diet by tossing together a quick salad for hot summer months, this chapter will win your heart!

Roasted Asparagus

The original finger food, roasted asparagus is simple, delicious, and elegant. It makes a great side dish for just about any meal.

 **DIFFICULTY**

Flavors: Green, salty, spicy, sour, rich

Equipment: A roasting pan, a small dish, and a whisk (a fork will do)

Ingredients

- 12 stalks asparagus (about pencil-sized)
- 1 tablespoon extra virgin olive oil
- 1/4 teaspoon black pepper
- 1/2 teaspoon lemon juice
- Dash of liquid smoke
- 1/4 teaspoon sea salt

Optional: 1 tablespoon nutritional yeast. You can replace the fine sea salt with a little coarse sea salt if you want a richer flavor.

Instructions

Preheat your oven on broil. Whisk together the oil, lemon, sea salt, smoke, and herbs. Add the asparagus to the pan and dress. Toss to ensure the stalks are well coated. Broil the asparagus for 4 to 6 minutes on the middle oven rack, turn and broil for another 6 minutes or until the asparagus is just staring to brown. Don't overcook. Remove from the pan and plate immediately. Taste and add salt as necessary. Plate with tongs and sprinkle with nutritional yeast or aioli. This is a side dish for 2. If you want to serve 4, double it.

Going further

This is a great and well-rounded side as is, but you can use it as a basic technique for roasting other vegetables. Add a dollop of Tarragon Aioli (page 64) to each serving for a little extra panache, color, and flavor.

Arugula, Artichoke & Fig Salad

Arugula (also known as rocket) is a great, peppery green. It adds flavor and color to this simple but full-flavored salad.

 **DIFFICULTY**

Flavors: Green, sour, rich, sweet, salty

Equipment: A large bowl, a small bowl, and a whisk (a fork will do)

Optional: If you don't like figs, you could also use dried red currants to replace the figs in this recipe (use 1/4 cup).

Ingredients

- 4 cups packed baby arugula
- 1 cup artichoke hearts, thoroughly rinsed and chopped (preferably jarred rather than canned)
- 6 dried calimyrna figs, stemmed and finely chopped

  Dressing
- 1 tablespoon extra virgin olive oil
- 1 teaspoon lemon juice
- 1/4 teaspoon black pepper
- 1/4 teaspoon sea salt

Instructions

Begin by preparing your ingredients. Add your dressing ingredients to the small bowl and whisk. Add your other ingredients to the large bowl, dress, and toss until well-combined. Taste and add salt as needed. Plate with tongs. This salad serves 2 comfortably. Double it for 4.

Going further

Preparing artichoke hearts from scratch is a real pain and requires good knife skills, but if you're eager to try it, God bless you and go for it. Otherwise, this is a very nice, simple salad with three main ingredients that taste great all by themselves and even better tossed together. It goes well by itself, but even better as a warmer or a side to a strong savory flavor.

Smoky Honeydew Melon Wedges

This is kind of a strange recipe, but if you've ever had honeydew and prosciutto, you'll get where it's going. This recipe adds a little fat, salt, and savory flavor to sweet, refreshing bits of honeydew.

 **DIFFICULTY**

Flavors: Rich, salty, sweet, savory

Equipment: A small bowl, a medium size bowl, and a roasting pan

Ingredients

- 2 cups honeydew melon, chopped into 1-inch cubes
- 1 teaspoon extra virgin oil
- Dash of liquid smoke
- Sea salt (1/4 teaspoon should do, but add more if you like it salty)

Instructions

Add the oil, salt, and liquid smoke to the small bowl and mix with a clean finger. Add the honeydew to the large bowl, dress and toss to combine. Let stand for about 5 minutes, and plate with tongs. These make a great *amuse bouche*, a great hors d'oeuvre, and a simple, cleansing appetizer. Toss these with some mixed greens for a nice salad.

The Basic Garden Veggie

Like the Caesar, the garden veggie is ubiquitous in American cuisines, but it's often made with iceberg lettuce, which lacks both flavor and nutrition. This recipe recommends romaine or just about any other leafy green instead. Complete with croûtons, this is a big salad that serves 4. Cut the recipe in half if it's just for 2 as a starter for a main course.

 **DIFFICULTY**

Flavors: Green, sweet, sour, rich, salty

Equipment: Two small bowls, a large bowl, a whisk (a fork will do), a baking sheet, and a pair of tongs

Ingredients

▶ 1 head of romaine lettuce, cored and leaves torn into bite-sized pieces
▶ 6 plum tomatoes, seeded, cored, and medium-diced (or 24 grape tomatoes, or 3 medium tomatoes)
▶ 1 red onion, peeled and finely chopped
▶ 2 carrots, trimmed and shredded (about 1/2 cup packed, shredded carrot)

Plus 1 additional cup vegetables of your choice

▶ 2 stalks celery, trimmed and diced;
▶ 1/2 small cucumber, seeded and thinly sliced in half rounds (skinned if you prefer);
▶ add 12 cremini mushrooms, stemmed and thin-sliced (preferably sautéed with garlic);
▶ for a hipper, more nutritious, and more colorful salad, add 1/2 cup raw beets, shredded, and 1/2 cup peeled and shredded raw daikon

Optional: You can substitute mesclun or spring mix if you prefer. If you substitute Boston, green, or red lettuce, you may need up to 2 heads to get a total of about 4 cups packed greens.

Croûtons

▶ 2 slices of whole wheat bread, or about 1 cup cubed bread if you use a baguette
▶ 1 tablespoon olive oil
▶ 1/2 teaspoon thyme
▶ 1/2 teaspoon basil
▶ 1/2 teaspoon oregano

Dressing

▶ 2 batches Simple Vinaigrette (page 48)
▶ 1 tablespoon minced fresh garlic

Optional: Instead of the vinaigrette, use the Caesar Dressing (page 60). Add 1 tablespoon nutritional yeast for extra flavor, nutrition, and body. Add 1 to 2 tablespoons Tarragon Aioli (page 64) to the vinaigrette and whisk thoroughly for something creamier. Add a tablespoon of pomegranate juice and a teaspoon of agave nectar. Don't be afraid to customize the dressing in a way that suits you. If you like, make a larger batch of vinaigrette and then experiment by mixing 1/2 or 1/4 of the vinaigrette with different flavors.

Instructions

Begin by preparing your ingredients. First, bake your croûtons. Preheat your oven to 350° F. Chop your bred into cubes (about 1-inch cubes will do), and toss with the oil and herbs. Bake on a baking sheet for 20 minutes or until the bread is thoroughly dried and toasted nice and brown. Add your salad ingredients to the large bowl. Whisk together the salad dressing to the small bowl. Add the dressing to the salad and toss to combine. If you prefer, add half of the dressing, taste, and add more as you like. Add the croûtons to the top and serve with tongs. This salad comfortably serves 4 as a side dish.

Going further

Everyone likes their salad a little bit different. Add some minced hot pepper or red pepper flakes to your dressing for extra heat. Add a little cilantro for some stronger green flavor. Replace the apple cider vinegar with lemon juice or with orange juice for something more citrusy. Grill your greens for some extra flavor. A garden salad is a great way to add a variety of fresh vegetables to your diet. Eat it the way you like it best!

Caesar Salad

A simple classic. There are more in-depth comments in the Caesar Dressing recipe (page 60).

Flavors: Green, sour, rich, sweet, savory, salty

Equipment: A whisk, fork or hand blender, a large bowl, and a couple of small bowls

Ingredients

- ▶ 1 batch Caesar Dressing (page 60)
- ▶ 1 medium-sized head romaine lettuce or about 4 cups loosely packed, torn leaves
- ▶ 4 plum tomatoes, chopped
- ▶ 1 red onion, chopped

Instructions

Begin by preparing your ingredients. Whisk your dressing in the small bowl. Cut off the bottom part of the core of your romaine and fan out the leaves. The yellow parts of the inner core of the romaine are the most bitter, and if you don't like these, discard. Tear the remaining leaves with your hands into bite-sized pieces and add to the bowl. Add your chopped tomatoes and onions. Dress and then mix to combine. Serve with tongs. This is a good-sized salad for 2 and will serve smaller portions to 4.

Going further

You could always grill your greens or add other vegetables (e.g., a little shredded carrot, some black kale chiffonade) to add color, texture, flavor, or nutrition, but this is a great salad as is. Add some homemade croûtons if you like (see The Basic Garden Veggie, page 86).

Clementine, Kalamata Olive & Collard Salad

This is a wonderful green salad that draws together a number of flavors and colors. The constituent elements of this dish create a number of flavor layers, which make this salad an experience of both flavor and texture.

 **DIFFICULTY**

Flavors: Rich, salty, sweet, sour, green, savory

Equipment: A small bowl, 2 large bowls, a roasting pan, and tongs if you have them

Ingredients

- ▶ 4 clementines, peeled, seeded, and sectioned
- ▶ 12 kalamata olives, pitted and chopped
- ▶ 1 bunch collard greens (4 to 6 leaves, or about 2 1/2 packed cups), coarsely chopped
- ▶ 2 tablespoons extra virgin olive oil
- ▶ 1 teaspoon lemon juice
- ▶ Dash of liquid smoke
- ▶ 1 teaspoon fresh cilantro, or fresh mint if you prefer, stemmed and minced
- ▶ Coarse sea salt (start with a pinch and add more to taste, the salad should be lightly salty)

Optional: Sprinkle some nutritional yeast into this salad for added flavor and nutrition. Coarse sea salt goes better in this salad than fine, but fine will work.

In place of collards, any sturdy green that roasts well (e.g., kale, black kale) should work in this salad. With a green like spinach or arugula, the texture and flavor won't really be strong enough if you roast. If you want to substitute either of those greens, arugula would probably go better with the other flavors, and you should use about 3 cups packed of baby leaves, no roasting.

Instructions

Begin by preparing your ingredients. Preheat oven to 400° F. Peel and section the clementine just like you would an orange. Remove any seeds and as much of the white pith as you can (or if you have experience sectioning an orange with a knife, go for it). Roll the collard greens up like you're rolling up a newspaper. Remove the stems and the top of the collard greens (about 1 inch above where the leaf starts to brand out, and about 1 inch from the top). Discard the stems. Cut the collards in 1/2-inch slices lengthwise, turn the collards or the board 90 degrees and chop until the collards are coarsely chopped. Pit and finely chop the olives, discarding the pits.

Stem and chop your cilantro or mint. Combine sea salt, olive oil, lemon juice, cilantro, and liquid smoke in a small bowl. Add the collards to the first large bowl. Add the oranges and olives to the second. Pour the dressing over the collard greens and mix until the greens are well coated. Pour the collards out on to the roasting pan and when the oven is fully heated, roast on the top over rack for about 5 to 8 minutes, or until the collards start to brown slightly. When ready, remove the collards from the oven and return to the first large bowl.

Let them stand for 5 minutes or until cool. Add the clementine and olives to the collards. Add the dressing, stir until all the ingredients are coated, and plate with tongs. This salad makes a good light lunch for 2 and serves 4 regular-sized portions. This salad goes well as an opener, a side salad, or a closer.

Going further

This salad goes well with rice or pasta. All of the ingredients are sturdy, which makes it a good salad for potlucks and parties. Add a little sriracha, jalapeño or other spice to add the only missing flavor for this dish. In particular, jalapeño goes well because of its wonderful citrusy flavor. Serve this in miniature pita bread sliced in half for a quick and full-flavored hors d'oeuvre, or a cracker or thin-sliced baguette for quickie canapés.

Carrot Salad with Agave Nectar, Walnuts & Golden Raisins

Simple, sweet, and beautiful, this is a great way to add carrots to your diet if you're not big on plain old sticks and dip.

 **DIFFICULTY**

Flavors: Sweet, sweet, sweet

Equipment: A large bowl, a small bowl, and a grater or mandoline

Ingredients

- ▶ 4 carrots, grated
- ▶ 2 tablespoons agave
- ▶ 1/2 cup golden raisins
- ▶ 1/4 cup walnuts, chopped
- ▶ 1 tablespoon lemon juice
- ▶ Sea salt (start with 1/4 teaspoon and add more to taste, but this salad should be sweet, not salty)

Instructions

Prepare your carrots by first removing the tips, but don't chop. Instead, grate them with a grater (thin) or julienne them using a mandoline (if you have a mandoline, you'll know what this means, but watch out for your fingers!). Add your shredded carrots and raisins to the large bowl. Whisk together the remaining ingredients in the small bowl. Dress the carrots and the raisins. Mix until thoroughly combined and let stand for 30 minutes.

Going further

This is a very simple recipe and is great just the way it is. But if you love to fiddle, add a little mint, a pinch of jalapeño and cilantro, or even chop a couple tablespoons of spinach for a beautiful green look and some additional flavor depth and nutrition. Experiment with blueberries, raspberries, cranberries, elderberries, goji berries, barberries, blackberries, Saskatoon berries, currants, or other fruits for extra color, flavor, nutrition, and texture.

Collard Green Noodles with Garlic,
Ginger & Tahini Sauce

Collard greens have a wonderful bright green flavor that really comes out with a sour, rich dressing. They're also quintessentially American, they look beautiful when served, and they're really, really good for you. If you grew up eating collard greens, this will be a new variation on a vegetable you already know. If you've never had collards, they have a wonderful, almost coffee-like flavor when they're properly prepared.

 **DIFFICULTY**

Flavors: Green, sour, rich

Equipment: A good sharp knife, a cutting board, one large bowl (able to hold 1 quart/1 liter water and one cereal-sized bowl), and a kettle or a pan capable of holding at least 8 cups water

Note: Collard greens may require a visit to your local HFS if you don't live where collards are common, as will tahini and possibly other dressing ingredients. Try to find collard greens with small stems. Otherwise, you'll be doing a lot of chewing.

Ingredients

▶ 8 cups boiling water for soaking the collards (unless you're roasting them), salted
▶ 6 to 8 good-sized leaves of collard greens (about 3 cups tightly packed)
▶ 1 batch Ginger, Garlic, and Tahini Dressing (page 60)
▶ Sea salt

Optional: Liquid smoke and 1 tablespoon olive oil if you roast the collards instead of soaking, and a dash or two of Tabasco, other hot sauce, or a pinch of cayenne for a little spice.

Instructions

Begin by preparing your ingredients. Bring your water to a boil (a kettle is fine for this). Wash the collards thoroughly. Arrange the leaves one on top of the other so that you have a stack of collards. Roll the leaves up tight width-wise like you're rolling up a newspaper. Cut off the stems (about 1 inch above where the leaves start to branch out from the stems) and discard. Chiffonade the collards width-wise in nice, thin strips about 1/8 inch or the size of thicker spaghetti noodles. You can experiment with larger strips if you prefer a wider noodle, but thinner's better for flavor and texture. Once you have sliced the collards, soak them for 10 minutes in a medium-sized bowl of hot, salted water (about a tablespoon of salt will do).

While your collards are soaking, mix the dressing. Whisk the remaining ingredients in the small bowl until you have a smooth, creamy dressing. Once your collard noodles have soaked, they should be a nice, beautiful green. You're ready to plate the dish. Drain the water and rinse them in a colander. Take a fork and twirl the collard greens like you're eating spaghetti. Slide them off the fork onto the plate. Add half of the collards onto each plate. Spoon half of the dressing onto each set of noodles. Add salt to taste. This serves 2 as a larger side dish, but doubles for 4.

Going further

This dish is salty, sour, and has a wonderful green (i.e., bitter) flavor. To add spice, add a couple of dashes of hot sauce to the dressing. To add sweet, instead of soaking the collards, chop them, toss them in a tablespoon of olive oil with a pinch of sea salt, and then oven-roast them at 450° F for about 10 minutes, or until some of them start to brown. A drop of liquid smoke in the dressing will add savory flavor. By roasting the collards with a little oil and smoke, you'll really be adding additional flavor layers that contrast discernibly with the dressing.

Roasted Kale

Roasted kale goes well with just about everything. It's good with potatoes, mushrooms, lentils, and chickpeas. It provides a simple green bed for seitan and tofu. It's highly nutritious, beautiful, and textured. It also tastes great. As vegetables go, there's none more reliable than kale.

 **DIFFICULTY**

Flavors: Green, salty, rich, savory

Equipment: A large bowl, a small bowl, a roasting pan or baking sheet, a whisk (a fork will do), and tongs

Ingredients

- ▶ 4 cups packed kale, stemmed and finely chopped
- ▶ 3 tablespoons olive oil
- ▶ 1 tablespoon lemon juice
- ▶ 1/4 teaspoon ground black pepper
- ▶ 1/4 teaspoon coarse sea salt
- ▶ Dash of liquid smoke

Instructions

Begin by preparing your ingredients. Preheat your oven to 450° F. Wash your kale thoroughly. Cut the stems about 1 inch above where your kale starts to flower out. Discard the stems. Finely chop the leaves and add them to the large bowl. Whisk the remaining ingredients in the small bowl for the dressing, dress your chopped kale with it, and mix thoroughly. Add your kale to the baking sheet and then bake for 10 minutes, or until your kale starts to brown slightly. Remove from the oven, and return the kale to the large bowl. Taste and add salt as necessary. Coarse salt is nice, but fine is fine. Let stand 5 minutes and then plate with tongs.

Going further

Roasted kale really does go well with just about everything. It can stand by itself as a side dish, or mix with virtually any other side dish for a wonderful warm salad. Sprinkle with a little nutritional yeast before plating to add flavor and nutrition. Replace some of the salt with a little tamari for a richer savory flavor, or add some hot pepper for a little heat. Swap the lemon juice for a little orange juice for a slightly sweeter flavor.

Red Bean & Black Rice Salad with
Spinach & Orange Peppers

Beans and rice are the world's great dietary staple and have long been a tradition in American cuisine. This recipe reinvents the classic with some bolder color choices and some more subtle and rich flavors. This is a very nutritious, beautiful, and flavorful salad. Don't let the lengthy preparation time deter you—this recipe doubles and keeps reasonably well. This is a big salad (a good lunch for 2) with plenty for lunch the following day if it's a side or appetizer.

 **DIFFICULTY**

Flavors: Savory, salty, sour

Note: You'll probably have to go to your HFS to get the miso and possibly to an Asian grocery to find the black rice. The rest you should be able to find at your local grocery.

Equipment: Two medium-sized pots, one capable of holding at least 4 cups liquid and the other at least 6 cups, a large bowl, and a small bowl for the dressing (a cereal-sized bowl will do)

Ingredients

▶ 1 batch White Miso and Hazelnut Butter Dressing (page 63)
▶ 2/3 cup uncooked red kidney beans or about 1 1/2 cups canned
▶ 1 cup uncooked forbidden black rice (2 cups cooked)
▶ 2 orange peppers, cored, seeded, and finely chopped
▶ 3 cups packed baby spinach, finely chopped
▶ 1 teaspoon extra virgin olive oil
▶ Sea salt (for the rice and beans, and to taste once the salad has been dressed)

Optional: Black rice is sweeter than brown. If you have to substitute, add a little organic sugar or agave nectar to the dressing—a pinch of sugar or 1/4 teaspoon agave nectar will be fine). Cayenne pepper will add some heat. You can also use canned beans in a pinch to greatly reduce the cook time (just be sure to rinse really well!).

Instructions

For the beans, bring the 3 cups water and the red beans to a slow boil on medium. Cover, decrease the heat to low and simmer for 2 1/2 hours, or until the water has been absorbed (see Preparing your Ingredients on page 9). When done, drain, rinse, and add to the large bowl.

For the black rice, about 45 minutes before the beans are ready, bring 2 cups water to a boil in one pan. Add a pinch of salt and a teaspoon vegetable oil. When the water has come to a boil, add the black rice and stir gently. Bring the contents back to a simmer. Turn down the heat to low. Cover and simmer for 15 to 20 minutes, or until all the water has been absorbed. Fluff with a fork and let stand in a covered pot for about 10 minutes and then add the rice to the salad bowl.

For the vegetables, roughly 20 minutes before the rice and beans are ready, carefully wash your spinach and peppers. Mince the spinach and add to the salad bowl (or if you prefer, just add the leaves to the bowl whole). Chop the peppers into about 1/4-inch dice and add to the bowl.

For the dressing, whisk the remaining ingredients in the small bowl, and then dress the salad ingredients in the large bowl. Toss until well combined. Taste and add sea salt as necessary. Plate with tongs. This salad serves 2 for lunch or smaller portions for 4.

Going further

Feel free to mix up the beans and grains in this salad. Brown rice, quinoa, and millet are satisfying alternatives to the black rice. White kidney beans, black beans, and others make similarly good alternatives. Just be mindful that other grains and beans have different cook times. To add a little green flavor, add a little lime zest to the dressing. To add some heat, add a dash of cayenne pepper or some minced jalapeño.

Roasted Red Potatoes with Chives

Who doesn't like potatoes? This dish roasts red potatoes accented by chives, a classic.

 **DIFFICULTY**

Flavors: Salty, sour, sweet

Equipment: A small bowl, a larger bowl, a baking sheet, tongs, a whisk (a fork will do), and a sharp knife

Ingredients

▶ 4 medium-sized red potatoes
▶ 1 tablespoon olive oil
▶ 1 tablespoon garlic
▶ 1 teaspoon white vinegar
▶ 1/4 teaspoon ground black pepper
▶ 1/4 cup packed fresh chives, minced
▶ Coarse sea salt

Optional: Chives can be hard to find when they're not in season. For a milder flavor, just use the greens of 2 scallions, minced. If you prefer a stronger onion flavor, use both the greens and the whites, but sprinkle them over the potatoes for the last 5 minutes of baking.

Instructions

Begin by preparing your ingredients. Preheat your oven to 350° F. Whisk the garlic, vinegar, oil, black pepper, and a dash of sea salt in the small bowl. Scrub and cut your potatoes into 1/2-inch dice. Put the potatoes in a large bowl, and dress. Put your dressed potatoes onto the baking sheet. Bake for about 30 minutes, or until the potatoes are browned and cooked through. You can tell a potato is cooked when it yields to gentle pressure from a fork. While your potatoes are roasting, mince your chives. When the potatoes are done, remove from the oven and return to your large bowl. Let the potatoes rest and cool for 5 minutes. Sprinkle with your minced chives. Taste and add coarse sea salt as necessary. Toss until well combined and plate.

Going further

This is a simple dish on which you can easily build. Add a little cumin for a more savory taste. Add a little red pepper for heat. Add some mustard for a little more sour and color. Swap the chives for scallions. Add some nutritional yeast for extra flavor and nutrition. This dish isn't particularly sweet, but potatoes are starchy, mostly glucose, and glucose is readily metabolized as sugar. This dish makes an excellent accompaniment to anything with spicy, green, and savory flavors.

Roasted Ginger Garlic Coleslaw

Is it weird to cook coleslaw? I dare to say no. This slaw is just right. It presents an Ethiopian twist to an American classic. Rumor has it that the Ark of the Covenant is kept in Ethiopia. I'm just saying, think about it.

 **DIFFICULTY**

Flavors: Sweet, salty, rich

Equipment: A large bowl, a small bowl, tongs, and a baking sheet or a roasting pan

Ingredients

Slaw
▶ 4 cups bagged coleslaw mix
Or if you want build your slaw from scratch
▶ 3 cups cored and shredded green cabbage
▶ 3/4 cups trimmed and shredded carrot
▶ 1/4 cup peeled and shredded white onion
▶ Coarse sea salt

Dressing
▶ 3 tablespoons extra virgin olive oil
▶ 1 tablespoon lemon juice
▶ 1 tablespoon minced fresh garlic
▶ 2 teaspoons minced fresh ginger
▶ 1/4 teaspoon ground black pepper
▶ 1/4 teaspoon sea salt

Optional: Add 1/4 teaspoon cayenne pepper for a spicier slaw. Add 1/4 teaspoon turmeric to the dressing for a sunny yellow color and 1/2 teaspoon finely ground fenugreek seeds to add that just-right flavor. If you don't have coarse sea salt, you can substitute fine.

Instructions

Begin by preparing your ingredients. Preheat your oven to broil. Whisk together the dressing in the small bowl. Add the slaw mixture to the large bowl. Dress the slaw and toss to combine. Add it to the roasting pan or baking sheet. Roast for 10 to 12 minutes or until the cabbage is starting to brown lightly (or a little more if you like it well browned). Remove from heat and let stand for 2 minutes. Taste and add sea salt as necessary. Plate with tongs.

Going further

This is an uncomplicated dish that pairs best with more complicated flavors. The flavor is simple and straightforward. This dish pairs well with spicy, green, and savory flavors. If you want to get your feet wet with this dish, just use bagged coleslaw mix; but if you want to go further, start shredding your own vegetables. Use purple cabbage instead of green, or purple carrots instead of orange. Add some black kale or collards chiffonade to broaden the color, flavor, and texture. Add a little cayenne or other pepper to add a little spice. I like to add chickpeas to mine, and potatoes are traditional, but this slaw is a good start as is. This makes a large side for 2, or smaller sides for 4.

Carrot & Black Kale Slaw
with Black-Eyed Peas

This is a simple pickled vegetable salad with some black-eyed peas tossed in. It's low-fat and mostly raw. The black kale in this dish is flat and a very dark green, unlike green or Russian kale. It's also called dinosaur or lacinato kale, but you'll be able to tell it from regular kale because it will be much less curly, looking more like collards.

 **DIFFICULTY**

Flavors: Sour, rich, salty, savory, green

Equipment: A small bowl, a larger bowl (preferably with a cover and, if not, some plastic wrap), a whisk (a fork will do), a colander, and a pan capable of holding at least 6 cups water with a tight-fitting lid

Ingredients

- ▶ 2 carrots, trimmed and shredded
- ▶ 1 bunch black kale (6 to 8 leaves or about 3 cups packed), chiffonade
- ▶ 1 medium red onion, thinly sliced
- ▶ 1/2 cup dark raisins
- ▶ 1 batch Simple Slaw Dressing (page 49)

Optional: Switch the red onion for vidalia for a milder onion. Add a fresh granny smith apple, cored and thinly sliced, 2 tablespoons walnuts, 1 teaspoon minced jalapeño, or all three for extra flavor and texture.

Instructions

Begin by preparing your ingredients. Shred the carrots into the larger bowl. Wash and stem the kale about 1 inch up from where the leaves flower out. Discard the stems. Cut the leaves width-wise in narrow strips about 1/4 inch wide. Whisk your dressing in the small bowl and pour over the other ingredients. Add the raisins and the sliced onion. Toss well to coat. Cover and let stand on the counter for a couple of hours until you're finished. Occasionally tossing the ingredients in the dressing will help the marinating process, but it's not absolutely necessary. When ready to serve, taste and add salt. Scoop a bit of slaw with your tongs, shake off the dressing slightly (or let drip dry for several seconds) and then add to the plate or a small bowl.

Going further

This is a beautiful salad with a lot of color, texture, taste, and nutrition. If you don't like raisins, you could slice some dried figs or add some dried cranberries or currants. You can also add a little heat with some minced jalapeño pepper or a dash of cayenne in the dressing. For a salad with more raw ingredients, add some thinly sliced apple instead (use a tart variety, such as granny smith). Add some walnuts to notch up the omega-3s and add a little crunch.

If you can't find black kale, you can also use collards, but this will make for a pretty chewy salad. You might want to roast the collards of soak them in bowling water to wilt them (see Collard Noodles, page 90, for ideas on technique). Or, you could use some shredded purple or savoy cabbage, but the flavor won't be quite the same.

Old-Fashioned Mock Egg Salad

This is a quick and easy-to-prepare alternative to egg salad.

 **DIFFICULTY**

Flavors: Rich, salty, savory

Equipment: A fork, a whisk or preferably a hand blender, a small bowl, a large bowl, and probably some plastic wrap

Note: You'll probably need to go to your HFS to get the nutritional yeast, the Vegenaise if you use it, and the various sea vegetables, gluten flour, etc.

Ingredients

▶ 1 batch Tarragon Aioli (page 64), but replace the tarragon with the following spices:
▶ 1 teaspoon mustard seed, ground
▶ 1/2 teaspoon turmeric
▶ 1/2 teaspoon ground cumin
▶ 1 pound firm tofu, drained and crumbled
▶ 1 small vidalia onion, peeled and minced (about 1/4 cup)
▶ 1/2 teaspoon sea salt

Optional: Add 1/4 cup rehydrated sun-dried tomatoes and about 1 cup minced baby spinach for a well-rounded lunchtime sandwich.

Instructions

Begin by preparing your aioli, adding the dry herbs listed above instead of the tarragon. Next, crumble the tofu with a fork into small pieces. Add the tofu to the large bowl and mix well with the aioli until well blended, cover, and refrigerate for 30 minutes (longer will allow a better mix of flavors). Taste and add salt as necessary.

Going further

This salad makes a good sandwich and a good hors d'oeuvre on crackers or tucked into half of a miniature pita with a little spinach and some sun-dried tomato. Customize your aioli with the herbs and spices you like. I like a little fresh dill in my mock egg salad. Strange but true.

Chipotle Mock Chicken Salad

Chicken salad is an American lunchtime staple. The nutritional yeast ensures a wealth of B vitamins, including B-12. It's also a family favorite and goes well with soup.

 **DIFFICULTY**

Flavors: Rich, salty, savory, green

Equipment: A fork, a whisk or preferably a hand blender, some aluminum foil, probably some plastic wrap, a small bowl, a medium bowl, and a large bowl

Note: You'll probably need to go to your HFS to get the nutritional yeast, the Vegenaise if you use it, and the various sea vegetables, gluten flour, etc.

Ingredients

▶ 1 batch Light Seitan (page 126), finely chopped

▶ 1 batch Tarragon Aioli (page 64)

▶ 1 additional teaspoon lemon juice

▶ 1 teaspoon dried thyme, rubbed

▶ 1 teaspoon dried savory, rubbed

▶ 1 teaspoon dried marjoram, rubbed

▶ 1 teaspoon ground cumin

▶ 1 teaspoon minced chipotle (or 1 tablespoon for a spicier salad)

▶ 1/4 teaspoon ground black pepper

▶ 1 stalk celery, trimmed and finely chopped

▶ 1/4 red onion, peeled and finely chopped

▶ 1/2 teaspoon sea salt

Optional: You can always leave out the chipotle if you don't like your mock chicken salad a little spicy, or swap it for a dash of liquid smoke and 1/4 teaspoon cayenne if you prefer. Add 1 teaspoon agave or maple syrup for a little sweetness, or add some chopped dates, raisins or dry currants to add sweet flavors and a little extra texture.

Instructions

Begin by preparing your ingredients. Prepare, cook, and tent the seitan first, following the basic recipe. When it has cooled to room temperature, prepare the aioli. Add the additional dry herbs listed with the tarragon to the aioli. Mince the celery and onion and add to the aioli after blending it, and stir them in to combine. When the seitan is done, chop it finely and add it to the large bowl. Add the aioli, celery, and onion mixture and stir until everything is well mixed. Cover and re-frigerate for 30 minutes (longer will allow a better mix of their flavors). Taste and add salt as necessary.

Going further

This simple salad is great for lunches, whether on regular whole wheat bread, wrapped in a pita or in a tortilla. Or pick up some miniature pita bread, slice in half, and stuff with various salads as hors d'oeuvres. Customize your aioli with the herbs and spices you like. I like my mock chicken salad on the spicy side, so I'll usually use a couple of teaspoons of chipotle. You can also reuse this aioli for a nice, spicy mayo. For a great mock chicken salad on the spicy side, reduce the Three-Pepper Whiskey Sauce (page 76) to about 1/4 cup before thickening, and then blend that with the aioli without adding any water.

Spicy Peanut & Mango Salad

This is a rich but tangy salad, best in the summer when ripe mangoes are easy to come by. It's inspired by a number of Thai salads. It goes great with a cold beer!

 **DIFFICULTY**

Flavors: Green, sour, rich, sweet, salty

Equipment: A paring knife, a large bowl, a small bowl, and a whisk (a fork will do)

Ingredients

▶ 2 to 3 ripe mangoes, peeled, stoned, and shredded (about 3 cups)
▶ 2 scallions, trimmed and minced
▶ 2 tablespoons chopped/crushed peanuts
▶ 1 tablespoon packed fresh mint, stemmed and minced
▶ 1 tablespoon packed fresh cilantro, stemmed and minced
▶ 1 tablespoon unsweetened peanut butter (sweetened is fine, but you may find the salad a little sweet)
▶ 1 teaspoon lime juice
▶ 1 to 2 teaspoons minced chipotle (use a full tablespoon for a spicier salad)
▶ 1 teaspoon green nori flakes
▶ 1 teaspoon minced fresh garlic
▶ 1/2 teaspoon minced fresh ginger
▶ 1/4 teaspoon sea salt

Optional: Replace the nori with some crumbled and reconstituted wakame for more of a sea flavor. Add 1 teaspoon minced lemongrass if it's in season and you can get it fresh. Add a pinch of sugar or a little agave nectar if you find your mangoes very sour (and you consider this a bad thing).

Instructions

Begin by preparing your ingredients. Add the scallion, mango, and sea salt to the large bowl. Let them stand for about 15 minutes. The mango will sweat as the salt begins to cook it very slightly, and you should have a little juice form. Pour off the resulting mango juice into the small bowl. Whisk the remaining ingredients in the small bowl with the juice. Dress the scallions and mango with it, tossing gently until well coated. Let stand or refrigerate for 20 minutes. Taste and add salt if necessary. Plate with tongs, and sprinkle with 1 tablespoon chopped peanuts for each serving. This makes a light side for 2. Double it for 4.

Going further

This is a great salad with lots of pronounced flavors. You could always add some mixed salad greens or spinach to widen out the nutritional profile, or add some julienned red pepper to add some color contrast. Mince some Light Seitan (page 126), if you have a little extra, for some additional texture and flavor.

Chickpea & Wakame Mock Tuna Salad

This is a more metaphorical interpretation of tuna salad, but it's easy to make and very flavorful. The wakame adds some wonderful salty green flavor and a sea taste. These also provide a great basis for mock tuna melts.

 **DIFFICULTY**

Flavors: Rich, salty, savory, green

Equipment: A pan capable of holding 4 cups liquid, a sharp knife, a fork, a whisk or preferably a hand blender, a small bowl, a large bowl, and probably some plastic wrap

Note: You'll probably need to go to your HFS to get the nutritional yeast, the Vegenaise if you use it, and the various sea vegetables, etc.

Ingredients

▶ 3 cups water
▶ 1 cup dried chickpeas, cooked and finely chopped (or about 2 1/2 cups canned chickpeas, rinsed and finely chopped)
▶ 2 tablespoons crumbled wakame
▶ 1 batch Tarragon Aioli (page 64), replacing the tarragon with 1 tablespoon nori flakes
▶ 1 tablespoon extra virgin olive oil
▶ 1/4 teaspoon sea salt

Optional: Wakame grown in the Atlantic is called alaria. You can also substitute kelp flakes if that's what you have, but use only about 1 tablespoon.

Instructions

Begin by preparing your ingredients. Start with the chickpeas. Bring the chickpeas and the water to a slow boil on medium heat, cover, decrease the heat to low, and simmer until the chickpeas are cooked through (this should take about 2 1/2 hours, but see the notes on beans in Preparing Your Ingredients, page 9).

When the chickpeas are cooked, you should have a little water left over. If you don't, add 1/4 cup, bring it to a simmer, add the wakame and let the chickpeas stand for 20 minutes until all the water has been absorbed or the wakame has been rehydrated. Simmer for a few minutes with the lid off stirring constantly if you need to boil off any excess water.

While your wakame is rehydrating, prepare your aioli following the basic recipe and add the extra olive oil before blending.

When the chickpeas and wakame are ready, drain and pulse blend them with the hand blender (or just chop finely if you prefer a little more texture,). Add the chickpea mixture to the large bowl and dress them with the aioli. Mix until combined, cover and refrigerate for 30 minutes (longer will allow a better mix of their flavors). Taste and add salt as necessary.

Going further

This salad is rich in texture and flavor. It makes for great sandwiches all by itself, but add 2 to 3 tablespoons of the Jalapeño Cheeze Sauce (page 68) over the mock tuna on toast (use half of the soy milk called for and do not reduce for a thicker sauce) and bake for spicy mock tuna melts.

Roasted Midwestern Succotash

Succotash is an American classic of beans and corn, beautiful and simple. Succotash has lots of variations, but traditionally, it's made with lima beans and corn, sometimes with red peppers, onions, or other vegetables. Sometimes it's boiled, and sometimes it's fried. But in the Midwest when I was growing up, it was always made with green beans and corn—usually straight from the can, but that's a terrible thing to do to these wonderful vegetables. This recipe roasts the corn in the husks, then roasts the corn with the beans.

 **DIFFICULTY**

Flavors: Sweet, salty, sour, rich

Equipment: A paring knife, a baking sheet, a small bowl, a large bowl, a pan capable of holding 8 cups liquid, and tongs

Ingredients

- ▶ 1 tablespoon vegetable oil (if you're roasting the corn)
- ▶ 3 ears corn (or about 2 cups kernels if you use canned or frozen)
- ▶ 2 cups green beans, trimmed and cut into 1/2-inch pieces
- ▶ 1 medium red onion, peeled and thinly sliced (about 1 cup onion)
- ▶ Coarse sea salt (coarse is preferred, but you can substitute fine sea salt)

Dressing
- ▶ 2 tablespoons extra virgin olive oil
- ▶ 2 tablespoons minced fresh garlic
- ▶ 2 teaspoons lemon juice
- ▶ 1/4 teaspoon ground black pepper
- ▶ Dash of liquid smoke
- ▶ 1/4 teaspoon fine sea salt.

Optional: Add 1/4 teaspoon cayenne pepper for a little additional spice.

Instructions

Begin by preparing your ingredients. Preheat your oven to 350° F. Pull the husks down to the end of the corn (but don't remove). Carefully remove the silk. Give the corn a good wash. Brush or rub the kernels with vegetable oil. Wrap each ear back up in its husk. Ensure that the ear is well wrapped with the husk. Once the oven is heated, put the husked corn in on an oiled baking sheet. Roast for 30 minutes or until the corn is done (varies by oven).

When the corn is done, pare off the kernels with a knife into a medium-sized bowl. Next, trim and cut your green beans. Peel and mince your onions. Add them all to the large bowl, and toss with the dressing. Add mixture to the roasting pan and roast for 10 minutes, or until the green beans are soft and starting to brown slightly. Remove from heat, and return to the large bowl. Taste and add coarse sea salt as necessary. Plate with tongs. This side dish serves 2 well, double it for 4.

Going further

As I mentioned, succotash has a lot of variations. To shave off some time, you can always use rinsed frozen or canned corn (making sure to let the frozen corn thaw properly). Add some diced red bell pepper, some scallions, a little agave nectar, some cayenne pepper, celery, whatever you like! Succotash is a basic vegetable dish that brings some simple color and flavor to the plate.

Brown Rice Risotto with Spinach & Sun-Dried Tomatoes

Risotto is a wonderful side dish. It's chewy, creamy, and easy to make (but very difficult to get just right). Like couscous and pilaf, it picks up flavor and color from its additional ingredients. But risotto is higher-maintenance than pilaf or couscous, and generally assumes you'll be spending time in the kitchen anyway! Traditionally, risotto is made with specific rices, but this recipe breaks all the codes of tradition by using short-grain brown rice instead.

 **DIFFICULTY**

Flavors: Sweet, salty, sour, rich

Equipment: A small bowl, 2 pans with tight-fitting lids capable of holding 4 cups liquid each, a whisk (a fork will do), and tongs

Ingredients

- ▶ 1 tablespoon extra virgin olive oil
- ▶ 1/4 teaspoon sea salt
- ▶ 1 tablespoon minced fresh garlic
- ▶ 1/2 teaspoon dried basil, rubbed
- ▶ 1/2 teaspoon dried oregano, rubbed
- ▶ 1/2 teaspoon dried marjoram, rubbed
- ▶ 1/2 teaspoon ground black pepper
- ▶ 1 cup short-grain brown rice
- ▶ 2 1/2 cups vegetable stock, simmered and added in 1/2-cup increments
- ▶ 1 tablespoon vegetable oil
- ▶ 1/4 cup vegan white wine

Dressing

- ▶ 2 tablespoons nutritional yeast
- ▶ 1 cup packed baby spinach, minced
- ▶ 1/3 cup sun-dried tomatoes, rehydrated and finely chopped
- ▶ Coarse sea salt

Optional: Add 1 tablespoon nutritional yeast and 1 tablespoon unsweetened soy milk at the end for a little extra flavor, nutrition, and creaminess, although this makes for a slightly runnier risotto better served in a bowl. If necessary, use 1/2 cup boiling water to rehydrate the tomatoes.

Instructions

Begin by preparing your ingredients. Bring the oil to heat on high. Bring your stock to a low simmer in the other pan. When it's ready, add the rice, the dry herbs, 1/4 teaspoon sea salt, and the garlic to the sauté pan and sauté for about 2 to 3 minutes or until the rice begins to brown very slightly. Then, add the white wine and let the rice absorb the wine (should take about 5 minutes). Add the nutritional yeast and sauté for 2 minutes. Add the first 1/2 cup of stock, cover, and simmer for about 15 minutes—do not stir. Add the second 1/2 cup and cover and simmer for another 15 minutes—again, do not stir. Add the third 1/2 cup of stock and cover and simmer for another 15 minutes—again, do not stir. At this point, your rice should be getting close to done.

Rehydrate your sun-dried tomatoes in the small bowl if using dried. After 20 minutes, drain and mince the tomatoes. In the last fifteen minutes, add your

remaining ingredients to the other small bowl. At the 45-minute mark, taste a small bite of your rice. If the rice is chewy but only slightly undercooked, add the fourth 1/2 cup of stock and your dressing, stir, and simmer for another 15 minutes, add your spinach and tomatoes, and simmer another 5 minutes. However, when you taste it at the 45-minute mark, if the rice is seriously undercooked, add the fourth 1/2 cup of stock and cook for another 15 minutes. Then taste again, and if it's still slightly undercooked add the fifth 1/2 cup of stock and your dressing, stir, and simmer for another 15 minutes. Add the spinach and tomatoes and simmer another five minutes. When the rice is fully cooked and softly chewy, add the nutritional yeast and/or the soy milk if you're using them. Taste and add salt as necessary. Cover and let stand 5 minutes to cool.

Plating: risotto is often a dish unto itself, but if you're preparing it as a side, it should be treated in a manner befitting its dignity and the amount of time and effort you invested in preparing it. As with pilaf, if you really want to get fancy, fill a small ramekin with your risotto and turn it over onto the plate. Flatten the risotto out slightly with a fork, add your main ingredient on top, and then top that with some microgreens.

Going further

This is a recipe that it may take you a few tries to get right. Risotto is deceptively complicated and requires experience to prepare correctly and predictably well. But when it's properly prepared, risotto is a culinary marvel. Its texture, color, flavor, smell, and mouth feel are all simply spectacular, and that only comes with practice. Once you've got the hang of basic risotto, you can be more creative with the additional accompanying flavors. Beans, nuts, seitan, fruits, and mushrooms are all excellent additions to risotto. These are traditionally cooked with the rice rather than added at the end, but that's more complicated and takes much more experience knowing when to add what.

Spicy, Smoky Quinoa
with Collard Greens

Quinoa is a traditional grain of the Southwest. Texture-wise, it's a bit like couscous but a little heavier. It also comes in a variety of colors: white, red, and blue are common. Unlike many other grains, quinoa is a complete protein. Just make sure to give it a good rinse first. This dish adds a bold green flavor and color with the collard greens and liquid smoke. A little bitter, a little spicy, this recipe reminds me fondly of my young adulthood.

 **DIFFICULTY**

Flavors: Sweet, salty, sour, spicy, rich

Equipment: A small bowl, a medium bowl, a large bowl, a pot with a tight-fitting lid capable of holding 8 cups liquid, a whisk (a fork will do), and tongs

Ingredients

- ▶ 2 cups water
- ▶ 1 cup quinoa
- ▶ 4 to 6 leaves of collard greens (about 2 cups stemmed and packed), finely chopped
- ▶ 1/4 teaspoon sea salt

Dressing

- ▶ 2 tablespoons extra virgin olive oil
- ▶ 1 tablespoon minced fresh garlic
- ▶ 2 teaspoons lemon juice
- ▶ 1 teaspoon onion powder
- ▶ 1 teaspoon ground cumin
- ▶ 1/2 teaspoon ground coriander
- ▶ 1/4 teaspoon ground cayenne pepper
- ▶ 1/4 teaspoon ground black pepper
- ▶ 2 dashes liquid smoke
- ▶ Sea salt (to taste)

Optional: 1/2 teaspoon fresh lemon zest, minced/grated. Or add 1/2 teaspoon fresh ginger minced. Add a little minced fresh cilantro if you like. Or add 1 to 2 tablespoons of Sour Cream (page 65) if you have extras and you want a creamier, more risotto-like side dish.

Instructions

Begin by preparing your ingredients. Stem your collards about 1 inch above where the leaves start to flower out and discard the stems. If you don't like the stems that remain in the leaves, fold each leaf in half so that the stem is exposed on the side like a spine, and slice it out with your knife. Then, roll the leaves up like a newspaper width-wise so that you have a long roll. Chiffonade in 1/4-inch slices widthwise. Turn the board or the collards 90 degrees and slice again. Or, you can throw your collards in a food processor and pulse chop for a minute if you prefer.

Rinse your quinoa thoroughly. Bring your water to a boil. Add 1/4 teaspoon sea salt and your quinoa, stir, cover, decrease the heat to low, and simmer for about 20 minutes. In the meantime, whisk together the dressing ingredients and set aside. At the 20-minute mark, add the collards stir to combine. Simmer for another 5 to 10 minutes or until all the liquid has been absorbed. Remove from heat, and dress the collards and quinoa with the dressing. Cover, and let stand another 5 minutes. Taste and add salt as necessary. Plate with tongs. This dish makes a larger side dish for 2 and serves 4 as a smaller side.

Going further

Quinoa has a slightly nutty flavor and a fluffy texture. It goes well as a side dish, but it also makes a nice porridge. If you don't like collards, mushrooms, onions, sun-dried tomatoes, raisins, arugula and other greens complement its texture and flavor well. Quinoa also presents very exotically if you use the red or blue/black varieties, and you can create a nice marbled effect by mixing colors of cooked quinoa.

Chickpea & Avocado Ceviche

Ceviche is commonly made with fish. In a fascinating example of food chemistry, the lime juice is what actually "cooks" the fish. Raw foodists beware! All those acidic ingredients you add to a dish slowly chew up the protein chains that constitute the food's enzymes. For this dish, chickpeas and avocado substitute for the fish, but there are some traditional ceviches that are made with beans. There's also no added oil to this dish, just wonderful fatty acids from the avocado.

 **DIFFICULTY**

Flavors: Sour, rich, salty, savory, spicy, green

Equipment: A small bowl, a larger bowl, a whisk (a fork will do), and a pan capable of holding at least 6 cups water with a tight-fitting lid

Ingredients

- 3 cups water
- 1 cup dried chickpeas
- 2 ripe avocados, pitted, skinned, and coarsely chopped
- 1 red onion, peeled, and finely chopped

  Dressing
- Juice of 2 medium-sized, ripe limes
- 1/2 teaspoon lime zest, minced
- 1 tablespoon cilantro, minced
- 1/2 teaspoon red pepper flakes (or 1/4 teaspoon ground cayenne pepper if that's what you have)
- 1/2 teaspoon ground cumin
- Dash of liquid smoke
- 1/4 teaspoon coarse sea salt

Optional: Coarse sea salt is preferred in this recipe, but fine will work. If you find the dressing a little too sour (depending on your tastes and on the limes), add a pinch of sugar or 1/4 teaspoon agave nectar. If you use canned beans, rinse them well and use 2 to 2 1/2 cups.

Instructions

Begin by preparing your ingredients. First, bring your water to a slow boil with the chickpeas. Cover and simmer on low until done (should take about 2 1/2 hours). When the chickpeas are ready, prepare the rest of your ingredients. Add the cooked chickpeas, chopped avocados, and the red onion to the large bowl. Whisk the remaining ingredients in the small bowl and then dress your ceviche. Let stand 5 minutes. Taste and add salt if necessary. Plate with tongs.

Going further

This salad is wonderfully full-flavored as it is. Chickpeas do pretty well in this salad, but you could always swap them for black beans for a more dramatic look.

Red Potato/Sweet Potato & Scallion Mash

Mashed potatoes are a common accompaniment to American dinners. But in spite of its starchy goodness, the potato has come under increasing criticism from nutritionists. This recipe combines sweet and red potatoes for a more colorful and healthier mash. This dish puts an emphasis on creating flavor layers (different, discernible elements of flavor combinations in a single dish). The sweet potatoes provide a sweet layer, with heat from the cayenne. The red potatoes provide a sour layer, with a little heat from the black pepper. There's also some textural variation. The sweet potatoes will be creamy. The red potatoes will be kind of doughy and chewy. Of course, you can prepare each half of this dish individually (just adjust your cook times).

 **DIFFICULTY**

Flavors: Sweet, salty, sour, spicy, green

Equipment: A baking sheet, a potato masher, two small bowls, two medium bowls, one large bowl, and an ice cream scooper (optional)

Ingredients

- 1 to 2 tablespoons vegetable oil (for roasting the potatoes)

Sweet potatoes
- 2 medium sweet potatoes (about 2 1/2 cups)
- 1 scallion
- 1/4 teaspoon sea salt
- 1 teaspoon lemon juice
- 1/2 teaspoon extra virgin olive oil
- 1/2 teaspoon minced fresh ginger (more to taste)
- 1/4 teaspoon dried cayenne pepper, ground
- 1/2 teaspoon ground cumin

Optional: Switch the cayenne pepper for black pepper for a less spicy dish, or add 1 teaspoon minced fresh jalapeño for something spicier. If you have fresh lemongrass, use 1/2 teaspoon, minced, instead of the 1/2 teaspoon lemon juice. Add 1 teaspoon minced fresh cilantro if you like.

Red potatoes
- 2 to 3 medium red potatoes (about 2 cups)
- 1 scallion
- 1/4 teaspoon sea salt
- 1/2 teaspoon extra virgin olive oil
- 1 tablespoon white vinegar

- 1 tablespoon minced fresh garlic
- 1/4 teaspoon ground black pepper (or to taste)
- 2 tablespoons nutritional yeast

Optional: You can use apple cider or malt vinegar if you prefer their taste over white vinegar with potatoes. If you have a little Sour Cream (page 65), nothing says you can't add a couple tablespoons in lieu of the vinegar, as well.

Instructions

An up-front note on potatoes: unfortunately, how long it takes to roast potatoes varies by size and freshness: longer for larger, fresher potatoes; shorter for smaller, older ones. You will need to check both sets of potatoes individually, and each potato individually if they are very different sizes. They may be done at different points. When they are done, remove them from the pan and reserve.

How can you tell when a potato is done? There are a lot of methods and these vary by cook. One of the best ways is to see if a fork easily pierces the potato without much resistance. Or you can give the potatoes a squeeze to see if they feel soft like a ripe avocado (use a damp, clean kitchen cloth that's not too thick). Of course, you can also use both methods, and this is recommended if you're not familiar with roast whole potatoes or sweet potatoes. This dish depends upon being able to tell when the wonderful sweetness of the sweet potatoes is starting to caramelize, and upon the fluff of the potatoes when they are fully and properly done.

With all of that on your shoulders, begin by preparing your ingredients. Preheat the oven to 400° F. Bake your scallions whole (as directed below) and then trim and mince. Wash and scrub the potato skins and scallions thoroughly. Puncture the skins of sweet potatoes and red potatoes in 3 to 4 places with a fork, going about 1/2 inch into the flesh. Brush potatoes with vegetable oil (shouldn't require more than 1 tablespoon). Add the red potatoes to the baking sheet and bake for 15 minutes. Add the scallions and the sweet potatoes and bake for 10 minutes. Remove the scallions and continue to bake the potatoes for another 30 to 45 minutes or until done.

When your scallions have baked and cooled, assemble the remaining ingredients. Mince both scallions and prepare your other herbs and spices. Put half the minced scallion in one of the small bowls along with the other dressing ingredients for the sweet potato. Add the remaining scallions to the other small bowl, and add all the dressing ingredients for the red potato. Mix each dressing individually and reserve until your potatoes are done.

When the potatoes are done, remove from the oven and allow both to cool for 10 minutes. Start with the red potatoes, and let the sweet potato cool further. Add the unpeeled red potatoes to a medium bowl and mash thoroughly with a potato masher. The skins will be difficult to mash entirely, and that's fine. Their texture is an important part of this dish (at least in New England!). Add the dressing for the red potatoes and mash further until thoroughly combined thoroughly. Taste and add salt as necessary.

For the sweet potato, slice off the tip of the potato and then carefully remove the loosened skin (the sweet potato will still be fairly hot). Add the peeled sweet potato to the second medium-sized bowl, dress and mash the sweet potato with a potato masher (or a fork) until thoroughly combined. Taste and add salt as necessary.

Add both the sweet potatoes and the red potatoes to the large bowl and mix with a wooden spoon until you achieve a marbled effect, but not so much that the two distinct potatoes are one mix (should take 4 to 5 stirs). To serve, spoon out carefully onto plates or scoop out with an ice cream scoop. Serves 2 with big portions, or smaller portions for 4.

Going further

This is a pretty elaborate side dish with a lot of flavor. It's also a good way for you to develop a habit of thinking about flavor layers. Flavor layers work by establishing two or more distinct and discernible flavors in a single dish. Typically, with simple cooking, you combine flavors with a main dish and a couple of complementary side dishes. This dish has two basic flavor layers in a single side and it provides a comparatively simple way for you to start thinking about more complicated plates. If you just want to keep it simple, though, this dish goes well with simple greens (think roasted kale) and savory flavors (e.g., seitan or tofu cutlets). To go more complicated, add a small dollop of Spinach, Arugula, and Walnut Pesto (page 52) to serve a richer mouth feel, a little extra flavor, and a little more green. Serve with a main dish that puts an emphasis on savory flavors and with a strong green side like roasted kale or romaine lettuce.

Brown Rice Pilaf with
Mushrooms & Onions

Pilaf is basically rice with stuff. Most Americans eat pilaf regularly and just don't know it. Historically, pilaf is a wonderful example of culinary transnationalism and syncretism. Pilaf started in Central Asia as pulao (mostly with nuts and fruit), and moved east to Southeast Asia and west to Europe, particularly to France where it became pilaf, typically with mushrooms and onions. Then it emerged in the United States as prepackaged, preflavored instant rice side dishes. This recipe takes you back to a time when cooks still flavored their own rice on their own terms.

 **DIFFICULTY**

Flavors: Sweet, salty, sour, spicy, rich

Equipment: One small bowl, one large bowl, a pot with a tight-fitting lid capable of holding 4 cups liquid, a whisk (a fork will do), and tongs

Ingredients

- 1 cup long-grain brown rice
- 2 cups vegetable stock (you can use water, but it will not be as flavorful)
- 1 tablespoon vegetable oil
- 1/4 cup button mushrooms, finely chopped (cremini, portobello, porcini, or black trumpet are also good)
- 1/4 cup onions minced (preferably shallots or vidalia)
- 1 tablespoon minced fresh garlic

Dressing

- 1 tablespoon extra virgin olive oil
- 1/2 teaspoon lemon juice
- 1 teaspoon thyme
- 1/2 teaspoon tarragon
- 1/2 teaspoon savory
- 1/2 teaspoon ground black pepper
- Sea salt (start with 1/4 if you're using stock or 1/2 teaspoon for regular water and add more as necessary)

Instructions

Begin by preparing your ingredients. Add the first tablespoon of oil to your pan and warm the oil on high. Add 1/4 to 1/2 teaspoon sea salt to the pan (noting whether you're using water or stock). When the oil is ready, add the onion and sauté for 3 minutes. Decrease the heat to medium-high. Add the garlic and the mushrooms and sauté for 5 minutes. Add the brown rice and sauté for 3 minutes until the rice starts to brown slightly.

Add the first cup of water or stock and bring the water to a boil. Be careful when you add the liquid, because you'll find that the oil may bring it to a boil much more quickly than you expect! Add the second cup of water when the water has settled down and bring the water to a low simmer on high. When the water has reached a light boil, decrease the heat to low, cover and let simmer for at least 45 minutes (or whatever your rice requires—some premium rices take 50 minutes). Typically, pilaf takes longer to cook than plain rice and water, so be prepared for it to take longer than the standard cook time for your rice.

In the meantime, whisk your other ingredients in the small bowl. When the rice is done, add it to the large bowl. Add your dressing, fluff the rice with a fork and to combine with the dressing. Taste and add salt as necessary. Cover your large bowl with a plate, let the rice stand another 10 minutes, and then serve.

Plating: pilaf is usually plated on the side, but it can be spread thin on the main part of the plate. If you really want to get fancy, fill a small ramekin with a your pilaf, turn it over onto the plate, add your main ingredient on top, and then top that with some microgreens and drip a sauce around the tower of food.

Going further

Traditionally, pilaf is made with stock, but it's not an absolute necessity. You're adding flavors with the mushrooms and onions, after all. Like couscous, pilaf is mostly about adding flavor and color to the rice. Traditionally, pilaf is a demure side dish, but there's no reason your pilaf can't reclaim its former beauty and texture. Cranberries, raisins, greens, tomatoes (sun-dried and regular), and other ingredients can all add flavor and color to your pilaf without violating any sacred principles.

Basic Crackers

A colleague suggested I include a cracker recipe in this book. And then I thought about all the wonderful things you could put in your crackers if you made them from scratch, end even cooler, what you could put on your crackers.

 **DIFFICULTY**

Flavors: Sweet and salty as a base

Equipment: A food processor, a medium bowl, a baking sheet (preferably at least 9 x 13 inches, or you may have to make multiple batches), a rolling pin, a ravioli cutter is nice to have, and if not, a pizza cutter, and some parchment paper (wax paper won't do)

Ingredients

▶ 1 1/4 cup whole wheat flour
▶ 1/4 cup ice-cold water (1/4 cup in reserve)
▶ 1/4 teaspoon sea salt (and more to taste)
▶ 2 tablespoons margarine

Instructions

Begin by preparing your ingredients. Add your dry ingredients to a bowl and mix. Cut the margarine into your dough (a food processor makes this a snap). Make a small well in the middle of the dry ingredients and add the liquids. Mix until dough forms, adding the reserved water if you need to do so, 1 tablespoon at a time. Allow your dough to rest covered while you preheat your oven to 350° F.

Next, break your dough into 2 even balls and roll it out (instructions vary below, so decide which cracker you're making) on a clean, lightly floured surface. For a basic cracker, roll the dough out in an oblong shape about 1/8 inch thick. Roll it out more thinly if you can, but this will take practice (your dough will probably tear the first few times you try to go thinner).

Cover your baking sheet with the parchment in a single sheet. Add the dough to the parchment paper. If you're going to cut your crackers cut off the sides to form the largest rectangle you can cut using the ravioli cutter. You can either cut the cracker at this point if you like squares or circles, or you can bake it whole and when the cracker is done, you can break it into rustic pieces. If you decide to cut your crackers, use the ravioli cutter to cut even strips in the dough (see below for varieties and sizes). Poke holes with a fork in your dough to avoid air bubbles.

Poke them in a pattern for cut crackers, or randomly to suit yourself with the one-big-cracker approach.

When the oven is ready, sprinkle the crackers lightly with a pinch of sea salt. Bake for 14 to 18 minutes (varies by cracker and by oven), or until the crackers are starting to brown lightly. Remove them from the oven and let them stand for 10 minutes to cool (preferably on a wire rack). Separate the crackers carefully or break your one large cracker into pieces suitable for dipping. If you want rounds instead of squares, cut them with a small drinking glass like you would other dough. Then ball up the remaining dough, roll it back out, and repeat.

Going further

Of course, the kind of crackers you might make and what you might top them with is entirely up to your imagination. Some suggestions:

The Herbs Galore. Add 2 teaspoons of the dried green herbs that you like to the dry ingredients. Roll out as thin as possible and cut into 1 x 1-inch squares or go rustic. Both are good. If you go rustic, go with a dip with sour, spicy, fermented, or fatty flavors (or all of these!). Top these with a little Sour Cream (page 65), very thinly sliced red onion, some thinly sliced cucumber, and a little black pepper.

The Pepper Jack. This is a good cracker all by itself. Add 1/2 cup nutritional yeast and 1 teaspoon black pepper to the dry ingredients. Roll out to 1/8 inch (less if you can) and cut into 1 x 1-inch segments. Top

these with a little Tarragon Aioli (page 64) and a thin slice of Light Seitan (page 126), or with a thin slice of Roasted Portobello, Pears, and Onion (page 117), and tie it up with some collard green chiffonade (see the recipe for Collard Noodles, page 90, for this technique). These crackers aren't as crisp as the basic recipe, but they're delicious.

The Sweet and Savory. This cracker is more of a sweetbread, but it's a nice basis for when more of a stale bread texture is called for with a canapé. Add 1 tablespoon dried onion flakes, 1 teaspoon savory and 1/2 teaspoon baking powder to the dry ingredients, and 1/4 cup agave nectar to the liquids. Cut into 2 1/2 x 1-inch squares. Top these with a little of the Tahini Cheese (page 154) or Sour Cream (page 65) and add some thinly sliced granny smith apples. Tie them with some toasted nori chiffonade for a nigiri sushi look and a savory accent, or sprinkle with a little sugar.

Of course, all of these crackers also do well with the White Bean and Parsley Dip (page 58), the Avocado Creton (page 57), the Artichoke and Caper Butter (59), the Kalamata Olive and Dill Pickle Tapenade (page 54), as well as any number of other toppings so long as you balance the flavors well. In terms of texture, you want a little creamy and a little chewy to complement the crunch of the cracker. You an also add your own ingredients: black sesame seeds, poppy seeds, or different flours (e.g., corn meal or teff) to get a drier texture.

Couscous with Arugula, Olives & Raisins

Couscous sounds foreign and exotic, but it's basically tiny grains of wheat pasta. It's good for you (when it's whole wheat) and it cooks in about 10 minutes without requiring attention. It's about as low-maintenance as you can get, and it has a nice nutty flavor and a soft, light, and chewy texture. This dish adds some flavor and color with wonderful, peppery arugula, sweet raisins, and sour olives.

 **DIFFICULTY**

Flavors: Sweet, salty, sour, spicy, rich

Equipment: A small bowl, a medium bowl, a large bowl, a pot with a tight-fitting lid capable of holding 4 cups liquid, a whisk (a fork will do), and tongs

Note: On the proportions of couscous to water: be careful to read any instructions on the couscous you buy if you buy it prepackaged. The amount of water required varies depending on the nature of the couscous. For couscous that does not come with directions, start with 1 1/2 cups of water and then 1/4 cup at a time until you have the texture you like.

Ingredients

- 1 cup dry, whole wheat couscous (not Israeli couscous)
- 1 1/2 cups boiling water (or vegetable stock, your choice)
- 1 cup of packed baby arugula, finely chopped
- 1 tablespoon extra virgin olive oil
- 1 tablespoon minced fresh garlic
- 1 teaspoon minced fresh ginger
- 12 kalamata olives, pitted and minced
- 1/2 cup thompson raisins

Dressing
- 1/4 teaspoon cayenne pepper (or more if you like it hot)
- 1/2 teaspoon ground cumin
- 1/4 teaspoon ground coriander
- Small pinch of ground cloves
- 1/4 teaspoon ground black pepper
- 1/4 teaspoon sea salt

Optional: If you prefer, use coarse sea salt, which is traditionally preferred.

Instructions

Begin by preparing your ingredients. Bring your water to a boil. Add 1/4 teaspoon sea salt and your couscous, stir until well combined, cover, and remove from heat. Let stand for 20 minutes. You may need to simmer on low for the first 10 minutes if your couscous isn't absorbing water. Check your couscous after the first 5 minutes to ensure it's absorbing water and if it's not, return it to heat and simmer covered on very low heat for 10 minutes, checking frequently.

When the couscous is done (and all the water has been absorbed), add the couscous to the large bowl. Chop the arugula and olives, and add with the raisins to the couscous. Whisk the remaining ingredients in the small bowl and then add the dressing to the large bowl. Stir thoroughly until well combined and let stand another 10 minutes. Taste and add salt as necessary. Plate with tongs. This is a filling side for 2, but double the recipe if you plan to serve 4.

Going further

Couscous is a simple-to-prepare canvas waiting for other ingredients to give it color and extra flavor. Experiment with the herbs and ingredients you like. For example, sun-dried tomatoes, pineapple, mushrooms, carrots, and seitan all work well. Because couscous is relatively neutral-tasting, it does well with a number of flavors and colors. Add a little mint or cilantro for some extra green flavor and color.

French-Style Roasted Green Beans with
Red Peppers & Onions

Red peppers make for a wonderful, colorful, and nutritious side. They're rich in vitamin C and other things that are good for you, and they're also easy to prepare. Fire-roasting peppers is the best way to prepare them, but that's difficult with an electric stove. This recipe cheats a little by oven roasting the julienned peppers instead with a little liquid smoke. Optionally, you can roast the peppers whole, remove the skin, and julienne the cooked pepper, but the skin has a lot of nutritional value. This approach is faster, and you'll have to oven roast the green beans and the onions anyhow.

 **DIFFICULTY**

Flavors: Savory, salty, rich, sweet, green

Equipment: A small bowl, a large bowl, a roasting pan, tongs, and a sharp knife

Ingredients

- ▶ 2 cups green beans, trimmed and chopped into 1-inch lengths
- ▶ 1 red pepper, cored, seeded, and julienned
- ▶ 1/2 small white onion, peeled and thinly sliced
- ▶ 1 teaspoon lemon juice
- ▶ 1 tablespoon extra virgin olive oil
- ▶ Dash of liquid smoke
- ▶ 1/4 teaspoon sea salt

Instructions

Begin by preparing your ingredients. Preheat your oven to 450° F. To prepare your green beans, trim and discard the tips, and then cut them into 1-inch pieces. Instead of mincing or dicing your red peppers (although dicing is fine for this recipe), slice them in long thin strips about 1/8 inch wide. Instead of dicing your onion, slice each half into long, thin strips as thin as you can make them (1/8 inch is also fine). Add these ingredients to the large bowl.

Next, whisk the remaining ingredients in the small bowl and then dress the peppers, beans, and onions and add them to your roasting pan (or baking sheet if that's what you have). Spread them as evenly as you can. Roast the vegetables for about 12 to 15 minutes, or until the peppers are bright red and spotted with brown. Let stand for 5 minutes to cool. Taste and add salt as necessary. You can plate your green beans and peppers immediately with tongs.

If the skin of the peppers bothers you, blanche them for 8 minutes in boiling, lightly salted water. Allow them to cool, and then peel; or roast them first, allow to cool, and then peel and julienne. This dish serves 2 as a larger side dish or 4 for smaller ones.

Going further

If you really want to get fancy, cut your green beans into their inch-long segments and then julienne them like the red peppers. Green beans are pretty common on the American table and, with red peppers and onions, make for a very flavorful and colorful side. Both main vegetables add a green flavor (even red peppers have a slight bitter flavor), some sweet, some sour, and, when roasted, some fat and salt flavor. The onion adds both a firmer sweet note than the pepper and a certain pungency to the dish.

You can, of course, enjoy the ingredients individually, but this is a beautiful and traditional American combination. This side will go well with a lot of dishes but will tend to shine most with savory flavors. Add herbs and other flavors to dress up this side dish. Yellow, orange, and purple bell peppers can be prepared in a similar way—just remember that green peppers are the least ripe, and therefore also the least sweet.

Basic Pasta from Scratch

Fresh pasta is, simply put, a million times better than rehydrated pasta. It's also simple, if somewhat time- and labor-intensive to make.

 **DIFFICULTY**

Flavors: Sweet, salty

Equipment: A large bowl, a rolling pin, a plate, and probably some waxed paper and plastic wrap; and if you want to make your noodles fresh: a colander, a pan capable of holding at least 8 cups water (larger preferred), and a ravioli or pizza cutter would be nice

Ingredients

- ▶ 2 cups durum semolina flour
- ▶ 2/3 cup warm water
- ▶ 1/4 teaspoon sea salt

Optional: You'll need at least 8 cups water and 1 tablespoon of sea salt if you want to cook your pasta immediately.

Instructions

Add the flour and salt to the large bowl and mix. Add the water and mix. When you have the dough, you're basically done. Making noodles is the hard part!

If you want to cook your noodles immediately, bring 8 cups salted water to a boil in a large pot. In the meantime, to make noodles, you'll probably need to break your dough into smaller balls. Start by breaking this dough in half, wrapping the pieces you're not rolling out in plastic so they don't dry out.

To make a basic fettuccine, roll out your dough out with a rolling pin on a clear, dry, and lightly floured surface until it's about 1/8 inch thick, fold over, and reroll. Repeat this twice and then roll out as thin as you can get it, less than 1/8 inch, to about 12 inches in diameter. Cut the circle into a large square by trimming the ends with a butter knife. Let the sheet air dry for 2 minutes and then cut the noodles into 1/4-inch thick strips. Use a ravioli cutter if you have one, a pizza cutter, or a knife. Pile them very loosely on a plate and roll out the rest of your dough. Of course, you can make other kinds of pasta if you'd prefer, but fettuccine is a good place to start.

When your noodles are ready, add them directly to the boiling water and stir gently to avoid clinging. Boil the noodles for about 3 to 5 minutes until done (they'll float and turn white when done). Do not overcook. Remove your noodles from the water and drain them in a colander.

Going further

Now that you have the noodles, what are you going to do with them? Obviously, noodles go well with all kinds of sauces. Better to prepare your sauce first and have it on a low simmer to sauce your pasta once it's done and drained. Labor intensive? It is, but the texture and flavor of fresh pasta really makes it worth it when you want something just right. Also, the basic recipe for pasta is, for all practical purposes, identical: flour and salt. But you can also add herbs and a little oil. A great way to get your feet wet with making your own pasta is to make your own lasagna (it's easy to cut a few strips precisely than a few dozen).

Roasted Portobello Mushrooms
with Pears & Onions

This is a traditional combination, combining wonderful sweet and savory flavors.

 **DIFFICULTY**

Flavors: Savory, sweet, salty, rich

Equipment: A small bowl, a large bowl, a roasting pan, a whisk, and tongs

Ingredients

- ▶ 4 large (4 to 5-inch) portobello mushrooms (if less than 3 inches in diameter, use 6)
- ▶ 1 pear, cored and thinly sliced (bartlett is preferable)
- ▶ 1 small red onion, peeled and thinly sliced
- ▶ 1 tablespoon unsweetened soy milk
- ▶ 1 teaspoon lemon juice
- ▶ 2 tablespoons olive oil
- ▶ 1/2 teaspoon ground black pepper
- ▶ 1/4 teaspoon sea salt
- ▶ 1 tablespoons nutritional yeast
- ▶ Coarse sea salt

Optional: 1 teaspoon minced Italian (flat-leaf) parsley to add a little green flavor and color

Instructions

Begin by preparing your ingredients. Preheat your oven to 450° F. Wipe the mushrooms clean, remove their stems, and slice them in about 1/8-inch strips. Wash your pear, cut it in half, and carefully cut the core out. Put the pear halves face down and slice in 1/8-inch strips. Peel and slice the onion as thinly as you can (1/8 inch is good). Add these ingredients to the large bowl.

In the small bowl, whisk the remaining ingredients except the nutritional yeast and coarse sea salt. Dress your mushrooms, onion, and pear slices. Toss thoroughly until well combined. Add them to your roasting pan and spread evenly in a thin layer. As best as you can, separate the pears from the mushrooms and onions.

Roast for about 30 minutes, or until the mushrooms are done and lightly browning. Remove the pan from the oven and let stand for 2 minutes. Heat the oven to broil and when the oven is ready, broil for 3 minutes. Remove the pan from the oven and add the mushrooms, pears, and onions to the large bowl. Let stand 5 minutes to cool. Taste and add coarse salt as necessary and toss lightly. You can use fine salt, but you won't get quite the same taste.

Plate carefully with tongs (your pears will be just about ready to fall apart) and sprinkle with nutritional yeast and the parsley if you're using it. Make a filling side dish for 2 or a small side for 4.

Going further

This is a fairly sweet and savory side. It goes well with sour, green, and savory flavors. It also makes a great sandwich filling.

Basic Yeast Dough

This recipe introduces you to basic dough. Exact recipes vary, but most doughs are variations on flour and water. Yeast doughs make great breads, bagels, pizza crusts, and other assorted baked items where the slight sour of the yeast adds flavor. Surprisingly, however, how to make a proper yeast dough is a serious matter of debate among bakers (mostly about whether or not to knead). This recipe suggests only very mild kneading.

 **DIFFICULTY**

Flavors: Sweet, salty, fermented

Equipment: A large bowl, a small bowl, and you may need a thermometer

Ingredients

- ▶ 2 1/2 cups hard whole wheat flour (reserve 1/4 cup)
- ▶ 1 cup warm water
- ▶ 1 teaspoon agave nectar
- ▶ 1 tablespoon vegetable oil
- ▶ 1 tablespoon yeast (use quick-rise if you're not accustomed to baking your own bread)
- ▶ 1/2 teaspoon sea salt

Instructions

Some recipes call for proofing the dough. You can if you like, but if your water is hot enough, it shouldn't be necessary. Instructions assume that you're proofing, but once you get the hang of judging water temperature, you should be fine. Heat your water (if you need to) to around 110° F and add it to the small bowl. Your tap water may or may not be hot enough. Add the agave nectar, the oil, and the yeast to the warm water and mix thoroughly with a wooden spoon or a finger (make sure it's clean!). Don't use a metal spoon. Measure out 2 1/2 cups flour and add all but 1/4 cup to the large bowl. If you want to add any dry herbs, add them to the flour at this point. Add the salt to the flour and mix. Add the 1/4 cup of flour to your yeast mixture and let it stand for 15 minutes. It should be all nice and bubbly, which means your yeast is active.

If your yeast is active, make a small well in your flour in the large bowl and pour your yeast mixture into the center. Slowly mix the flour with a wooden spoon or your hands (again, making sure they're clean!). Stir gently until it's well combined. The dough should be soft, supple, and neither particularly moist nor particularly dry. Cover the dough with a moist, warm towel and leave it in a warm place. After 30 minutes, check that it's rising. Squish it

back down by pressing gently with your hands to push out the air. Cover again with moist warm towel. After another 30 minutes, your dough is basically ready for use. Sprinkle a clean, flat surface with a little flour. Remove it from the bowl, and press down on the dough firmly with your palms. Turn the dough over and fold in half once. Press firmly again with your palms.

If you like kneaded dough, knead for about 5 to 10 minutes (if you're rolling out the dough for pizza and whatnot, knead). If you're philosophically opposed to kneading bread dough, you're done. If you're not sure, try both ways a couple of times and come to your own decision about which bread you like better. No-kneading usually generates a lighter, fluffier loaf. Kneading usually results in a chewier, heartier, more condensed loaf.

Going further

Now you can make pizza, bagels, bread, whatever you like with your dough. Double this recipe to make a nice-sized loaf that will last a few days. Dough can be somewhat tricky. The amount of water varies a bit depending on the nature of the flour. Be careful using soft flours, pastry flours. Their resulting texture is somewhat different, as is the amount of water they need (same goes for ancient wheats, spelt, etc.). It may also take you a few tries to get the amount and temperature of the water right. If you add herbs, add dry ones to the flour. Dough was the first thing I ever learned to make from scratch almost 20 years ago, and I'm still working on it.

Basic Pastry & Baking Powder Doughs

Pastry and baking powder doughs are good for pies and other dishes that require a little more neutrality to the taste of the dough. Not everyone likes the fermented taste of dough in strawberry pie. But doughs that don't involve yeast are also great for those times when you want a quick dough, one that's guaranteed to rise, a flakier dough, or a dough that's good for a lot of wet ingredients. If you want a quick puff pastry dough (a dough not covered in this book), but don't want to go to the effort, use phyllo. You can buy it frozen at many grocery stores and most health food stores.

 **DIFFICULTY**

Flavors: Sweet, salty, rich

Equipment: A large bowl, a small bowl, and a pair of butter knives (a fork will do), a rolling pin, and probably some waxed paper

Ingredients

- ▶ 1 1/2 cups whole wheat flour
- ▶ 4 to 8 tablespoons ice-cold water (use as little as possible)
- ▶ 1/2 cup vegetable shortening (or suet)
- ▶ Sea salt (a pinch will do for dessert pie dough, 1/4 teaspoon will do for savory uses)

For baking powder dough add

- ▶ 1 teaspoon baking powder to the dry ingredients
- ▶ 1 tablespoon vinegar to the wet ingredients

Instructions

Begin by preparing your ingredients. Measure out and add the flour to the large bowl. Add the margarine to the flour. What's difficult about pastry dough is cutting the margarine into the flour. Use a pair of butter knives or a food processor to cut the margarine into the flour until you have what amounts to small pebbles. This will take you several minutes with knives, or a few seconds with a food processor. You can try using a fork, but you may have some difficulties with this.

When you've successfully cut the margarine into the flour, make a small well and add the cold water (it really should be ice-cold to avoid melting your margarine). Mix carefully with your hands. Add water until your dough comes together in a nice ball. When your dough has come together, let it rest in a cold place for about 30 minutes, and your dough will be ready to use.

For a baking powder dough, add the vinegar to the liquid ingredients, add the baking powder to the dry ingredients, and repeat the same process.

Going further

You may wonder why you would use one kind of dough over another. Obviously, yeast dough is sour, which makes it less useful for sweet pastries. Pastry dough tends to be more "all-purpose" and can be used for sweet dishes (e.g., pie) or savory (e.g., bureka). Sometimes you'll want an airier, thicker crust (e.g., pizza) or sometimes you'll want a thin, flaky one (e.g., baklava). The short answer is, it depends on what the flavor of the final dish will be and what texture of chew you'd like in the final dish, but some dishes are more often prepared with particular types of dough.

Regardless of the type of dough you use, you'll almost certainly want to roll your dough out and do something fancy with it, which will vary by the recipe (see the runza, pizza, and pie recipes in later chapters). Depending on the nature of the dough, either flour a flat, dry surface and roll your dough out with a rolling pin, or roll your dough out between wax paper. Typically, for pies and other pastries, you'll want to use wax paper. For pizza pockets and other baked savories, a floured surface will probably be fine. If you're baking a pie, you'll probably want to add some sweetener to your liquid ingredients (or granulated sugar to your dry ingredients), and you want some fermented/sour flavor to your dough, add a tablespoon of vinegar to the liquid ingredients.

Getting Past the Recipes:
What Makes a Good Side Dish, a Good Appetizer & a Good Salad?

To the "plate partners" of this chapter in their brave struggle to be taken seriously as more than just filler before or with the main course, I salute you all! But in all seriousness, side dishes are an important part of the plate. In fact, small plate approaches like tapas and mezze are becoming trendier both in the home and at the restaurant, in part because people want more and different flavors in a single sitting than meat, potatoes, and two (often relatively tasteless) vegetables. But the role that side dishes play is still largely to support the central part of the plate, whatever that is. Unlike an appetizer, which tends to be most successful when it provides a full set of flavor all by itself, side dishes can be perfectly simple—so long as they're complementary to the center of the plate.

So, the real question with preparing good side dishes is, what does it mean to be complementary? And the most accurate answer is that it depends. In a nutshell, though, you can plan your plates in a number of ways. For example, you could plan them all around complementary colors (you'll notice, for example, that I do a plethora of combinations of orange and green). You can plan them around complementary flavors. I tend to pair green and sweet side dishes with savory main dishes and a sour or spicy sauce. You can plan them around a locale (e.g., all New England or Southern) or you can plan them around your guests. None of these are the wrong way to do it. But your best plates will probably be those that take all of these factors into account.

As the defining side dish of American cuisine (after potatoes, of course), salads are a study in contrasting textures, flavors and colors. What makes a great salad? Variety. Experiment with the fruits, roots, nuts, shoots, herbs, oils, juices, vinegars, and other stuff that interests you. But another question is, what's an *amuse bouche*?

"Salad" is a classic starter in American cooking, but it's also a side dish and sometimes it's the whole meal. Sometimes it's an appetizer, sometimes an hors d'oeuvre, and sometimes it's something just to amuse your mouth while you wait for your food (that's what an *amuse bouche* is). It all depends. How do you know which kind of salad to serve when and with which fork?

For the most part, the old rule of civilized society with respect to eating your salad first and with the outside fork are getting further and further removed from modern cuisine. Why? Partly because it was never really a hard-and-fast rule in the first place. Salad sometimes finishes a meal, depending on where you are. Partly because what constitutes salad has never been a really stable category of ingredients, and partly because our concept of salad is changing. What holds fruit salad and Caesar salad together into a stable culinary category except that it's not meat and it's not potatoes? Not much, really (and when you consider the ontological status of potato salad, it starts to look like salad is anything that isn't meat—wink, wink).

Ideas about salad are changing as Americans eat a wider variety of fruits and vegetables. Nevertheless, you can still think of your salad as a set of flavors. The fuller the set of flavors, the better it will work as an appetizer. The lighter it is, the easier it will be to have a few bites before the main appetizer, or as part of a course of various appetizers, which makes the salad a good amuse bouche. But most of all, don't be afraid to push salad into entirely new directions. Salad's focus on contrast and diversity is what makes salad truly great from a culinary perspective and what makes it the dish of the future.

Vincent Guihan | New American Vegan

Chapter 5:
Seitan & Potatoes, and Other Soon-to-Be-Traditional Favorites

Don't listen to those crazy side dishes. Main dishes are what truly shine! Sure, all great actors need their supporting players and extras, but can some wilted kale really compete with stuffed and roasted squash with a velvety rosé? This chapter addresses the center of the plate. Recipes start with simple dishes like cutlets with mushroom gravy and proceed to more complicated dishes like pot pie.

Nowhere is "faux" more obvious than in the plant-based reinvention of a traditional dish, and nowhere does real flavor shine better than in a dish prepared with multiple flavor layers accented by the appropriate set of "plate partners." On the other hand, there's also nothing like putting everything together in a single pan and eating what comes out of it. Many traditional plant-based dishes are prepared this way and these types of dishes have long been the hallmark of American cuisine. This chapter also includes some one-dish wonders like pizza and runza (the hot pocket). If you like to eat kale or collard greens every single day, like I do, but want to mix it up a little with more imaginative or more traditional main dishes, this is the chapter.

Basic cutlets:
a note on working with seitan and tofu

Many of the recipes in this section are plates built from the simpler recipes for sauces, sides and salads in the earlier chapters. The following recipes for seitan can usually be used interchangeably with tofu cutlets, but where this isn't the case, I've made note. This recipes walks you through the basics of working with tofu and seitan, high-protein foods that can be substituted into many of the dishes with which many Americans are already familiar.

Tofu is simple and straightforward and only requires a little knife work to get started, but it takes some time to marinate. With seitan, you can control the flavor and texture from the very beginning of the dish and no marinade is really required. Both are simple, flavorful, flexible, easy to store, clean, environmentally friendly, and relatively inexpensive. What's not to like? Best of all, animals aren't used to make it appear on your plate, unless you compel your kids to help you prepare dinner.

Will the tofu and the seitan taste like meat? Not really. They'll have a texture and flavor similar to the finished dish, which is largely determined by the way the dish is prepared and by all the accenting flavors. What seitan and tofu do is provide a texture with only a modest amount of flavor—basically what amounts to a blank culinary canvas. So, while they are meat replacements in a very vague sense, they're not meat replacements in the same way that chicken is not a beef replacement. They're just a simple, flexible savory flavor that can be prepared, cut, and accented in ways that show off the chef's skills.

In fact, in that regard alone, seitan is far more flexible than any animal body, since it can take on a variety of textures and flavors from the outset of the dish. Tofu is slightly less flexible, of course, and so, it gets short shrift in this cookbook. Further, you can improve the absorbency of tofu by freezing it overnight, but that's a somewhat lengthy process. It's not that I don't like tofu. When prepared properly, tofu is excellent. It's just that seitan is a little more flexible and gluten flour can sit on your shelf for a while.

Dark Seitan Cutlets

These are little rounds of brown, seitany goodness. They also make a good burger—just break them into 3 to 4 patties and flatten them out more.

Flavors: Savory, salty, rich

Equipment: A small bowl, a larger bowl, a whisk (a fork will do), and a sharp knife

Note: You'll probably need to go to your local HFS for the gluten, the nutritional yeast, the teff, and the optional Worcestershire sauce. (Remember, most mainstream Worcestershire sauces have animal ingredients.)

Ingredients

- ▶ 3/4 cup gluten flour
- ▶ 1 tablespoon teff flour
- ▶ 1 teaspoon flax meal
- ▶ 2 tablespoons walnut butter (or 3 tablespoons chopped walnuts ground to butter consistency)
- ▶ 2 tablespoons nutritional yeast
- ▶ 1 teaspoon ground cumin
- ▶ 1/2 teaspoon ground coriander
- ▶ 1/4 teaspoon ground black pepper
- ▶ 2/3 cups cold water
- ▶ 2 tablespoons tamari
- ▶ 1 tablespoon catsup
- ▶ Dash of liquid smoke

Optional: Add 1/2 teaspoon ginger, 1 teaspoon Worcestershire sauce, or even some fresh orange zest to the liquid ingredients for a little extra flavor. You can swap the walnuts for tahini, but your dark seitan won't be as dark.

Instructions

Begin by preparing your ingredients. Add all of your dry ingredients to a medium bowl and mix thoroughly to combine. Add all of your liquid ingredients to a small bowl and whisk until well combined. Make a well in the flour and add the liquid ingredients to the medium bowl. Mix with a wooden spoon or your fingers until dough forms. Don't knead! Note, this will be wet dough. That's the way you want it to be—no need to add flour. Your seitan is now ready to be cooked.

To cook most of the seitan cutlet recipes (refer to the specific recipes for different instructions), preheat your oven to 300° F. Break your seitan into 2 cutlets for larger cutlets, or into either 4 round patties for small burgers or 4 oblong cutlets if you prefer smaller portions. Smoosh the cutlets into rounds about 1 1/2 inches thick and 3 inches across. I use a ramekin to shape them and then just dump them out.

Next, lightly oil an 8 to 12-inch piece of aluminum foil with 1/2 teaspoon oil per cutlet (or spray with nonstick if that's your thing), and wrap each cutlet individually. The amount of foil you'll need will depend on the size of your cutlets. Cook the cutlets for 30 minutes on the bottom (the part of the package with the most folded up foil). Flip and cook for another 30. With smaller cutlets, reduce your cooking time to 25 minutes and 20 minutes each side. Remove from the oven and tent (leave in the foil) for 10 minutes.

To sear the cutlets, heat 1 tablespoon vegetable oil on medium-high and brown by frying both sides lightly for 3 to 5 minutes.

Going further

This is a fun recipe. It's a great way to make burgers or something fancier. Or cook it, slice it, and toss it into a stir fry with broccoli.

Light Seitan Cutlets

These are light-colored and paired with some traditional herbs, but they don't really taste like chicken. They're a flexible, lightly savory wheat meat alternative with plenty of flavor all by themselves.

 **DIFFICULTY**

Flavors: Savory, salty, rich

Note: You'll probably need to go to your local HFS for the gluten and the nutritional yeast.

Equipment: A small bowl, a larger bowl, a whisk (a fork will do), and a sharp knife

Ingredients

- ▶ 3/4 cup gluten flour (regular whole wheat flour won't work)
- ▶ 1/2 teaspoon sea salt
- ▶ 1 tablespoon corn flour
- ▶ 1 teaspoon flax meal
- ▶ 2 tablespoons nutritional yeast
- ▶ 1 teaspoon tarragon
- ▶ 1/4 teaspoon ground black pepper
- ▶ 1/2 teaspoon savory
- ▶ 3/4 cup cold water
- ▶ 2 tablespoons tahini
- ▶ 1 teaspoon minced fresh garlic
- ▶ Dash of liquid smoke

Optional: Add a pinch of thyme, sage, or other dry green herbs or a little fresh lemon zest to the light cutlets for a little extra flavor.

Instructions

Begin by preparing your ingredients. Add all of your dry ingredients to a medium bowl and mix thoroughly to combine. Add all of your liquid ingredients to a small bowl and whisk until well combined. Make a well in the flour and add the liquid ingredients to the medium bowl. Mix with a wooden spoon or your fingers until dough forms. Don't knead!

Note: this will be wet dough. That's the way you want it to be—no need to add flour. Your seitan is now ready to be cooked.

To cook most dishes with seitan cutlets, preheat your oven to 300° F (refer to the specific recipes for different instructions). Break your seitan into 2 cutlets if you're have a big, manly appetite for protein like I do, or into either 4 round patties for burgers or 4 oblong cutlets if you prefer smaller portions. Smoosh the cutlets to 1/4-inch thickness for most of the recipes (the schnitzel and the Florentine will be thinner, and you may want to make your burgers slightly thinner). Try to avoid thinning the edges (this makes the seitan dry more quickly at the ends and results in some toughness). Cup the cutlets with your palms so that you have ends that are about the same thickness as the cutlet generally is.

Next, lightly oil an 8 to 12-inch piece of aluminum foil with 1/2 teaspoon oil per cutlet (or spray with nonstick if that's your thing), and wrap each cutlet individually. The amount of foil you'll need will depend on the size of your cutlets. Cook the cutlets for 30 minutes on the bottom (the side of the package with the most folded up foil). Flip and cook for another 25 minutes. With smaller cutlets or for the Seitan Schnitzel and Seitan Florentine, reduce your cooking time to 25 minutes and 20 minutes each side. Remove from the oven and tent (i.e., leave in the foil) for 10 minutes. Trim any slightly overdone edges before serving.

To brown the cutlets, heat 1 tablespoon vegetable oil on medium-high and brown by frying both sides lightly for 3 to 5 minutes.

Going further

In fact, there are a number of different ways to prepare seitan from this point onward, but you now have the basics.

You can mix and match herbs as much as you like. Don't be afraid to customize your seitan the way you want it with the flavors that you like. What you want in a good dough is the gluten, a drying agent (the corn, teff, or chickpea flours), some fat (the tahini, walnuts, or olive oil), and other flavors (whether it's dried herbs or other sauces in small amounts). The rest is really up to you. Some recipes recommend boiling, some pan-frying, some roasting in foil.

Most of the seitan in this book will involve roasting in foil, although in some cases, you'll simmer and then roast. Different preparation techniques produce slightly different textures. Boiling produces a more rubbery, moist seitan. Roasting, a slightly denser, chewier texture. In some cases, you'll want a nice moist center and chewy outside and this is where a little simmering and a little roasting come in handy. Seitan is a simple way to replace meat dishes in plant-based cooking because you can prepare it just the way you like, but really it is a way to supersede and reinvent main dishes altogether.

Tofu Cutlets

Tofu is a wonderful and flexible canvas waiting for any cook to paint. Tofu is fast and flexible: it can mimic a number of textures fairly easily and it absorbs flavors well. The flavor of good tofu is very slight but pleasant. It shouldn't taste like water or have no taste at all. Asian markets usually have the best.

 **DIFFICULTY**

Flavors: Savory, salty, rich

Note: You'll probably have to visit your local HFS for the agave nectar.

Ingredients

- ▶ 1 pound extra firm tofu (pick a block about 2 inches thick if you have a choice, and don't buy silken tofu).
- ▶ 3 tablespoons tamari
- ▶ 1 teaspoon brown mustard
- ▶ 1 teaspoon agave nectar
- ▶ 1 tablespoon minced fresh garlic
- ▶ 2 tablespoon extra virgin olive oil
- ▶ 1/4 teaspoon ground black pepper
- ▶ Dash of liquid smoke

Optional: You can always substitute sugar for the agave or add a tablespoon prepared catsup if you prefer (catsup usually has a lot of sweetener). Trying replacing some of the tamari with 1 teaspoon red miso and 1 tablespoon water. Or, just use the marinade you like!

Instructions

Begin by preparing your ingredients. Next, slice the tofu. Press your hand gently down on the tofu. With your knife, carefully cut through the center of the tofu. Cut each half into quarters, and each of those quarters into eighths. You should have squares that are about 1/4 inch thick (although it depends on the shape of your original block of tofu). Now, you'll need to marinate your tofu. Add the tofu to a medium-sized bowl. Whisk the marinade ingredients in a small bowl, add to the tofu, and toss to combine. Cover the bowl and let stand for 15 minutes on the counter or, if you prefer, 2 to 4 hours in the refrigerator.

To cook the tofu cutlets, preheat your oven to 400° F and roast your tofu cutlets on a baking sheet with all of the marinade for 10 to 15 minutes (or until lightly browned). Flip the cutlets and roast for another 10 to 15 minutes or until lightly browned. Remove from the oven and sauce.

Going further

This is a quick and simple introduction to tofu. It makes a simple main plate by itself, but you'll probably want an additional sauce to accompany it. You can always slice the tofu thin for a more "shaved" approach, or thicker for a burger approach. In both cases, you may need more tamari and cook times will vary.

Lemon & Herb Cutlets

A traditional combination of fresh lemon and the green flavors of herbs adds a lot of flavor to tofu and seitan. If you don't like the extra lemon, you can always leave it out.

  DIFFICULTY

Flavors: Savory, salty, rich, sour, green

Equipment: A small bowl, a larger bowl, a baking sheet, tongs, a whisk (a fork will do), and a sharp knife.

Ingredients

- 1 batch Tofu Cutlets (page 128) or 1 batch Light Seitan (page 126)
- Sea salt (a little sprinkle before serving)
- 2 teaspoons fresh-squeezed lemon juice (organic lemon preferred)
- 2 to 4 thinly sliced lemon wedges for garnish

Additional ingredients for the seitan
(in addition to those already called for):

- 1 teaspoon dry oregano, rubbed
- 1/4 teaspoon dry rosemary, rubbed
- 1 tablespoon minced fresh garlic

Additional ingredients for the marinade
(in addition to those already called for):

- 1 teaspoon dry oregano, rubbed
- 1/4 teaspoon dry rosemary, rubbed

Optional: 1/2 teaspoon lemon zest, 1 tablespoon fresh mint, or cilantro for garnish. Add an additional teaspoon of the liquid ingredients of the seitan to the tofu marinade for a more permeating taste of lemon (although if you do, be sure to taste and adjust the amount of lemon juice in the final dish to your taste).

Instructions

Begin by preparing your ingredients. For the seitan, preheat your oven to 300° F. Break your assembled dough into equal halves. With your hands, carefully flatten the seitan into a smooth, oblong shape. Bake and tent following the Basic Cutlets recipe. Unwrap and sprinkle with a pinch of sea salt as necessary.

For the tofu, preheat your oven to 400° F. Grease the baking sheet. Place your tofu cutlets on the sheet and then pour the remaining marinade over the cutlets as evenly as you can. Bake on the middle oven rack for about 15 minutes. Flip the cutlets carefully with a fork and then with a spoon, pour remaining marinade over the cutlets. Bake for another 15 minutes, or until the cutlets have browned and most of the moisture has been absorbed. Remove from heat and let stand 10 minutes. Taste and sprinkle with a little salt as necessary.

Drizzle 1 teaspoon lemon juice equally over the servings and garnish with lemon wedges. If you're adding the cilantro or mint, sprinkle these over the cutlets before adding the lemon juice and the lemon wedge on top.

Going further

This dish already has a number of flavors. Pair it with Roasted Red Potatoes (page 94) and Roasted Kale (page 91) or collards for a simple plate. Pair it with pilaf or risotto for a more complicated one.

Cutlets Cacciatore

A traditional favorite with mushrooms and peppers. Tofu and seitan work equally well in this dish.

  DIFFICULTY

Flavors: Savory, salty, rich, sour, spicy

Equipment: A small bowl, a larger bowl, a pan capable of holding at least 6 cups water with a tight-fitting lid, a baking sheet, tongs, a whisk (a fork will do), and a sharp knife

Ingredients

▶ 1 batch Tofu Cutlets (page 128) or 1 batch Light or Dark Seitan (page 126, 125)

▶ About 1 pound pasta of your choice: linguine, fettuccine, and spaghetti are all fine

▶ Or, 2 cups short- or long-grain brown rice

▶ Water (about 12 cups for pasta, 4 cups for rice)

▶ Sea salt (1 tablespoon to salt the water for pasta, 1/4 teaspoon to salt the water for rice)

Sauce

▶ 2 batches of Tomato Herb Sauce (page 66)

▶ 1 additional teaspoon oregano

▶ 1 additional teaspoon basil

▶ 1/2 teaspoon sage

▶ 1 additional tablespoon garlic

▶ 1 large white onion, peeled and finely chopped

▶ 1 green bell pepper, seeded, cored, and finely chopped

▶ 1/4 cup wine (red or white, although white is more traditional)

▶ Sea salt (a pinch or to taste)

Note: Add the oregano, basil, and sage to the tomato sauce when you add the rest of the dry herbs in that recipe.

Optional: Typically, the tofu and seitan would be breaded lightly with flour for this dish. If you want to flour your tofu or seitan, you'll need about 1/2 cup whole wheat flour, a pinch of sea salt, about 2 teaspoons total of the dry green herbs you like, about 1/2 cup unsweetened soy milk and 1 tablespoon vegetable oil.

Instructions

Begin by preparing your ingredients. If you're making rice, you'll want to put it on when your cutlets come out of the oven. If you're making pasta, put it on when you set your sauce to simmer.

First, make the cutlets. For the seitan, preheat your oven to 300° F. Prepare, bake, and tent the cutlets following the Basic Cutlets recipe. Unwrap and slice each piece into 8 equal slices, or if you prefer smaller bites, cut the 8 slices in half for 16 equal pieces.

For the tofu, make the Basic Cutlets recipe. Preheat your oven to 400° F. Lightly oil the baking sheet. Place your tofu cutlets on the sheet and then pour the remaining marinade over the cutlets as evenly as you can. Bake on the middle oven rack for about 15 minutes. Flip the cutlets carefully with a fork and then with a spoon, pour remaining marinade over the cutlets. Bake for another 15 minutes or until the cutlets have brown and most of the moisture has been absorbed. Remove from the oven. Let stand 10 minutes to cool.

While your cutlets are cooling the first time around, begin the tomato sauce. Prepare it in a medium bowl and add the extra herbs and spices. Add 1 tablespoon olive oil to the pan and bring to heat on high. Add your onion and sauté for 6 minutes. Decrease the heat to medium-high and add your green pepper and sauté for 3 minutes. Your pan should be starting to brown. Add 1/4 cup wine and deglaze the pan for 2 to 3 minutes or until the white wine has reduced by about 1/2. Add the Tomato Herb Sauce, and return to a simmer. Cover the pan with the lid ajar. Cook and reduce by about 1/4 to 1/3 (depending on how thick you like your sauce). In the meantime, prepare your seitan or tofu (and breading if you're breading either).

If you're breading your cutlets, when they are done and cool enough to handle, dip each piece into the soy milk and then roll into the flour mixture until well-coated. Brush each cutlet with vegetable oil. Add to the baking sheet and bake for another 5 to 8 minutes, flip and bake another 5 to 8 minutes or until the cutlets have browned. Or, heat the oil in a frying pan and fry the cutlets on medium-high heat, turning until all sides are brown, which should take a couple of minutes per side. Remove from the oven or the pan and add to the sauce when it has reduced and simmer for another 10 minutes. Remove from heat and let stand 5 minutes.

Going further

This is a simple but flavorful dish. To keep it simple, serve with brown rice. For a more complicated plate, serve with Roasted Portobello Mushrooms with Pears and Onions (page 117) and risotto or pilaf.

Cutlets a l'Orange

Citrus and seitan go really well together. This is a reinterpretation of a common French dish that become popular in the United States with the influx of *haute cuisine*. The citrus gives it a simple, fresh flavor.

  DIFFICULTY

Flavors: Savory, salty, rich, sour, spicy

Equipment: A small bowl, a larger bowl, a baking sheet, tongs, a whisk (a fork will do), and a sharp knife

Ingredients

▶ 1 batch Dark Seitan (page 125), or Tofu Cutlets (page 128)
▶ For the seitan, add 1 teaspoon ginger to the liquid ingredients
▶ 1 batch Orange Sauce (page 70)

Optional: Dark Seitan is preferred for this recipe, but the light variety will also work. The dark just provides a little more color and flavor contrast.

Instructions

Begin by preparing your ingredients.

For the seitan, preheat your oven to 300° F. Prepare, bake and tent your cutlets following the Basic Cutlet recipe. Unwrap, and plate (or brown a little if you like).

For the tofu, preheat your oven to 400° F. Grease the baking sheet. Place your tofu cutlets on the sheet and then pour the remaining marinade over the cutlets as evenly as you can. Bake on the middle oven rack for about 15 minutes. Flip the cutlets carefully with a fork and then with a spoon, pour remaining marinade over the cutlets. Bake for another 15 minutes or until the cutlets have browned and most of the moisture has been absorbed. Remove from heat and let stand 10 minutes.

To plate and sauce, prepare your sauce about 10 minutes from the completion of tofu or seitan cutlets. When both are ready, add the seitan to the middle of the plate and with a tablespoon, and drip sauce over the cutlets. Use about 4 to 6 tablespoons sauce per plate. With side dishes, plate the cutlets to the center/side, preferably the left side. If you're serving with Roasted Kale, consider plating the greens in a flat, smooth and circular layer, laying the cutlets over the top and then saucing the cutlets. What's important with plating is arranging the plate in a way that's inviting, promotes visual contrast, and really draws attention to the effort you've put into your work.

Going further

This flavors of this dish are primarily sour and citrusy. So, this dish goes well with greens as a side dish. For some simple extra carbs, serve with roasted potatoes. For a fancier plate, serve with pilaf.

Whiskey Seitan

This dish has whiskey!

 DIFFICULTY

Instructions

Begin by preparing your ingredients.

Flavors: Savory, salty, rich, sour, spicy

For the seitan, preheat your oven to 300° F. Break your assembled dough into 2 equal pieces (or 4 for smaller cutlets if you prefer). Prepare, bake, and tent as directed in the Basic Cutlets recipe. Unwrap and plate or brown in the oven if you like.

Equipment: A small bowl, a larger bowl, a baking sheet, tongs, a whisk (a fork will do), and a sharp knife.

For the tofu, preheat your oven to 400° F. Lightly oil the baking sheet. Place your tofu cutlets on the sheet and then pour the remaining marinade over the cutlets as evenly as you can. If your sauce is already prepared, add 1 to 2 tablespoons to the marinade if you like. Bake on the middle oven rack for about 15 minutes. Flip the cutlets carefully with a fork. With a spoon, pour any remaining marinade over the cutlets. Bake for another 15 minutes or until the cutlets have browned and most of the moisture has been absorbed. Remove from heat and let stand 10 minutes.

Ingredients

▶ 1 batch Tofu Cutlets (page 128) or Light Seitan (page 126)

▶ 1 batch Three-Pepper Whiskey Sauce (page 76)

To plate and sauce, prepare your sauce about 10 minutes out from the completion of your tofu or your seitan cutlets (or if you prefer, before you get started). When both are ready, add the seitan to the middle-left of the plate and with a tablespoon, drip sauce over the cutlets. Use about 4 to 6 tablespoons sauce per plate. If you're plating with side dishes, plate the cutlets to the center/side, preferably so that it is on the right side of the plate for the eater. If you're serving with Roasted Kale (recommended!), consider plating the greens in a flat, smooth, and circular layer, laying the cutlets over the top and then saucing the cutlets. Again, what's important is to make the plate look inviting and to really bring all the effort you've put into your work to a beautiful finish.

Optional: I often swap the whiskey for cognac which makes a good substitute if you have cognac on-hand more often than whiskey. Sprinkle with a teaspoon or so of minced cilantro for a little green color and flavor.

Going further

The sauce is sweet and spicy (and brown). So, this dish goes well with green, sour, and savory flavors. To keep it simple, serve this with roasted mushrooms, roasted kale, and roasted potatoes. For a more elaborate plate, serve with Brown Rice Pilaf (page 108) and French-Style Green Beans, Red Peppers, and Onions (page 114).

Corned Seitan & Cabbage

A holiday favorite for Irish Americans everywhere. This is really a seitan-only recipe. Tofu cutlets won't work as well. Corning is basically the addition of coarse sea salt. As a consequence, the seitan will be lightly salty. Add a little less salt to the vegetables for a more traditional plate or reduce the tamari even further and salt your vegetables to your taste.

  DIFFICULTY

Flavors: Savory, salty, rich, sour, spicy, green

Equipment: A small bowl, a larger bowl, a pan capable of holding at least 6 cups water with a tight-fitting lid, a baking sheet, tongs, ramekins, a whisk (a fork will do), and a sharp knife

Ingredients

- ▶ 1 batch Dark Seitan (page 125) but reduce the tamari by 1 tablespoon
- ▶ Add 1 tablespoon extra virgin olive oil
- ▶ Use about 1/4 teaspoon coarse sea salt

Vegetables

- ▶ 2 medium potatoes (avoid baking potatoes), in 1/2-inch dice
- ▶ 1 cup water for steaming the potatoes
- ▶ 1 batch Roasted Ginger Garlic Coleslaw (page 95)
- ▶ 1 additional carrot, trimmed and shredded
- ▶ 1 additional white onion, peeled and thinly sliced
- ▶ 1 additional tablespoon extra virgin olive oil added to the dressing
- ▶ 1 extra pinch of fine sea salt
- ▶ Coarse sea salt to taste (1/2 teaspoon total should do)

Optional: Leave out the ginger if you prefer a more traditional taste.

Instructions

Dice and steam the potatoes for 30 to 40 minutes or until done. Make the coleslaw recipe and add the potatoes and onions, an extra tablespoon olive oil, and a extra pinch of fine sea salt. If you are baking the cabbage, potatoes, etc. together with the corned seitan, preheat your oven to 400° F. Bake on the middle rack for about 30 minutes. Flip the foil packages and bake for another 20 minutes. If you are just baking the cutlet and making the coleslaw separately, preheat to 300° F. Bake on the middle rack for about 20 minutes. Flip the foil packages and bake for another 20 minutes. If you simmer your seitan (see notes below), add an additional 10 minutes to your bake time (5 minutes each side).

Otherwise, prepare, cook, and tent the seitan following the basic recipe, noting the additions and subtractions listed above. Instead of smoothing out your seitan, break into two pieces, and push each down into a small ramekin. Tap out each piece of seitan on a clean cutting board so that you have a nice, rounded cutlet. Add all of your ingredients (except the seitan) and mix until well combined. Place the cutlet and half of your vegetables into about 12 to 18 inches of foil and wrap. Repeat with the other cutlet.

When the seitan is done and cooling (leave it wrapped), spread the cabbage and potatoes on a lightly oiled baking sheet or roasting pan. Increase the oven temperature to broil. Broil until lightly browned (3 to 8 minutes, depending on how cooked the vegetables are). If you want a roasted flavor for your seitan, add it to the cabbage and potatoes for the last 5 minutes of cooking. Do not over-broil! When done, let stand about 5 minutes to cool. Plate with the cutlet in the center and the potatoes, cabbage, and carrots circled around it.

Going further

If you want a juicier cutlet, lightly simmer these fresh from the ramekins in lightly salted water for about 10 minutes and then roast. This is a full, beautiful, and flavorful plate when you're done, but if you want a little extra flavor, add some roasted mushrooms as a side. If you serve this to Irish-American friends or family, be sure to remind them that "traditional corned beef and cabbage" was never a traditional dish of the Irish but a concoction that immigrants threw together because they found themselves in a new and unfamiliar place, ready to meet the challenges of the New World head on. New traditions are a wonderful way to build communities.

Cutlets with Pomegranate
Jalapeño Sauce

This is a simple favorite with lots of bold flavors. Seitan is preferable in this dish, but you can also use tofu.

  DIFFICULTY Instructions

Flavors: Savory, salty, rich, sour, spicy

Equipment: A small bowl, a larger bowl, a baking sheet, tongs, a whisk (a fork will do), and a sharp knife

Ingredients

▶ 1 batch Tofu Cutlets (page 128) or Dark Seitan (page 125)
▶ 1 batch Pomegranate and Jalapeño Sauce (page 69)

Begin by preparing your ingredients.

For the seitan, preheat your oven to 300° F. Prepare, bake, and tent your seitan following the Basic Cutlets recipe. Unwrap and cut each cutlet into 8 equal slices and plate.

For the tofu, make the Basic Cutlets recipe using the basic marinade. Preheat your oven to 400° F. Lightly oil the baking sheet. Place your tofu cutlets on the sheet and then pour the remaining marinade over the cutlets as evenly as you can. Bake on the middle oven rack for about 15 minutes. Flip the cutlets carefully with a fork. With a spoon, pour remaining marinade over the cutlets. Bake for another 15 minutes or until the cutlets have browned and most of the moisture has been absorbed.

In the meantime, prepare your sauce. Taste and add salt as necessary. When the tofu or seitan is done, plate and then spoon sauce over the top, coating well.

Going further

This dish adds some very bold spicy and sour flavors. Pair it with some Roasted Kale (page 91) or collards and some potatoes for a simple plate or with some succotash and pilaf for a more complicated one.

Seitan Schnitzel

In American terms, this is a seitan-fried steak, or maybe it's a country-fried steak. I'm all confused, as I'm not sure what's substituting for what now. Regardless, it's not deep-fried, so I've gone with schnitzel. But for those who like a nice breaded crunch, this is a great dish. Use light seitan for a more proper schnitzel or dark for a more of a country-fried seitan.

 DIFFICULTY

Flavors: Savory, salty, rich, sweet, spicy

Equipment: A hand blender or food processor, a sharp knife, a small bowl, a saucer or other wide and shallow dish, tongs, wax paper is nice to have, a pastry brush will be useful, a baking sheet, and a whisk

Ingredients

- ▶ 1 batch light or Dark Seitan (page 125)
- ▶ 1/4 cup unsweetened soy milk
- ▶ 1 cup breadcrumbs (panko if you can find them, or use two slices lightly toasted whole wheat bread)
- ▶ 1/2 cup whole wheat flour (cornstarch will also work)
- ▶ 2 tablespoons vegetable oil (1 for blending, 1 for brushing)
- ▶ 1 tablespoon unsweetened soy milk
- ▶ 1/2 teaspoon ground black pepper
- ▶ 1/4 teaspoon sea salt

Optional: Any additional dry herbs, for example, dried onion powder or dried garlic powder, cayenne pepper, and tarragon are all good ways to season your breading. If you like it really plain, you can dial back the black pepper.

Instructions

Begin by preparing your ingredients. Prepare the seitan following the Basic Cutlet recipe, but carefully flatten your seitan to even thinner proportions (aim for 1/8 inch). If you have a smaller appetite, break the cutlets into 4 and reduce the cook time by 5 minutes each side. Preheat your oven to 300° F and bake for 25 minutes on the middle rack, flip, and bake for another 20 minutes. Your cutlet will be slightly underdone, and that's fine.

When the seitan is done, remove from the oven and let it rest 10 minutes, heat your oven to 450° F. While the seitan is cooling, whirl the bread, sea salt, soy milk, and 1 tablespoon of the vegetable oil in a food processor or crumb the bread with a knife and whisk in a small bowl. If you don't have a pastry brush, add the second tablespoon of vegetable oil to the bread and whirl along with everything else.

Next, add the soy milk to the saucer. Dip the seitan in it until it is well coated, then dip it in the flour until it is well coated. Set aside to dry (about 10 to 15 minutes will do). Dip the floured seitan in the soy milk again and then dip it into the breadcrumb mixture and roll to coat. You may need to pack the breading down with your fingers, and if you do, do so over the wax paper. Repeat with the second cutlet.

When both cutlets are ready, lightly oil the baking sheet and the cutlets. Brush with the second tablespoon of vegetable oil. Bake for 10 to 12 minutes or until the breadcrumbs start to brown lightly. Remove from the oven and turn carefully with tongs and return to the oven to cook another 10 to 12 minutes. Remove from the oven, and plate carefully with tongs.

Going further

Serve this schnitzel with some Sour Cream (page 65). A dollop on top or in a side ramekin works well. This dish also goes well with the Simple Mornay Sauce (page 80) or any of the gravies in Chapter 3. For a simpler plate, serve it with roasted sweet potatoes and black kale. For a fancier plate, serve it with Borscht (page 30) and Red Potato/Sweet Potato and Scallion Mash (page 106). This dish also goes well on a bun with some fries with a little Tarragon Aioli (page 64).

Seitan a la King with Fresh Fettuccine

This was a classic in the Midwest when I was growing up. With red peppers, mushrooms, white sauce (usually made from a roux), and pasta, traditionally, this is a richer, heavier dish. My recipe modernizes and lightens it, but without sacrificing the comfort factor. It also goes well with rice.

  DIFFICULTY

Flavors: Savory, salty, rich, sweet, green

Note: You'll need to get various ingredients from the HFS for the seitan, the nutritional yeast, etc.

Equipment: A sauté pan capable of holding 8 cups liquid, a whisk, a small bowl, a small pan capable of holding 4 cups liquid, and a large pan capable of holding at least 8 cups

Ingredients

▶ 1/2 to 1 batch Light Seitan (page 126)
▶ 1 batch Pasta Dough (page 116)
▶ 1 to 2 batches Simple Mornay Sauce (page 80)
▶ 1 tablespoon vegetable oil
▶ 1 medium-sized vidalia onion, peeled and finely chopped
▶ 1 red bell pepper, cored, seeded, and diced (1/4-inch dice preferred)
▶ 1 green bell pepper, cored, seeded and diced (1/4-inch dice preferred)
▶ 8 cremini or button mushrooms, stemmed and thinly sliced (1/8 inch is preferred)
▶ 1/4 cup vodka
▶ 1 teaspoon lemon juice
▶ 1/4 teaspoon ground black pepper
▶ 1 tablespoon nutritional yeast
▶ Sea salt (start with 1/4 teaspoon and add more to taste)

Note: This recipe varies a little bit depending on whether your pasta will be a side dish or a main dish and how well sauced you prefer your a la king. Traditionally, this dish is saucier than regular pastas with red sauce, more like an alfredo, but not quite as thick. For a lighter side dish, use 1 batch of sauce and 1/2 batch of seitan (or make a full batch and just use one of the cutlets, reserving the other for whatever you want). For a well-sauced main entrée or as a bigger appetizer for 4, use a full batch of seitan and 2 batches of the Simple Mornay Sauce (you'll have a little leftover sauce).

Optional: You can replace the vidalia onion with 4 scallions if you prefer some green.

Instructions

Begin by preparing your ingredients. When the seitan is done, cut into 1/2-inch cubes. If you like, brown your cubes using 1 tablespoon vegetable oil (see the Basic Cutlets recipe, page 126, for details) and set aside. Once your seitan is done and cooling, prepare your noodles. Roll, cut, and cook your fettuccine according to the basic recipe. Cook, drain, and rinse your fettuccine thoroughly with cold water.

Once your noodles and seitan are ready, prepare your sauce. Whisk together and prepare a double batch of the Simple Mornay Sauce and set aside. In the sauté pan, bring 1 tablespoon oil to heat on high. Add 1/4 teaspoon sea salt to the pan. Add the onion and sauté for 3 minutes. Reduce to medium-high and add the red and green peppers and sauté for 3 to 5 minutes. Add the mushrooms and sauté for 6 to 8 minutes. When the pan starts to brown slightly, sauté for another 2 minutes, and then add the vodka and lemon juice to deglaze. Sauté for another 2 minutes, and add your Mornay Sauce. Add the nutritional yeast and black pepper. Bring the sauce to a simmer and reduce to low. Remove the seitan from the foil and chop into 1/2-inch dice. Add to the sauté pan and simmer for another 5 minutes. Remove from heat. Taste and add salt as necessary. It should be slightly salty, since your noodles will not be.

To plate, roll the fettuccine up with a fork, and then add to the plate in small nests. Ladle sauce over the top and sprinkle with the nutritional yeast. Or, add the fettuccine to a pasta bowl, ladle in sauce, and then toss to combine. Serves 2 for dinner or 4 as a side dish.

Going further

Traditionally, this dish is higher in fat than it is in this recipe. If you want to add fat, add a tablespoon of macadamia nut butter to the sauce. Because it's a fairly heavy dish, you should pair it with light greens with some sour dressing. This dish goes well with the Garden Veggie (page 86), some chopped spinach and artichoke, and even the Caesar Salad (page 87). Of course, you can also always add a little chopped spinach or arugula while the sauce is cooling to add color, flavor, and nutrition (I add 1 tightly packed cup to this recipe).

Seitan Florentine

This cookbook wouldn't be complete without at least one stuffed seitan recipe. You can use this technique to mock a number of dishes: seitan Kiev, seitan cordon bleu, and to make a number of other types of roulades. This dish is also one of my favorites. Traditionally, this dish is made with spinach, which is a great way to have it, but it's also good with arugula. I usually make it with black kale.

   **DIFFICULTY**

Flavors: Savory, salty, rich, sour, sweet

Equipment: A small bowl, a larger bowl, tongs, a whisk (a fork will do), and a sharp knife

Ingredients

- ▶ 1 batch Light Seitan (page 126)
- ▶ 1 batch Simple Mornay Sauce (page 80) or the sauce of your choice
- ▶ 6 button mushrooms (about a half cup), stemmed and finely chopped
- ▶ 2 cups packed baby spinach (or greens of your choice, but if you use kale, use 1 1/2 cups)
- ▶ 1/4 red onion, minced
- ▶ 1 tablespoon olive oil
- ▶ 2 tablespoons white wine
- ▶ 1 tablespoon nutritional yeast
- ▶ 1 tablespoon macadamia nut butter, cashew butter or tahini
- ▶ 1/2 teaspoon lemon juice

Instructions

Begin by preparing your ingredients. Then sauté your vegetables. Bring oil to heat in the pan. Add a pinch of sea salt. Add the chopped onions and sauté for 3 minutes. Add the mushrooms and sauté for 5 minutes. Add the white wine to deglaze the pan and sauté another 2 minutes. Decrease the heat to medium-high. Add the greens and sauté until the volume as a whole has been reduced by about 1/2. This will take you about 3 minutes with spinach, or 5 to 7 with black kale. Add the lemon juice, nutritional yeast, and nut butter and mix to thoroughly combine. Remove from heat and let stand for about 5 minutes.

While your sauté is cooling, preheat your oven to 350° F and prepare your seitan using following the basic recipe. Break your seitan into two equal balls (for two cutlets, and you may have leftovers). Instead of flattening out to an oblong shape, carefully roll your seitan out a little further. You can roll it between wax paper if that's more comfortable for you, or just use your hands. The dough can be a little tricky, but assuming it's nice and moist, you shouldn't have too many problems.

When your sauté is cool and your seitan is flat, take one cutlet and hold it in your left palm (reverse if you're left-handed). Spoon half of the mixture into the center of your palm. Carefully pull the dough around the filling. You may have to flatten the dough with your fingers. If you've made pupusas, this will be old hat. When you have a little ball of dough with the filling safely tucked inside, bring both of your palms together gently to flatten into a nice roundish-oblong shape. Close any remaining seams as best as you can with your fingers. It's not a serious problem if you have small holes in the dough, but do your best to close them for your presentation.

The other way to prepare a "stuffed" seitan is to smooth out the filling on the rolled out seitan and roll it up into a roulade. This technique is best when you have filling that's nice and smooth (e.g., duxelles, or minced kalamata olives and spinach). You can use this technique with spinach and mushrooms if you chopped your mushrooms finely enough. When you have your seitan and it's filling all nice and snug, wrap in foil and bake for 25 minutes, flip, and bake another 20 minutes.

Remove the seitan from the oven and let it stand for 10 minutes in foil. Prepare your sauce while the seitan cools. When the sauce is ready, unwrap and plate in the center or center-left of your plate if you have side dishes. Drizzle the sauce over your cutlet—about 4 to 6 tablespoons sauce per plate, or more if you like.

Going further

This is a relatively simple technique and you can stuff your seitan with just about anything you like. Side with Roasted Red Potatoes (page 94) for a simple plate, or with Brown Rice Pilaf (page 108) and French-Style Green Beans with Red Peppers and Onions (page 114) for a fancier one. Or get crazy. Stuff your seitan with some mashed potatoes, and plate the greens and mushrooms. It's entirely up to you!

Stuffed Pizza with Spinach, Sun-Dried
Tomatoes & Seitanic Sausage

Stuffed pizza has always been my favorite. It's the most difficult to make, but it's also the richest and most fun!

Flavors: **Sweet, salty, sour, rich, green, spicy**

Equipment: **A couple of bowls, a food processor (or a hand blender), a rolling pin, a stainless steel or cast iron frying pan or pie tin, a pizza cutter, and a pie wedge is nice to have**

Ingredients

- 1 batch Yeast Dough (page 118)
- 1 tablespoon extra virgin olive oil
- 1 teaspoon fine corn meal
- Sea salt (start with a pinch and add more to taste)
- 1 batch Tomato Herb Sauce (page 66)

Filling
- 1/2 batch Seitan Schnitzel (page 136), coarsely chopped
- 1 tablespoon extra virgin olive oil
- Pinch of sea salt
- 1/4 cup sun-dried tomatoes, rehydrated and finely chopped
- 1/2 cup hot water
- 1 pound firm tofu, drained and pressed
- 1 batch Spinach, Arugula, and Walnut Pesto (page 52)
- 1/4 cup nutritional yeast
- 1 teaspoon arrowroot powder
- 2 additional tablespoons minced fresh garlic
- 1 additional tablespoon extra virgin olive oil, or 2 tablespoons if you want a heavier filling
- 1 additional teaspoon lemon juice
- 1 tablespoons dried oregano, rubbed
- 1/2 teaspoon sea salt (add more to taste

Optional: **To keep things simple, replace the pesto with 1 1/2 cups chopped spinach and cashews if you prefer.**

Instructions

Begin by preparing your ingredients. Make your seitan first. Prepare, tent, and cool the seitan following the basic recipe with faux-sausage alterations (page 136). When your seitan is out of the oven, preheat your oven to 400° F.

Once the seitan has started, begin your dough and let it rise in a warm place. When you flip the seitan at 30 minutes, reconstitute the sun-dried tomatoes in 1/2 cup hot water for 30 minutes. Drain the tomatoes, chop, and set aside. Begin the tomato sauce using the pizza sauce variation of the recipe (page 66). Next, prepare the filling. Prepare the pesto. Blend the tofu, the pesto, and the remaining filling ingredients. Add the sun-dried tomatoes and stir to combine.

When your sauce, dough, and toppings are ready, break the dough into two parts, roughly 2/3 and 1/3 of the total amount. Sprinkle the pan with corn meal. Roll the bottom, larger crust out to at least 11 to 12 inches in diameter (depending on the size of your pan). Roll the smaller, top crust out to around 10 inches (depending on the size of your pan—you want to ensure that the top crust fits over the bottom like a pie crust would).

Lightly oil your frying pan or pie tin, and sprinkle with corn meal and a pinch of sea salt. Add the bottom crust to the pan as if you were adding a pie crust. Chop your seitan into 1/2-inch dice, and toss with 1 tablespoon extra virgin olive oil and sea salt (and any extra pepper and agave nectar you might like if you like your sausages sweet and/or spicy). Brush the crust with olive oil. Add about 4 to 6 tablespoons of sauce in a smooth, even layer, then add the seitan. Spoon the tofu filling on top and smooth with a spoon into an even layer. Add the top crust and pinch closed, seam and trim the edges with a knife the way you would a pie.

Add to the oven and bake for 20 minutes. Remove from the oven and poke holes in the top of the crush with a fork. Return to the oven and bake for another 10 to 15 minutes or until the crust is starting to brown lightly. Remove from the oven, add the tomato sauce to the top crust, and sprinkle with nutritional yeast and oregano. Return to the oven and bake another 5 minutes. Remove from the oven and let stand for 10 minutes or until the pizza has cooled but is still warm. Cut and serve as you would a pie.

Going further

Be forewarned, stuffed pizza is the most difficult. If you want to add vegetables to a stuffed pizza, their moisture will come out during the cooking process and that can affect your crust (even if it has been thoroughly oiled. So, if you do add vegetables, make sure you cook them thoroughly until they have expelled a fair amount of their moisture before adding them to your pie. That's amore!

Thin-Crust Margharita Pizza

I came up with these recipes one night when I was sitting on my old balcony and the moon hit my eye just so. That's not even remotely true. Truthfully, however, pizza was the very first dish I ever learned to cook completely from scratch. Unlike much of the rest of the world, Chicagoans take pizza very, very seriously. In Chicago, pizza ranges from fast food to a gourmet meal and comes in a number of varieties, thin-crust, thick-crust (especially pan) and stuffed. This is a simple basil and sauce combination with a nice, thin crust.

 **DIFFICULTY**

Flavors: Sweet, salty, sour, rich, green

Equipment: A few bowls, a rolling pin, a pizza cutter, and a 14-inch pizza pan or a pizza stone if you have one

Ingredients

- ▶ 1 batch Yeast Dough (page 118)
- ▶ 1/2 to 1 batch Tomato Herb Sauce (page 66)
- ▶ 1 teaspoon fine corn meal
- ▶ 1 tablespoon plus 1 tablespoon extra virgin olive oil
- ▶ 1 cup packed basil, stemmed, and chiffonade
- ▶ 2 tablespoons nutritional yeast
- ▶ 1 teaspoon dried oregano
- ▶ Sea salt (start with a pinch and add more to taste)

Note: If you like your pizza saucier, make a whole batch of Tomato Herb Suace and be sure to note the variations to the basic recipe for pizza sauce. You may have to reduce it by 1/2 depending on the water content of your tomatoes.

Instructions

Begin by preparing your ingredients. First, prepare your dough, and while it's rising, prepare your sauce according to the recipe. When you have your sauce and dough ready, prepare your toppings and preheat the oven to 450° F.

Sprinkle your pan with the corn meal. Roll the crust out as evenly as you can to a circle 14 inches in diameter. Brush the crust with 1 tablespoon oil. Add the sauce in a thin, smooth layer to within 1/2 inch of the edges. Bake for 15 minutes and remove from the oven.

While the pizza is baking, chiffonade the basil. At the 15-minute mark, remove the pizza from the oven, and then sprinkle with basil, nutritional yeast, and oregano. Drizzle 1 tablespoon olive oil over the top. Return to the oven and bake for another 5 minutes. Remove from the oven, let stand for 10 minutes to cool, and cut into rectangles.

Going further

You can make your pizza with any toppings you like. Artichokes, olives, peppers, seitan pepperoni, and seitan sausage all go well on a pizza. You can even use prepackaged plant-based cheeses if you like (these often melt much better if you grate them and toss them with a little vegetable oil before sprinkling them on top). The margharita is a classic because of its simplicity, color, and light flavor, but there's no rule that you have to use a white or a red sauce. You can make a rosé. You can even branch out and use one of the other sauces in Chapter 3

Combination Pan Pizza with
Green Peppers, Mushrooms & Onions

Pan pizza is also very popular in Chicago and is one of the styles of pizza for which the city is known. Traditionally, pan pizza gets its name from being cooked in a pan. Seriously, you can use a cast iron or stainless steel frying pan, or a pie tin if you have one large enough.

 **DIFFICULTY**

Flavors: Sweet, salty, sour, savory, rich, green

Equipment: A couple of bowls, a rolling pin, a stainless steel or cast iron frying pan or pie tin, a pizza cutter, and a pie wedge is nice to have

Ingredients

- ▶ 1 batch Yeast Dough (page 118)
- ▶ 1/2 to 1 batch Tomato Herb Sauce (page 66)
- ▶ Extra virgin olive oil
- ▶ 1 teaspoon fine corn meal
- ▶ 1/2 white onion, peeled and thinly sliced
- ▶ 8 cremini mushrooms, stemmed and thinly sliced
- ▶ 1/2 green pepper, cored, seeded, and chopped
- ▶ 2 tablespoons nutritional yeast
- ▶ 1 teaspoon dried oregano, rubbed
- ▶ Sea salt (start with a pinch and add more to taste)

Instructions

Begin by preparing your ingredients. First, prepare your dough, and while it's rising, prepare your sauce according to the recipe. When you have your sauce and dough ready, prepare your toppings and preheat the oven to 400° F.

While your sauce and dough are cooking, prepare your green pepper, mushrooms, and onion. Slice the vegetables as thinly as you can and toss them with a tablespoon of olive oil and a pinch of sea salt. Lightly oil your pan and then sprinkle it with corn meal and a pinch of sea salt (you can also add a pinch or two of onion powder if you're adventurous and like a seasoned crust). You can also sauté your vegetables first if you prefer. Sprinkle a pinch of salt into the bottom of the pan as well.

Next, roll the crust out as evenly as you can to a circle 12 inches in diameter. Add the crust to the pan and brush lightly with olive oil (the crust will roll up the sides of your pan slightly, and that's fine). Add the sauce up to the edges. Add the vegetables on top in a light and evenly spaced layer. Bake for 20 minutes and remove from the oven. Sprinkle with nutritional yeast and oregano. Drizzle a tablespoon of olive oil over the top. Return to the oven for another 5 minutes. Remove from heat, let stand for 10 minutes to cool and cut into slices for thick crust. Add 1/4 cup diced fresh pineapple to give this more of a West Coast feel.

Going further

Pan pizza is slightly less flexible than thin crust in terms of the amount and types of toppings. There's less crust to work with and that typically means fewer ingredients. But, on the other hand, you can flavor your crust more easily than with thin crust, and if you like crusty pizza, pan pizza is hard to beat.

Spinach, Arugula & Walnut Pesto Stromboli
with Kalamata Olives & Sun-Dried Tomatoes

The stromboli is a uniquely American reinterpretation of the calzone, which is like a pizza but folded over and sealed up like a hand pie. Traditionally, the stromboli is longer, thinner, and usually made with a white sauce rather than a red one. You can also leave out of the tofu filling and make this as a thin-crust pizza instead.

 **DIFFICULTY**

Flavors: Sweet, salty, sour, rich, green

Equipment: A few bowls, a rolling pin, and a baking sheet. You can also use a pizza stone if you have one.

Ingredients

- ▶ 1 batch Yeast Dough (page 118)
- ▶ 1 tablespoon extra virgin olive oil
- ▶ 1 teaspoon fine corn meal
- ▶ Sea salt (start with a pinch and add more to taste)

Filling

- ▶ 1/2 cup sun-dried tomatoes, finely chopped
- ▶ 1/2 cup kalamata olives, pitted, and minced
- ▶ 1/2 batch Spinach, Arugula, and Walnut Pesto (page 52)
- ▶ 1/2 brick firm tofu (approximately 1 cup)
- ▶ 1/4 cup nutritional yeast
- ▶ 1 additional teaspoon lemon juice
- ▶ 1 additional tablespoon minced fresh garlic
- ▶ 1 additional tablespoon extra virgin olive oil
- ▶ 2 teaspoons dried oregano, rubbed
- ▶ 1/4 teaspoon sea salt (or to taste)

Optional: Make 1/2 batch Tomato Herb Sauce with the pizza sauce variation (page 66) for a dip or a finishing sauce.

Instructions

Begin by preparing your ingredients. First, prepare your dough, and while it's rising, get the rest of your ingredients together. Pit and mince your olives and finely chop your sun-dried tomatoes without reconstituting. Finally, prepare your sauce following the basic recipe, and then blend it with the tofu, additional nut butter, 1/4 teaspoon sea salt, nutritional yeast, lemon juice, and garlic until smooth. Add the olives and the tomatoes and stir to combine. Taste and add salt if necessary (the filling should be salted just right for your taste or very lightly salty).

When you have your sauce and dough ready, prepare your toppings and preheat your oven to 450° F. Split the dough into quarters and roll the crust out to circles 6 inches in diameter. Brush the crust lightly with oil, and spread 1/4 of the filling on top. Roll up each stromboli and seam the way you would a tortilla. Fold the tops and bottom of the dough in about 1 inch. Then fold the right side inward and over the filling. Fold the left side over. Seam the filling in as best as you can and shape into a long, smooth cylinder. Repeat for the other strombolis. Bake with the seam side down.

Sprinkle the pan with corn meal, and add each stromboli to it. Sprinkle each stromboli with a little sea salt if you like. Add to the oven and bake on the middle rack for about 15 to 20 minutes or until your crust is starting to brown lightly. Remove from the pizza from the oven and let stand for 10 minutes to cool. Plate carefully.

Going further

Strombolis are simple to make, and you can stuff them the way you like. Because the dough is sealed, pick ingredients that either absorb moisture if you use ingredients that release moisture, or sauté them thoroughly before adding. These keep for a few days and make a nice lunch. Two strombolis will serve 2 people as a reasonable main dish, and you can always double the recipe.

Tofu & Kale Hot Pocket

This dish is based on the runza, the proud Central European predecessor to the hot pocket. Today, the runza remains a fast food in some areas of the United States. It's a great and simple lunch that you can eat with your hands, goes well with a few sides for a simple dinner. You can even make little mini ones for hors d'oeuvres if you like. This dish has a number of similar European and American cousins, though, like the calzone, bureka, stromboli, and others. Although these dishes vary individually, they're wonderful, simple yeast dough stuffed with stuff. This recipe makes 2 pockets, but there's no reason you couldn't double it and make several lunches for the week.

 **DIFFICULTY**

Flavors: Savory, salty, rich, sweet, sour, green

Equipment: A sharp knife (although a food processor is also good), 2 baking sheets (or a sheet and a roasting pan), 2 large bowls, 2 small bowls, a brush, and a saucer for the soy milk.

Ingredients

- ▶ 1/2 batch Yeast Dough (page 118)
- ▶ 1/2 brick tofu (about 1/2 pound), crumbled
- ▶ 2 cups kale, minced
- ▶ 1/2 vidalia onion, minced
- ▶ 1 tablespoon corn meal

Dressing

- ▶ 2 tablespoons tamari
- ▶ 2 tablespoons catsup
- ▶ 2 teaspoons mustard (yellow or brown, but brown is preferred)
- ▶ 1 tablespoon garlic
- ▶ Sea salt (start with 1/4 teaspoon and add to taste)

Or use one of the following:

- ▶ 1 batch Ginger, Garlic, and Tahini Dressing (page 60) whisked with 2 tablespoons water;

- ▶ 1/2 cup Tarragon Aioli (page 64);
- ▶ 1/2 batch Tomato Herb Sauce (page 66), reduced by 1/2;

Optional: 1 tablespoon unsweetened soy milk

Instructions

Begin by preparing your ingredients. Preheat your oven to 450° F. Make your dough in the large bowl. While it rises, crumble your tofu with a fork and mince your kale, or give them a whirl in a food processor. Add them to the other large bowl. Whisk together the dressing of your choice and pour it over the tofu and kale and mix until well combined. Roast the kale and tofu for 20 to 30 minutes, stirring with a fork every 10 minutes, or until the moisture has been absorbed and both the kale and tofu are well cooked. Remove from the oven and add the mixture back to the large bowl. Taste and add salt as necessary. Your filling should be slightly salty, since your dough will not be.

Reduce your oven temperature to 400° F and roll out your dough. Knead the dough for five minutes. Break the dough in half and roll out each piece to approximately 8-inch circles on a floured cutting board.

Brush the dough with a tablespoon vegetable oil. Add half of the filling in the center. Squish it down gently with a clean hand. Fold up the runza like a burrito, pulling the edge facing away from you toward you, folding in the left and the right edges, and then rolling the whole loaf over. Be careful to seam it up properly and not to let your filling escape, and then shape it like a bun. Repeat with the other loaf.

Sprinkle the corn meal onto your second baking sheet in a thin layer. Add the runza carefully to the pan and bake for 15 minutes. Remove from the oven and brush with the unsweetened soy milk (if you're using it). Return to the oven and bake another 5 to 10 minutes until the crust is lightly browned. Remove from the oven and let stand at least 10 minutes to cool before serving.

Going further

This is a simple dish with lots of potential. Add a little tomato sauce and some pizza toppings for a quick calzone. Just fold it in half and seam rather than rolling it up. Add a little white sauce and some roasted portobello, pears and onions (see the recipe in Chapter 4) and roll it up like a newspaper for a stromboli. Or, change the ingredients. If you don't like kale, use spinach, arugula, collards, or all three. If you don't like tofu, use some chopped cooked chickpeas or some steamed and chopped potatoes. Use seitan. Or use the black lentil and artichoke mixture in the pot pie recipe further on in this chapter. What's important is that your ingredients not be too wet, so if you use a lot of mushroom and onion, roast them thoroughly first. It's also important not to overstuff your dough, so only use 1 to 1 1/2 cups packed filling for each dough.

Mushroom & Collard Green Pot Pie

This is a simple and rich-tasting pot pie full of vegetables, white gravy, and flaky pastry. This makes for a good holiday meal or for a dinner party when you want to serve something more traditional. Although you can use a single pie dish, your presentation won't be as elegant as it would be for individual portions.

 **DIFFICULTY**

Flavors: Savory, salty, rich, sweet, sour

Note: You'll probably need to get the miso and nutritional yeast at your local HFS.

Equipment: A frying pan capable of holding 8 cups liquid, 2 4-inch ramekins or a 9-inch glass pie dish, a medium bowl, a small bowl, a hand blender (a whisk or a fork will do), and a pie wedge for serving

Ingredients

Shell
▸ 1 batch Pastry Dough (page 120)

Filling
▸ 2 tablespoons vegetable oil
▸ 1/2 teaspoon ground cumin
▸ 1 teaspoon paprika
▸ 1 tablespoon dried tarragon, rubbed
▸ 1/2 teaspoon thyme
▸ 1/2 teaspoon savory
▸ 1/4 teaspoon dried ground cayenne pepper (or black pepper if you prefer something less spicy)
▸ Dash of liquid smoke
▸ 1 cup peeled and finely chopped red onion
▸ 2 tablespoons minced fresh garlic
▸ 1 teaspoon minced fresh ginger
▸ 1 cup trimmed and finely chopped carrot
▸ 1 cup trimmed and finely chopped celery
▸ 8 medium button or cremini mushrooms, stemmed and sliced
▸ 4 leaves collard greens, stemmed and finely chopped
▸ 1/2 teaspoon sea salt

Gravy
▸ 1 cup water
▸ 1 tablespoon white miso
▸ 2 tablespoons nutritional yeast
▸ 1 tablespoon tahini
▸ 1 teaspoon tamari
▸ 1 tablespoon lemon juice

Thickener
▸ 1 tablespoon water
▸ 2 teaspoons arrowroot powder

Optional: 1/4 cup rehydrated sun-dried tomatoes, 1/4 cup chopped artichoke hearts, or 1/4 cup kalamata olives. You can also replace the gravy with one you prefer, for example the Jalapeño Cheeze Sauce (page 68) or the Simple Mornay Sauce (page 80).

Instructions

Begin by preparing your ingredients. Make your pie crusts using the basic recipe (page 120) and let the dough rest while you prepare the rest of the dish.

Stem your collards about 1 inch above where the leaves start to flower out, discard the stems, and chop finely. Trim, chop, and mince the rest of your remaining vegetables. When the filling ingredients are ready, bring your vegetable oil to heat in the frying pan on high. When the oil is hot, add the dry herbs, 1/4 to 1/2 teaspoon sea salt (you'll probably need to add salt later if you only use 1/4 teaspoon at this point), and the liquid smoke and sauté for 2 minutes. Add the onion and sauté for 3 minutes. Add the garlic and ginger and sauté for 2 minutes. Add the carrots and sauté for 2 minutes. Add the celery and sauté for 2 minutes. Add the mushrooms and collards and sauté for another 5 to 10 minutes.

In the meantime, blend or whisk together your gravy ingredients. When your pan is starting to brown lightly, add the gravy and deglaze the pan. Add any of the optional ingredients. Cook for another 3 minutes. In the meantime, whisk together your thickener. Add to the pan, constantly stirring. When the gravy has thickened, remove the pan from heat and set aside. Taste and add salt if required.

While your filling cools, prepare your pie shell and preheat your oven to 350° F.

If you're using ramekins, divide the dough into 2 equal parts. Divide the each part into 1/3 and 2/3-sized pieces. Roll out the 2/3 sized pieces for the bottom part of the crust in the ramekin. For a 4-inch ramekin, roll out to approximately 8-inch circles. Add the bottom crust to the ramekin and brush with a little vegetable oil. Roll out the second crust to about 5-inch circle and cut it into 1/2-inch slices with a knife or with a ravioli cutter if you have one. Add half of the vegetable mixture to the first ramekin, and add the 1/2-inch slices of dough over the top, crisscrossing in a lattice, with a 1/2-inch space between each piece of dough. Repeat with the other ramekin. Poke 3 to 5 holes in the top crust with a fork.

If you're using a regular pie dish, divide the dough in slightly uneven portions (somewhere between a half-and-half split and a two-to-one split). Roll out the larger piece for the bottom crust, and the smaller piece of the top crust, using the same process, but 12-inch and 10-inch circles, respectively, instead. Fill the whole pie with the vegetable mixture, cover, and seam the pie like you would any other. Poke 3 to 5 holes in the top crust with a fork.

When the oven and pot pies are ready, bake on the middle rack for 10 minutes. Remove the pies from the oven and brush the crusts with the unsweetened soy milk. Return to the oven and bake for another 10 minutes, or until the crusts are nice and brown. Remove from the oven. Let stand 10 minutes to cool, cut, and serve.

Going further

If you've made one pot pie, you've pretty much made them all. Change the legumes, change the spices, change the mirepoix. Use yellow, red, orange, green, and jalapeño peppers with some red beans and corn meal for a pepper pot pie. Use white sesame seeds, onions, white beans, and some spinach for an elegant white pot pie. What's important to this dish is the right amount of moisture (too moist, and your crust won't cook properly) and the binding (no legumes, and you'll have to figure out something else to hold it together).

If you choose to add the optional ingredients, this is a pretty well rounded pie. Having said that, some roasted potatoes, some asparagus and other sides won't hurt it in the slightest. For a fuller plate, add some Roasted Red Potatoes (page 94) and French-Style Green Beans, Red Peppers and Onions (page 114) or succotash (page 101). For a fancier plate, this dish goes well with the Red Potato/Sweet Potato and Scallion Mash (page 106).

Chickpea & Coconut Burger

This is a simple and filling chickpea burger for when you want something more home-made and more flavorful than the store-bought veggie burger. This will make 4 reasonably sized patties or 2 super-sized burgers and will keep in plastic wrap for a few days in a refrigerator. But because of the chemistry of the burger, they don't microwave well. If you want to reserve a couple of burgers, make them up to the patty point, wrap them in plastic, and refrigerate. They'll keep a few days.

DIFFICULTY

Flavors: **Savory, salty, rich, spicy**

Equipment: **A hand blender (you can make do with a whisk and a potato masher), a pan with a tight-fitting lid capable of holding 6 cups water, a sauté or frying pan, a larger bowl, a baking sheet, tongs, and a spatula will also be helpful**

Ingredients

- 1 cup dried chickpeas (or about 2 to 2 1/2 cups canned)
- 3 cups water
- 1 tablespoon vegetable oil
- 1 small red onion (about the size of a lemon), peeled and finely chopped
- 1 teaspoon turmeric
- 1 tablespoon ground cumin
- 1 teaspoon ground coriander
- 1 tablespoon dried tarragon
- 1 teaspoon dried savory
- 1/2 teaspoon ground black pepper
- 1 tablespoon minced fresh garlic
- 1 teaspoon minced fresh ginger
- 1 teaspoon minced fresh chipotle
- 1 teaspoon prepared brown mustard
- 1 tablespoon tamari
- 1 teaspoon lemon juice
- 1/4 cup desiccated, unsweetened coconut
- 2 dashes of liquid smoke
- 2 tablespoons coarse yellow corn meal
- 1/4 cup pecan butter (peanut, cashew, almond, macadamia, or walnut butter will also work)
- 2 tablespoons nutritional yeast
- 1/4 teaspoon sea salt

Instructions

Begin by preparing your ingredients. Bring the water and the chickpeas to a slow boil in the pan on medium heat. Reduce to low, cover and simmer for 2 1/2 hours or until the chickpeas are cooked through and the water has been absorbed. Drain and rinse your chickpeas and add them to the large bowl. Add the nutritional yeast, the nut butter, the coconut, and the corn meal to the chickpeas.

When your chickpeas are done, bring 1 tablespoon vegetable oil to heat on high in your frying pan. Add all of the dry spices except for the nutritional yeast and sauté for 1 minute. Add the onion and sauté for 3 minutes. Decrease the heat to medium-high and add the ginger and garlic and sauté for 3 minutes. Add the tamari, liquid smoke, chipotle, mustard, and lemon juice and deglaze the pan. Sauté for and additional 2 minutes and remove from heat. Let stand for 5 minutes to cool.

Next, pour your spice mixture over the chickpeas. Blend everything with a hand blender until smooth. You can also mash with a potato masher or the back of a wooden spoon. Taste and add salt as necessary—your burger should taste good to you at this point. Now is the best time to add more seasoning if you want it a little spicier or saltier.

Wait for the chickpea mixture to cool (time will vary, but 30 minutes should be good). Preheat your oven to 400° F. Take about 1/2 to 3/4 cup of the mixture, form a ball, and press and shape with your palms to form patties with your hands. Patties should be about 3 inches in diameter and about 1/2 inch thick. If you want thicker burgers, you'll need to cook them longer (add an extra 10 minutes for 1-inch burgers, and expect your outside to be a little crispier).

Lightly oil the baking sheet. Add your patties to the oiled sheet, and when your oven is ready, bake for 15 minutes, flip, and then bake for another 15 minutes. When your chickpeas start to brown and the edges begin to crisp, they're ready. Remove from the baking sheet and allow to cool on a plate for 5 minutes. Serve as cutlets or with the buns of your choice.

Going further

This makes a nice chickpea burger that is moist on the inside and a little crispy on the outside. You can experiment (e.g., cooking longer, removing the coconut and corn meal) to get different textures. Replace the coconut with ground flax meal and the pecan butter for walnut butter for more omega-3s. Replace the corn meal with gluten flour for a slightly chewier texture. Change the spices to give it a different flavor.

Make some Kalamata Olive and Dill Pickle Tapenade (page 54) or Mango Chipotle Salsa (page 62) or just some Tarragon Aioli (page 64) to serve on top. You could even make your own buns for these, and if you have time, go for it. Break the dough recipe in Chapter 4 into 4 equal pieces, sprinkle with a little corn meal and bake for about 20 minutes. This burger goes well with greens and sweet potatoes or with a little Black Kale and Carrot Slaw (replace the 3 cups black-eyed peas with 1 cup raisins).

Mango Chili with
Tahini Cheese & Cilantro

I wrestled with where to put the chili in this book. Is it a soup? Is it a meal? Is it a side dish? I went with meal! This is a bold, very spicy chili. It deserves to be in with the rest of the mains. It will serve 4 as a main dish, and more if you're serving it as a side. This chili isn't especially spicy, though. It's also not an exact replica of chili made from dry chili mix. If you want something more like that, replace the cumin, coriander, and paprika with a couple tablespoons of chili powder (and you may need to dial back the salt by 1/2 teaspoon, depending on your particular chili mix). Add the minced jalapeño to increase the pique.

DIFFICULTY

Flavors: Savory, salty, rich, sour, sweet, fermented, green, spicy

Equipment: A few small bowls, a large bowl, a sauté pan, 2 large pans capable of holding at least 12 cups liquid (you can get by with one), and a ladle

Ingredients

- 1 cup black or green lentils (black preferred)
- 2 cups water
- 4 ripe mangoes, peeled, stoned, and chopped
- 4 large ripe tomatoes, cored, seeded, and chopped
- 2 tablespoons vegetable oil
- 2 teaspoons paprika (Hungarian preferred)
- 1 tablespoon ground cumin
- 1 teaspoon ground coriander
- 1/2 teaspoon ground cayenne pepper
- 1/2 teaspoon ground black pepper
- 2 medium yellow or white onions, finely chopped
- 2 carrots, trimmed and coarsely chopped (or finely chopped if you don't like bigger chunks)
- 2 stalks celery coarsely chopped (or finely chopped if you don't like bigger chunks)
- 8 medium-sized cremini or button mushrooms, stemmed and thinly sliced
- 1 tablespoon minced fresh garlic (or 2 if you like your chili good and garlicky)
- 1 tablespoon white vinegar or apple cider vinegar
- 1 tablespoon agave (you may need a little more if your mango isn't entirely ripe)
- 1/4 cup peanut butter
- 1 teaspoon sea salt
- 1 teaspoon minced cilantro for garnish

Tahini cheese
- 1 batch Nori Tahini Spread (page 50) minus the nori
- 1 teaspoon turmeric

Optional: 1 large jalapeño, cored, seeded, and minced.

Instructions

Begin by preparing your ingredients. Start with your lentils. Add the lentils and water to the small pan and bring to a slow boil on medium heat. Decrease the heat to low, cover, and simmer for 30 minutes.

Next, prepare your mango and tomatoes. Add the peeled, stoned, and chopped mango and the cored, seeded, and chopped tomato to a large bowl and liquefy with a hand blender until nice and smooth.

Next, heat the 2 tablespoons oil on high until is it ready. Add 1/4 teaspoon sea salt to the pan. First add all of your dry spices for the chili to the oil and sauté for 2 minutes. Next, add the onion and sauté for 5 minutes. Decrease the heat to medium-high and add the carrot and sauté for 3 minutes. Add the celery and sauté for 2 minutes. If you are adding the jalapeño, add it now. Add the garlic and sauté until the vegetables start to brown. Sauté for 2 to 3 minutes once the vegetables are browning. Add the mushrooms sauté for another 5 to 8 minutes. This will probably overload your pan a little, and that's fine. This chili cooks everything together. Sauté until your pan starts to brown lightly and then sauté for 2 more minutes.

Add 1/2 cup of the mangoes and tomatoes to the pan and deglaze. Add the remaining mangoes and tomatoes, and bring the whole pan to a simmer on medium heat. Add your agave, peanut butter, and white vinegar and stir to combine thoroughly. Reduce by about 1/2, and when the lentils are done, add them to the pot. Cover loosely and simmer the chili on low (or medium-low, depending on your stove and the thickness of the bottom of your pan) for 30 minutes to 1 hour, stirring occasionally to avoid burning (the longer your chili cooks, the better!).

When your chili is ready, whisk together the tahini cheese following the basic recipe, but replace the nori flakes with the turmeric. Remove the chili from heat and let stand 15 minutes. Taste and add salt as necessary. Stir thoroughly and ladle the chili into bowls. Garnish further with minced cilantro (1 scant tablespoon per bowl) by sprinkling it in a nice green layer in the center of the bowl. Dollop 1 tablespoon cheese on top of the cilantro. The recipe should provide you with several servings of the tahini cheese, but you may need to double if you're serving several small bowls of chili).

Going further

If you're not hot on mango, or it's out-of-season or hard to get in your area, just add 4 extra tomatoes. You can also bake some cooked macaroni with this dish to make one of my childhood favorites: chili mac! You don't have to stick to mirepoix vegetables. Add peppers, zucchini, whatever you like. Or, if you prefer red kidney, white, or black beans, just make them separate and add to the chili as you see fit! This dish goes well with rolls, crusty bread, some plain brown rice, or a tofu dog.

Hot Grilled Portobello Steak
Sandwich with Gravy

When I was a kid in Chicago, my father would take us to the local greasy spoons on Cermak, where there were several family-owned, family-run places. Without fail, he'd get a hot turkey or a hot chicken sandwich. This recipe is a reinterpretation of those dishes. For a more appropriately faux-fowl version, use a little Tarragon Aioli (page 64) and some Light Seitan (page 126).

 **DIFFICULTY**

Flavors: Savory, salty, rich, spicy

Equipment: A hand blender (you can make do with a whisk), a pan with a tight-fitting lid capable of holding 6 cups water, a larger bowl, and a baking sheet

Ingredients

▶ 1 to 2 batches of any of the gravies in Chapter 3 (or 1 to 2 cups gravy of your choice)

▶ 4 to 8 portobello mushrooms, stemmed and thinly sliced (see note)

▶ 1 small red onion, peeled and thinly sliced

▶ 2 tablespoons water

▶ 1 tablespoon tamari

▶ 1 teaspoon lemon juice

▶ Sea salt

▶ 4 slices whole wheat bread

Optional: Make 2 batches of gravy if you want more for your potatoes, or if you want to make a triple-decker sandwich, or if you like your gravy really thick (in which case, make a double batch and reduce by 1/4). More gravy seldom hurts. If you're using the Red Lentil, Red Onion, and Red Wine Gravy (page 74), you really only need 1 red onion total. If you want to add the texture of red onion, thinly slice half the onion and sauté it with the mushrooms.

Note: The number of mushrooms depends on how thick you like your sandwich and how large your portobellos are. For portobellos bigger than about 4 inches, 4 mushrooms should do for 2 sandwiches if you want something light. I usually use 3 larger portobellos, myself, but I love mushrooms. If your portobellos are smaller, use 6 to 8, depending on how small they are.

Instructions

Begin by preparing your ingredients. First, prepare your gravy and leave it on low to keep warm. Next, bring the oil to heat in your pan on high heat. Add 1/4 teaspoon sea salt. Add the sliced onion and sauté for 4 minutes. Slice the portobellos into 1/8-inch slices and add the portobello mushrooms and sauté for 8 to 12 minutes, or until the portobello slices are cooked through and the pan is starting to brown. Decrease the heat to medium-high and add the lemon juice, tamari, and water to deglaze the pan. Sauté for another 2 minutes. Remove the mushrooms from heat.

Taste and add sea salt as necessary. Add any reduction remaining to your gravy.

When the mushrooms and gravy are ready, toast your bread very lightly. You want to dry it slightly so that it will absorb the gravy a little more readily, but not to the point that the bread is browning. Layer the mushrooms equally between the two sandwiches with tongs. Ladle piping-hot gravy over the mushrooms onto the sandwich open-faced. Add the top layer of toast, and push down on the sandwich firmly with a clean palm. Ladle your gravy over the top.

Going further

This is a fairly easy recipe that goes well with greens and mashed potatoes, sweet or regular. Traditionally, this dish is made with white bread, and the heat of the gravy melts the bread. So, make sure your gravy is hot. You could even make your own buns for these, and if you have time, go for it. Make the dough recipe on page 118 into a loaf and bake for about 20 minutes. For a simpler plate, serve with the Roasted Red Potatoes (page 94) and Roasted Kale (page 91). For a lighter lunch plate, make the Carrot and Black Kale Slaw (page 96).

Fiery Portobello, Green Apple
& Green Pepper Adobo

Spicy, sour, rich all around, this is a great dish but not for the faint of heart. The sauce is a beautiful, rich red, and the green peppers and portobellos round out the flavor. Serve it with rice and some water! Or if you really like your food spicy, simply serve it on a sandwich bun.

 **DIFFICULTY**

Flavors: Spicy, savory, salty, rich, sour, sweet

Equipment: A larger bowl, a hand blender, a baking sheet, and tongs

Ingredients

Portobellos

- ▶ 1 medium white onion, peeled and thinly sliced (about 1 cup)
- ▶ 1 green apple, cored and thinly sliced (preferably granny smith or another sour apple)
- ▶ 2 green bell peppers, cored, seeded, and thinly sliced
- ▶ 4 to 6 large portobellos, stemmed, wiped clean, and thinly sliced
- ▶ 1 to 2 tablespoons fresh cilantro, minced (more if you really like cilantro)
- ▶ Sea salt

Adobo

- ▶ 4 small/medium tomatoes, cored and chopped (about 1 1/2 cups crushed tomatoes)
- ▶ 2 to 3 tablespoons minced chipotle
- ▶ 2 tablespoons extra virgin olive oil
- ▶ 3 tablespoons fresh lime juice, or 2 tablespoons white vinegar if you prefer

- ▶ 1 to 2 tablespoons minced fresh garlic
- ▶ 1 tablespoon tamari
- ▶ 1 tablespoon agave nectar, or 2 teaspoons sugar if that's what you have
- ▶ 1 teaspoon ground cumin
- ▶ 1 teaspoon dried oregano, rubbed
- ▶ 1/2 teaspoon ground black pepper
- ▶ 2 dashes liquid smoke
- ▶ 1/2 teaspoon sea salt

Note: The portobellos should be about 4 to 5 inches in diameter. Use 6 to 9 if you can only find smaller ones. A couple of tablespoons of chipotle should be enough for most, but 3 tablespoons will better suit spicier palates. If you like it really spicy, add in a little habañero. Try to slice everything between about 1/4 and 1/8-inch thick. Thinner is usually better, but if you slice your mushrooms too thinly, they may break when you toss them with the marinade. You don't have to worry about that with the other ingredients.

Optional: Add some orange wedges and/or thinly slice 1/2 an avocado and add the slices at the end for a little extra flavor and color. You can always dial back the chipotle and black pepper if you prefer your food less spicy (but you'll always want to decrease the white vinegar, and then you may as well just make the Cutlets Cacciatore). Add 1 teaspoon dark cocoa to deepen out the flavor if you don't find the green peppers add enough bitter flavor to balance out the rest of the dish.

Instructions

Begin by preparing your ingredients. Add the adobo ingredients to a large bowl and blend until smooth. Add the green peppers, mushrooms, onions, and apple slices to the large bowl and marinate for at least 30 minutes. Toss gently to coat. If you can, marinate the mushrooms, peppers, and onions for a couple of hours on the countertop, or longer covered in the fridge if possible (overnight is best) and then add the apple about 20 to 30 minutes before you're ready to cook. A longer marination will give the finished dish a more balanced flavor. What's happening in terms of the food chemistry is that the acids in the pepper (as well as the salt and lime juice) are cooking the other ingredients. That allows the flavors to mix a little better, and it takes some of the bite out of the hot pepper while retaining most of its flavor.

If you only marinade for 30 minutes, however, toss gently again at the 15-minute mark. When ready, preheat your oven to 400° F. Add the vegetables (but not the marinade) to the baking sheet, and roast everything on the middle rack for 40 minutes, until the portobellos are nice and soft and cooked through. At the 20-minute mark, remove from the oven and turn the ingredients gently with tongs. Return to the oven.

While the mushrooms are roasting, add the remaining marinade to a small saucepan and heat on high. When the sauce comes to a simmer, decrease the heat to medium and cook until the sauce is reduced by about 1/2 or becomes the consistency of jarred tomato sauce, whichever is thicker. You'll probably have about 1/3 cup sauce, depending on how long you marinate the vegetables.

Plating: take a couple of tablespoons of adobo and paint each plate in a wide, thin circle. Taste the portobellos and sprinkle with sea salt if necessary. Then, plate the roasted vegetables with tongs in a nice cone-shaped stack in the middle of the adobo circle. Finally, spoon a little adobo over the top. Garnish with minced fresh cilantro and, if you like, avocado or nutritional yeast. This dish serves a light main plate for 2.

If you serve this as a sandwich (a great way to have it) use 4 good-quality hot dog buns. Paint each with about 1 tablespoon sauce. Then stuff each bun with 1/4 of the vegetables. Bake each sandwich on the baking sheet at 400° F for about 5 minutes to ensure the sauce melts the bun a little. Then sprinkle with your cilantro.

Going further

Roasted potatoes, rice, and leafy greens all make good side dishes. Given the spiciness, collard greens, rapine, and bitter melon in particular complement the strong flavors of the adobo. You could also make this with the Light Seitan (page 126), thinly sliced tofu, or Dark Seitan (page 125) if you prefer. But the portobellos keep this nice, simple, and light.

Jambalaya

Jambalaya is a beautiful, flavorful Southern dish. Traditionally, this dish is prepared like paella or risotto (everything cooked together), but more and more you'll see it served as sauce over pasta to reduce the complexity of preparing the dish and to keep the colors of the peppers, which dull with cooking.

This recipe makes a finished dish that's primarily focused on the tofu or seitan. For a more rice-focused dish, double all of the other ingredients (this will serve 4 for a full plate or 8 for side dishes).

 **DIFFICULTY**

Flavors: Savory, salty, rich, sour, spicy, green

Note: You'll probably have to go to your HFS or a Japanese grocery to get the kelp and wakame. These add a little "sea" flavor to the dish but aren't absolutely necessary.

Equipment: A small bowl, a larger bowl, a pan capable of holding at least 6 cups water with a tight-fitting lid, a baking sheet, tongs, a whisk (a fork will do), and a sharp knife

Ingredients

- ▶ 1 batch Tofu Cutlets (page 128) or Light Seitan (page 126)
- ▶ 1 teaspoon kelp flakes
- ▶ 1 teaspoon extra virgin olive oil for browning

Rice

- ▶ 1 tablespoon vegetable oil
- ▶ 1 large white onion, peeled and finely chopped
- ▶ 1 tablespoon minced fresh garlic
- ▶ 1 green bell pepper, seeded, cored and chopped fine
- ▶ 1 red bell pepper, seeded, cored and chopped fine
- ▶ 1 teaspoon lemon juice
- ▶ 2 small tomatoes, cored, seeded, and chopped

- ▶ 1 tablespoon crumbled dried wakame sea vegetable
- ▶ 2 cups water, salted with 1/4 teaspoon sea salt and brought to a boil
- ▶ 1 cup long-grain brown rice

Dressing

- ▶ 1 tablespoon extra virgin olive oil
- ▶ 1 teaspoon lemon juice
- ▶ 1 teaspoon ground cumin
- ▶ 1/2 teaspoon ground cayenne pepper (or white pepper if you have it)
- ▶ 1/4 teaspoon ground black pepper
- ▶ 1 teaspoon dry oregano, rubbed

Optional: Add an extra 1/2 teaspoon cayenne pepper or 1 tablespoon minced fresh jalapeño pepper with the garlic for extra spice!

Instructions

Begin by preparing your ingredients. Prepare your seitan or tofu (and breading, if you're breading either).

For the seitan, follow the basic seitan recipe but add the kelp flakes to the dry ingredients and replace the tahini with walnut butter. Heat your oven to 300° F. Bake and tent as directed in the Basic Cutlets recipe. Unwrap and slice each cutlet into 8 equal pieces, and then into 1/2-inch cubes. Brush or toss with 1 teaspoon extra virgin olive oil. Add the pieces to a baking sheet and bake for another 5 minutes, flip and bake another 5 minutes or until lightly browned. Remove from the oven, allow to cool.

For the tofu, make the Basic Cutlets recipe, except cut your tofu into 1/2-inch cubes instead of rectangles (so that you have about 30 cubes). Add the additional kelp to the marinade, and marinate the tofu in it for at least 30 minutes, preferably, as long as possible. Preheat your oven to 400° F. Grease the baking sheet. Place your tofu cutlets on the sheet and then pour the remaining marinade over the cutlets as evenly as you can. Bake on the middle oven rack for about 15 minutes. Flip the cutlets carefully with a fork and then with a spoon, pour remaining marinade over the cutlets. Bake for another 15 minutes or until the cutlets have browned lightly and most of the moisture has been absorbed. Remove from the oven.

Once you have your seitan or tofu underway, start the rice. For the rice, add the oil to the pan and bring to heat on high. Add 1/4 teaspoon sea salt to the pan.

Add your onion and sauté for 3 minutes. Decrease the heat to medium-high. Add your garlic and sauté for 2 minutes. Add your green and red pepper and sauté for 5 to 7 minutes. Your vegetables will start to brown the pan, and that's fine. Add 1/4 cup white wine and deglaze the pan. Sauté for another 3 minutes or until the white wine has reduced by about 1/2 or absorbed. Add the water, rice, tomatoes, wakame, and lemon juice to the pan. Bring the liquid to a simmer and stir to combine. Decrease the heat to low, cover, and simmer for 30 to 50 minutes or until the rice is done (this varies a lot with the type of long-grain rice and will take longer than it typically would).

When the rice is done, whisk together remaining dressing ingredients. Dress the rice and toss to combine. Let stand 10 minutes to cool. Add sea salt to taste. Spoon out the rice onto dinner plates and then plate your cutlets on top in a stack with tongs. Serves 2 with a full plate, 4 for side dishes.

Going further

It has become more and more common for jambalaya to be plated with fettuccine. If you prefer a pasta to rice, sauté the sauce ingredients but don't add the water and rice. Just remove from heat, add the seitan or tofu when done, simmer for about 10 minutes, and then plate over the pasta. Add 1 to 2 cups minced spinach or arugula to the rice about 5 minutes before finishing in order to round out the nutritional value.

Mom's Wheat Loaf with
Spicy Tomato Coulis

This is a simple and straightforward wheat loaf. Not only does it taste great, it's good for dinner parties when you want just the right 1950s postwar kitsch factor. Be sure to make this in an apron and black horn-rimmed glasses. Now, if you're not looking to serve 6, that's fine. You can make this wheat loaf and slice it for sandwiches throughout the week!

 DIFFICULTY

Equipment: A baking pan (3 x 9-inch will do), some aluminum foil, a serving platter, a gravy boat, and a hand blender

Ingredients

Loaf
▶ A triple batch of Dark Seitan (page 125)
▶ 2 ripe, medium-sized tomatoes, cored and seeded

Coulis
▶ 1 batch Tomato Herb Sauce (page 66)
▶ Add 1/4 teaspoon black pepper or cayenne pepper to the sauce (black for milder heat, cayenne for something hotter)
▶ Sea salt (to taste)

Optional: 1 tablespoon white vinegar and 1 teaspoon agave nectar for the sauce.

Instructions

Begin by preparing your ingredients. Crush your tomatoes by blending them with a hand blender. (You can use a fork if you're really determined and your tomatoes are good and ripe). Replace 1 cup water in the seitan recipe with 1 cup crushed tomatoes.

When ready, preheat your oven to 350° F. Wrap the seitan in foil and bake in the baking dish for 2 hours. At the 1-hour mark, flip the seitan over and return to the oven. Remove the wheat loaf from the oven and from the pan. Let cool (still wrapped in foil) for 15 minutes.

Next, prepare your tomato sauce and add the additional pepper to it. Remove the wheat loaf from foil, and slice in 1/2 to 1-inch rounds, depending on how thick you like your slices. Plate the loaf and the slices carefully on a nice serving dish.

You can serve the coulis in a side dish (a gravy boat would be fabulous) or drizzle some over the loaf. If you're serving guests, sauce on the side is usually preferable unless it's integral to the dish or you really know your guests' culinary tastes well.

Going further

I have to admit, my mother never made meatloaf when I was growing up. I never really felt left out. But this dish still makes up for that, and it goes well thin-sliced in sandwiches. If you like this dish but don't really have to feed 6 people, try replacing the portobellos in the Hot Grilled Portobello Sandwich (page 156) with slices of this wheat loaf. Or, serve slices on buns or bread with a little White Bean and Parsley Dip (page 58), a little tapenade (page 54), or even a little faux cheeze and Nori Tahini Spread (page 50).

To vary the wheat loaf itself, add 1 to 2 tablespoons ground kalamata olives to the liquid ingredients to replace some of the walnuts. Or, if you're really looking more for slices, you could make the Light Seitan (page 126) instead and use 1 cup unsweetened soy milk instead of the crushed tomatoes. If you really want to get fancy, prepare the loaf and then glaze it with the strawberry chipotle or maple mustard sauces, or bake it with the orange sauce or pomegranate barbecue sauce. This dish also goes well with the Three-Pepper Whiskey Sauce (page 76) or the Red Lentil, Red Onion, and Red Wine Gravy (page 74). For a fancier plate, serve with Collard Green Noodles (page 90) and Red Potato/Sweet Potato and Scallion Mash (page 106).

Spinach & Cheeze Tortellini

For fresh stuffed pasta, this is a relatively simple and fun dish to make. It also tastes great and, like so many fresh pastas, has a much better flavor and texture than store-bought. This recipe takes a little dexterity, but more important, practice. It will take several tries before you get the hang of it and can measure the size of the dollop of filling to the size of the piece of dough. Some of your tortellini won't make it, and that's fine. You'll be making about 3 to 4 dozen of these depending on how large your pieces of dough and your dollops are. Your last ones will be more successful than your first! If you're new to pasta, you can also make these as ravioli, which can be a little easier. There are notes on this at the end of the instructions.

 **DIFFICULTY**

Flavors: Savory, salty, rich, sweet, green

Note: You'll have to get some of your ingredients at the HFS (e.g., the nutritional yeast, maybe the nut butter).

Equipment: A sauté pan capable of holding 2 quarts of liquid, a large pan capable of holding at least 12 cups liquid, a whisk, a small bowl, and a large bowl

Ingredients

- ▶ 1 batch pasta (page 116)
- ▶ 12 cups salted boiling water
- ▶ 2 tablespoons extra virgin olive oil (1 for the sauté, 1 for the tofu)
- ▶ 1/2 brick of firm tofu (approximately 1 cup)
- ▶ 2 tablespoons cashew butter (or macadamia butter)
- ▶ 2 tablespoons plus 2 tablespoons nutritional yeast
- ▶ 1 teaspoon lemon juice
- ▶ 1 tablespoon minced fresh garlic
- ▶ 1/2 small red onion, peeled and minced
- ▶ 2 cups packed baby spinach
- ▶ 1/4 cup white wine
- ▶ 1/4 teaspoon sea salt

One of the following

- ▶ 1 batch Tomato Herb Sauce (page 66) reduced by about 1/2 for something traditional;

- ▶ 1 batch Simple Vinaigrette Dressing (page 48) with no mustard, an added tablespoon minced garlic, some coarse sea salt, 1 tablespoon nutritional yeast, and black pepper to taste;
- ▶ 1 batch Spinach, Arugula, and Walnut Pesto (page 52) for something beautiful and green; or the sauce you like with stuffed pasta.

Instructions

Begin by preparing your ingredients. First, choose your sauce and prepare it. Second, prepare your filling. Add the tofu, a tablespoon of the extra virgin olive oil, the lemon juice, and the nut butter and blend with a hand blender until smooth. Next, bring the tablespoon of the oil to heat in the sauté pan on high. Add the minced onion and sauté for 3 minutes. Add the garlic and sauté for 2 minutes. Add the spinach and sauté for 3 to 5 minutes until the pan starts to brown. Add the white wine and deglaze the pan. Sauté for another 3 minutes while the wine reduces. Remove the pan from the heat and add the onions, garlic, and spinach to the bowl with the tofu. Blend the filling a bit with a hand blender until smooth but not liquefied. Add 2 tablespoons nutritional yeast and mix. Your filling should be moist, but not runny. Add 1 to 2 additional tablespoons nutritional yeast if your filing is too moist or 1 tablespoon water if it's too dry. (It should be roughly the

Vincent Guihan | New American Vegan

consistency of ricotta cheese.) Taste and add salt to your taste (the filling should be neither too salty nor under-salted).

When you have your sauce and your filling ready, make and roll out your pasta dough. Roll it out as thinly as you can without it tearing, slightly thicker than construction paper but thinner than 1/8 inch. You may need to do the dough in 2 to 3 batches depending on how large of a surface you have. Instead of cutting noodles, cut 1 1/2-inch squares in the pasta. Flare all sides of your square by squeezing with your thumb and forefinger.

To stuff your pasta, add slightly less than 1 teaspoon of filling to the center of each square. Smooth the filling from a ball into a cylinder by rolling it gently in the dough with your fingers. Fold the square in half into a triangle, covering your cylinder. Carefully pinch the sides so that the filling is sealed in. Take the two long ends of the triangle and wrap them around your ring finger and seal the dough so that you have what looks like a headband. Repeat until you have used all of your pasta. You may have to reroll some scraps.

When your tortellini are ready, bring the 12 cups salted water to a boil and add your tortellini. You may have to add your tortellini in 2, possibly 3 batches depending on the size of your pan. If you do them in batches, use a slotted spoon, a slotted spatula, or a wooden spoon to remove cooked tortellini and rinse each batch with cold water when done. Add to a plate or bowl (depending on the viscosity of the sauce) and ladle sauce over the top. Sprinkle with a little nutritional yeast or some oregano. This recipe serves 2 as a full plate and 4 as a side dish.

If you decide to go with ravioli, roll the pasta as thin as you can get it without tearing, just like the tortellini. You can make each of the ravioli

one at a time, or cut 2 (or 4) precise, roughly equal-sized rectangular sheets of dough. You can use a baking sheet to do this, just set it on top of the dough and cut around it.

Add a little less than a teaspoon or so of filling, placing the dollops equidistant from each other about 1 1/2 to 2 inches apart, so that you have one large sheet of pasta with a lot of little dollops of filling. Cut the second sheet to be slightly larger (an extra 1/2 inch on all sides should be enough) and lay the second sheet as precisely as you can over the filling and the first sheet. And then cut the ravioli into its own individual square. Trim any edges that are oversized. You can make a nice seam by pressing down firmly with a fork on the edges.

If you prefer circular or semicircular ravioli, you can cut with a drinking glass about 2 1/2 inches in diameter. Most rocks glasses or wine glasses will do. Pinch the edge with your thumb and forefinger all around the circle. Add a little bundle of filling to the middle, and then carefully fold the ravioli in half over the filling. Pinch closed so you have a good seam. Again, you can run over this seam with a fork for a little extra decoration. When your ravioli are ready, prepare them the same way you would the tortellini.

Going further

Making tortellini involves a lot of work, but fresh pasta is worth it. And now that you know how, you can make tortellini, ravioli, and other dishes with the stuffings of your choice. What's important is that the stuffing be fairly homogeneous. It can be difficult to make a stuffed pasta with a lot of oddly shaped, firm ingredients. Mushrooms, potatoes, some greens, nuts, and even berries make good stuffed pasta ingredients for those reasons. Experiment with the stuffings and sauce combinations that you like best!

Yet Another Mac & Cheeze with
Spinach & Sun-Dried Tomatoes

This is a relatively involved macaroni and cheese. If you want to keep it simple, you can always just make the pasta and the sauce. Of course, macaroni and cheese varies substantially from household to household, sometimes coming from a box and sometimes homemade. Many vegans take this dish very seriously, and this isn't meant to replace anyone's favorite. It's merely a humble, flexible offering for those who are new to the plant-based version of this dish. You'll notice that there are several basic sauce recommendations, with varying levels of yellow coloring as well as thickness. Try out several and find the one you like the best.

 **DIFFICULTY**

Flavors: Sweet, salt, rich, fermented

Equipment: A couple of small bowls, a couple of large bowls, a kettle is nice for the water, a hand blender, a food processor, and a glass baking dish—9 x 13-inch will do—or 4 small (3-inch) ramekins or 2 larger ones able to hold a similar volume

Ingredients

Pasta
- 9 cups water
- 1 tablespoon sea salt
- 2 1/2 to 3 cups dry macaroni, small shells, or penne pasta*
- 1/2 cup sun-dried tomatoes
- 2 cups packed baby spinach, finely chopped
- 1 to 1 1/2 cups sauce from a recipe below (or mix and match!)

*For shells and macaroni, use about 2 1/2 cups (especially if you use rice pasta, which tends to result in more cooked pasta than wheat). For penne, you can get away with about 3 cups.

For a traditional yellow sauce
- 1 1/2 cups unsweetened soy milk (reserve 2 tablespoons for the thickener noted below)
- 1/4 cup nutritional yeast
- 1 tablespoon lemon juice
- 2 tablespoons tahini
- 1 tablespoon tamari
- 1 tablespoon minced fresh garlic
- 1 teaspoon minced fresh ginger
- 1/2 teaspoon agave nectar
- 1/2 teaspoon turmeric
- 1 teaspoon paprika (Hungarian preferred)
- 1 teaspoon onion powder
- Dash of liquid smoke
- 2 tablespoons unsweetened soy milk (to thicken)
- 2 teaspoons arrowroot powder
- 1/4 teaspoon sea salt

Optional: Add 1 tablespoon minced fresh jalapeño or 2 tablespoons Mango Chipotle Salsa (page 62)

For a simple, lighter white sauce
- 1 batch Simple Mornay Sauce (page 80)
- 1/2 cup unsweetened soy milk
- 1/4 cup nutritional yeast
- 1 additional tablespoon nut butter (your choice, not peanut)
- 1 additional tablespoon nutritional yeast
- 1 tablespoon minced fresh garlic
- 1 teaspoon onion powder
- 1/4 teaspoon ground black pepper
- Sea salt

For a sour cream and onion style sauce
- 1/2 batch Sour Cream (page 65)
- 1 additional tablespoon nut butter (your choice, not peanut)
- 1/4 cup nutritional yeast
- 4 scallions, trimmed and minced (same a few teaspoons greens for garnish if you like)

- ▶ 2 teaspoons dried onion powder, ground

For the optional topping
- ▶ 2 slices whole wheat bread
- ▶ 2 tablespoons vegetable oil
- ▶ 1 teaspoon paprika

Optional: You can use up to 3 cups of pasta if you don't like your macaroni and cheese really saucy. You could always make noodles from scratch, but for this dish I like to use brown rice macaroni or shells. Any pasta that cups sauce and bakes well should work. Add some sautéed mushrooms if you like.

Instructions

Begin by preparing your ingredients. Bring water to a boil with salt in a kettle if possible. Reserve 1 cup to rehydrate your sun-dried tomatoes if using dry-packed (about 20 minutes in a small bowl should do). Add the rest to your pan with the salt. Prepare your pasta following instructions and cook for the minimum amount of time. If you don't have a kettle, then bring your water to a boil in the pan and then carefully ladle out a cup for your tomatoes.

While the pasta is cooking, prepare your sauce. For all of the sauces above except for the yellow sauce, prepare using their respective basic recipes, adding the additional ingredients before blending or thickening. Add a tablespoon of water to dilute if you need to.

To prepare the yellow sauce, assemble all of the ingredients, less the soy milk and arrowroot powder for thickening, in a small pot and mix until well-combined. Bring to a boil and gently simmer for about 5 minutes. Be careful to avoid letting your soy milk boil over. In the meantime, whisk the arrowroot powder and the reserved soy milk in a small bowl

until the arrowroot is dissolved. Remove the sauce from heat and add the arrowroot mixture and stir vigorously until the whole sauce thickens (should only take a minute; you may have to return your sauce to low heat for a few minutes for it to thicken).

When the pasta is ready, it should be al dente (still slightly firm but not chewy). Drain immediately, add to a large bowl, and sauce the pasta. Add the spinach to the pasta and sauce. Stir to combine. Drain and mince the sun-dried tomatoes, and add to the large bowl. Stir to combine. Taste and add salt as necessary. Let stand 5 minutes for the spinach to wilt and for the mac to cool. Serve either in your larger baking dish or in individual ramekins for a more elegant touch.

If you're baking this dish, preheat your oven to 350° F. Add your mac and cheeze either to your baking dish or to 4 ramekins. Whirl your bread slices in a food processor with 1 tablespoon vegetable oil to crumb, sprinkle over the top, and then sprinkle with paprika. Bake for about 10 minutes or until the bread crumbs are lightly browned. This serves 4 as a side dish, or provides a plateful to 2.

Going further

There are lots of ways to make this classic comfort food. Add 2 tablespoons minced olives or sauté some mushrooms with your spinach for extra texture and flavor. Serve this with Collard Noodles (page 90) for a simple but elegant plate. For plating, I like to plate the ramekin in the center of a dinner plate, and then drape some collard noodles over the top (imagine a head of bad '80s hair) but this requires the outside of your ramekin to be nice and clean!

Holiday Cutlets with
Mushrooms, Potatoes & Stuffing

This is a holiday dish, complete with seitan, greens, vegetables, potatoes, stuffing, etc. It's a pretty big meal, but once you get the hang of whipping all the ingredients together, it's fairly low-stress and low-maintenance compared with a traditional holiday dinner. Relax. Put your feet up. Have a beer, a glass of wine, or a whiskey while your dinner bakes away—or have all three! It's a holiday!

If you're stuck at someone's nonvegan holiday dinner, just prepare and reheat in the oven. This serves 4, with big, full holiday plates with leftovers! Halve the recipes for 2.

  DIFFICULTY

Flavors: Savory, salty, rich, sour, spicy, sweet, green, fermented

Equipment: A few large bowls, a few medium bowls, a few small bowls (or at least one of each if you don't mind washing as you go), 1 or 2 pans capable of holding at least 6 cups water, a steamer, 2 to 3 baking sheets (depending on size), a whisk, a hand blender, some aluminum foil, and probably plastic wrap (if only for the leftovers)

Ingredients

- ▶ 2 batches of Light or Dark Seitan (page 126)
- ▶ or 2 batches of Tofu Cutlets (page 128)

Any of the following side dishes

- ▶ 1 batch Roasted Red Potatoes with Chives (page 94)
- ▶ 1 batch Midwestern Succotash (page 101)
- ▶ French-Style Green Beans with Red Peppers, and Onions (page 114)

Gravy

- ▶ 1 batch Red Lentil, Red Onion, and Red Wine Gravy (page 74) or use the gravy of your choice. There's no reason you have to use a traditional gravy recipe. Many of the more savory sauces in Chapter 3 will work well!

Glaze/sauce in addition to the gravy (optional)*

- ▶ 1 batch Black Currant Horseradish Sauce (page 75)
- ▶ or 2 batches Maple Mustard Sauce (page 79)

*These will stretch to 4 servings assuming you'll only want a few tablespoons of sauce for the main dish. Double if you want more.

Stuffing

- ▶ 2 slices of whole wheat bread, crumbed
- ▶ 4 cremini mushrooms, wiped clean, stemmed, and finely chopped
- ▶ 1 small carrot, trimmed and finely chopped
- ▶ 2 tablespoons extra virgin olive oil
- ▶ 1/4 cup vegetable stock
- ▶ 2 tablespoons chopped walnuts (you can substitute peanuts or cashews if you prefer)

- ▶ 1 small red onion, peeled and finely chopped (about 1/2 cup)
- ▶ 1 tablespoon tamari
- ▶ 1 teaspoon dried tarragon, rubbed
- ▶ 1/2 teaspoon dried savory, rubbed
- ▶ 1/2 teaspoon dried sage, rubbed
- ▶ 1/4 teaspoon ground black pepper
- ▶ 4 dried calimyrna figs, stemmed and finely chopped, or 1/4 cup raisins
- ▶ Sea salt (start with a pinch and add more to taste)

Optional: It's your holiday. Eating food you don't really want on your holiday is just plain wrong. Replace the potatoes with Red Potato/Sweet Potato Mash (page 106).

Instructions

Begin by preparing your ingredients.

Start the seitan about 1 1/2 hours before you plan to eat. Or start the tofu about 1 hour before you plan to eat.

Start the stuffing about 1 hour before you plan to eat.

Start the potatoes about 45 minutes before you plan to eat.

Start the gravy about 40 minutes before you plan to eat.

Start the succotash or the green beans and red peppers about 35 minutes before you plan to eat.

Start the mushrooms about 30 minutes before you plan to eat.

Start the glaze/sauce about 10 minutes before you plan to eat.

Prepare, tent, and cool your seitan, or prepare your Tofu Cutlets using the Basic Cutlets recipe, and when underway start your stuffing.

For the stuffing, lightly toast the bread for about 5 minutes and then grind in a food processor or chop with knife until you have a fine dice. Add them to a medium bowl. Toss the bread, olive oil, dry and fresh herbs, carrots, raisins, and onions until combined. Add the stock and then mix to combine. Spoon the stuffing into foil, and then carefully wrap (like the seitan). Make sure you have a tight seam otherwise your stuffing with dry out.

Bake the stuffing on the middle rack bake for 30 to 45 minutes with the seitan or until done (your stuffing should be moist, but not wet, and your vegetables should be softening but not entirely soft). At the 20-minute mark, check the stuffing to ensure it isn't drying out. If it is, remove from the oven, return the ingredients to the bowl, and add 2 tablespoons water. Rewrap, return it to the oven, and bake for another 20 minutes and check again (you may need to bake longer).

Prepare each additional side dish separately as per instructions in the basic recipes.

Roasted Acorn Squash Stuffed with Wild Rice,
Pinto Beans, Cranberries & Collards

This is a wonderful dish for presentation, and acorn squash has a wonderful, creamy texture. I often use puréed roasted acorn squash with some nutritional yeast in dough to simulate cheese. Because of the effort, this is a good dish for a small dinner party. You can also save yourself some time and stress by using leftover sauces with this dish. It goes well with a little Tarragon Aioli (page 64), or a little Mango Chipotle Salsa (page 62) and Sour Cream (page 65).

 **DIFFICULTY**

Flavors: Savory, salty, rich, sweet, green

Equipment: Three pans capable of holding at least 4 cups liquid with tight-fitting lids, a sauté pan, a baking sheet (or 2, depending on the size), a whisk (or a hand blender), several small and medium bowls, and probably a cleaver

Ingredients

Squash
- 2 acorn squashes (about 1 to 2 inches larger than a large grapefruit), halved and seeded
- 1/2 teaspoon sea salt
- 2 tablespoons vegetable oil

Stuffing
- 2/3 cup dry pinto beans (or 1 1/2 cups canned pinto beans, rinsed)
- 2 cups water
- 1 batch Brown Rice Pilaf (page 108), substituting 1/2 cup brown rice for wild rice
- 1/4 cup vegetable oil
- 1 small red onion, peeled and finely chopped (or 1 medium red onion, reserving 1/4 cup for the pilaf recipe)
- 2 tablespoons minced fresh garlic
- 2 dashes liquid smoke
- 1/2 cup dried cranberries, thoroughly rinsed and minced
- 2 tablespoons nutritional yeast
- 5 to 8 leaves of collard greens, trimmed and finely chopped (about 2 packed cups)
- Coarse sea salt (start with 1/2 teaspoon and add more to taste)

Sauces
- 1 batch Tomato Herb Sauce, fully cooked following the option for a pasta sauce (page 66)
- 1 batch Simple Mornay Sauce (page 80)
- Sea salt

Optional: If you prefer, make two batches of the Tomato Herb Sauce and add a couple of table-spoons Sour Cream (page 65) or Tarragon Aioli (page 64) if you want something a little quicker. If you don't have wild rice, you can always stick to just long-grain brown. If you do use wild rice, be sure to pick a longer cooking brown rice (e.g., basmati) to match the cook times, or be sure to add your brown rice later to the cooking cycle.

Instructions

Because of the complexity of this recipe, a brief schedule:

The beans, if you start from scratch, will take about 2 to 3 hours (depending on whether or not you soak). You can start the squash when the beans have an hour or less remaining.

The squash will take about 1 hour.

Once you have the squash in the oven, start your pilaf.

At about the 30-minute mark, start your sauces.

At the 45-minute mark, start your collards and cranberries.

Begin by preparing your beans. Bring 2 cups water to a boil in the small pan with your pinto beans on medium. Cover, and simmer on low until the water is absorbed and the pinto beans are cooked through (should take about 2 hours, but keep an eye on your beans to ensure they don't overcook).

Preheat your oven to 350° F. Cut your squashes in half and remove any seeds and any discolored, over ripe flesh. Brush the inside with vegetable oil and sprinkle with a pinch of sea salt. Rub oil on the outside as well. Poke the flesh with a fork in a few places and place cut-side down on the baking sheet. Bake on the middle rack of your oven for about 45 to 60 minutes, turning the squash over at the 25-minute mark, or until it is cooked and the flesh is lightly browned.

Note: The length of time the squash will take to cook will vary by the size of your squash and your oven—keep an eye on it as it cooks! When it is ready, remove it from the oven and let it stand for 10 minutes to cool. The squash is done when the flesh is soft and lightly browned.

Once you have started your squash, prepare your pilaf following the basic recipe (page 108).

Next, prepare your sauces. Make the Tomato Herb Sauce (page 66). Prepare the Simple Mornay Sauce (page 80). When both are ready, you can either mix your sauces for a rosé, or keep them separate for a more elegant plate. If you keep them separate, you'll need to keep both sauces warm, but it will provide you with some discrete flavors and some nice color contrast. Return the sauce(s) to a simmer.

Once your sauces are on the go, bring the vegetable oil to heat on high. Add 1/4 teaspoon sea salt to the pan. Add the onion and sauté for 3 minutes. Decrease the heat to medium-high and add the garlic and liquid smoke. Sauté for 2 minutes. Add the chopped collards and the cranberries and sauté for 8 minutes, or until the collards are nicely wilted. Remove from heat. Toss with the nutritional yeast.

When the beans, rice, collards, and cranberries are all ready, add them to a large bowl and mix to combine. Taste and add salt as necessary.

Plate the squash and spoon the mixture into it. You'll probably have more filling. I overstuff my squash and let the filling fall out over the side onto the plate (it's both a good way to use the extra and to represent the bounty of the harvest). Drape about 1/2 to 3/4 cups sauce (or use a similar amount of the sauces if you decide to keep them separate) over each half of the squash with your trusty tablespoon.

The recipe serves 4 well, but you could pair with some roasted asparagus for a light side dish.

Going further

This is a simple, elegant, and classically American meal. You can always twiddle the sauce to your liking, but this is a beautiful plate for fall when squash is in season. Ripe acorn squash is a mix of orange and green, and the roasting only highlights the color. For a brighter red, swap the pinto beans for red beans. If this dish isn't enough, for a simple plate, serve it with some grilled asparagus or any of the green salads in Chapter 4. For a fancier, fuller plate, serve it with Succotash (page 101) or French-Style Green Beans with Red Pepper, and Onions (page 114), and make some fresh bread using the dough recipe in Chapter 4.

Getting Past the Recipes:
Addressing the Center of the Plate

The door is now wide open for you to experiment. Make seitan cordon blue. Make yourself a Salisbury faux steak. Make a faux chicken-fried steak, a faux cheese steak, or a faux turducken (just don't make a tomucken that involves yuba, mushrooms, and seitan—I'm going to include a recipe for that in my next book). But don't forget all the great traditional meals in American cuisine that were prominent before the era of fast food convinced us that speed was more important to a meal than nutrition, elegance, or compassion. More important, don't be afraid to adjust your ideas around what constitutes the center of the plate a little more. Maybe it's not a "meat replacement" at all, but a nice vegetable curry with some rice, or maybe a vegetable stew. The culinary expectations of coursed dinners with centers of the plate are rules that do not have to apply to a new, contemporary cuisine. You can stick with these paradigms or you can dump them. You can use them ironically when you want or you can follow some of the rules and not others. Vegans shouldn't repeat traditions because they're traditions; they should repeat them because they're morally sound, meaningful, useful, and most of all (at least when it comes to cooking) fun.

Chapter 6:
When Vegan Desserts Attack!

Why anyone would want to read this chapter is self-evident. Recipes start with simple frozen-fruit sorbets straight from freezer to hand blender to dish and move on to puddings, mousses, and more. Desserts are a wonderful way to finish your meal, and not all desserts have to be heavy, overly sweet, and not good for you.

Horchata Risotto Rice Pudding

This is wonderful, simple stovetop rice pudding, made almost the same way you make risotto. I love rice pudding, and I usually make mine with rice milk, but I add a little ginger for extra flavor. It reminds me of horchata, a creamy rice milk very common in Chicago. Although many restaurants in North America add dairy to it, it's traditionally just rice and spice in the New World versions. Originally it was made with tigernut, and it has similar roots in almond milks in Europe. Horchata was the first nondairy milk I ever drank. The first time I had it was in a small restaurant in Wicker Park. I've loved it ever since.

Flavors: Sweet, rich

Note: You'll probably have to get the agave nectar and possibly the arrowroot from your HFS.

Equipment: A saucepan capable of holding at least 8 cups liquid, a medium bowl, and a whisk (a fork will do)

Ingredients

- ▶ 1/2 cup short-grain brown rice
- ▶ 1 cup water
- ▶ 1 tablespoon nut butter (macadamia, almond, or cashew preferred)
- ▶ 1 1/2 cups vanilla rice, soy, nut, or hemp milk (Natura brand vanilla rice milk preferred)
- ▶ 1 tablespoon minced fresh ginger
- ▶ 1 teaspoon ground cinnamon
- ▶ Small pinch of sea salt
- ▶ 1/2 cup agave nectar
- ▶ 1 teaspoon arrowroot powder
- ▶ 2 tablespoons soy milk or other nondairy milk (for the thickener)
- ▶ 1 teaspoon agave (if you have a sweet tooth, but you shouldn't need it)

Optional: You can use long-grain brown rice for this recipe, but it will take longer to cook and won't have quite the same creamy texture. For a little citrus flavor, add 2 tablespoons fresh-squeezed orange juice and 1 teaspoon minced orange zest to the thickener. Add 1/4 cup raisins for a traditional accompaniment. If you want a purple rice pudding, use black rice instead (adjust your preliminary cooking time).

Instructions

Begin by preparing your ingredients. Bring the water to a boil in the pan on high heat and add the rice. Return to a simmer, reduce to low, cover, and steam the rice for 45 minutes, or until done and all the water has been absorbed.

In the meantime, whisk together the liquid ingredients (except the arrowroot and the soy milk for the thickener) with the cinnamon, zest, and sea salt in the medium bowl. When the rice is done, add 1/3 of the mixture to the pan, return the rice to a simmer, cover, and cook for 30 minutes. Stir every 10 to 15 minutes to avoid sticking. At the 20-minute mark, add another 1/3 of the mixture to the pan. Return a simmer on medium heat, return the heat to low, cover, and cook for another 20 minutes. Stir every 5 to 10 minutes. At the 40-minute mark, add the last 1/3 of the mixture to the pan. Return a simmer on medium heat, return the heat to low, cover, and cook for another 10 minutes, stirring every 5 to 10 minutes to avoid sticking. Whisk together the arrowroot and soy milk for the thickener and add to the pan. Stir until the mixture thickens.

Remove from heat, and pour your pudding into a container, ramekins or martini glasses. Cover with plastic wrap if necessary. Chill for 4 hours, garnish with a sprinkle of cinnamon and an orange wedge if you like and serve. The orange wedge is a nice touch if you're serving in martini or rocks glasses. This serves 2 nice-sized desserts.

Going further

Add some crushed pistachios or some orange zest to deepen the flavors, colors, and textures of this dish. Sprinkle with a dash of cayenne pepper when serving for some bold color and a little heat.

Americano Ice

"Ice" is a kind of all-purpose term to describe frozen desserts in American cooking that make use of water rather than dairy. Technically, this is a granita, which is a bit like sorbet but tends to be a little more icy and granular in its texture and chemistry (chunkier is one way to describe it). Unlike sorbet, as a technique of preparation, larger ice crystals form, giving a granita its unique texture. Typically in North America granita is served as a drink, but this recipe is more traditional.

 **DIFFICULTY**

Flavors: Sweet, sour, green

Equipment: A medium-sized bowl (preferably with a cover; if not, then use a little plastic wrap), martini glasses or dessert bowls, and 2 tablespoons

Ingredients

▶ 1 cup water
▶ 1/4 cup agave nectar
▶ 2 shot of espresso, chilled (or 6 tablespoons very strong coffee)

Optional: Double the espresso if you like a strong coffee taste.

Instructions

Whisk your ingredients in a medium-size bowl. Return to the freezer and chill covered for 4 hours, scraping with a fork every 15 to 30 minutes (freezers may vary in terms of the length of time required). When well frozen, scoop the granita with a tablespoon. Cup and smooth the scoop with the other tablespoon. Switch the spoonful into the other spoon and then switch back. Add to the dish. Repeat until you have half of the granita in one cup and half in the other. The purpose of this technique is to produce a smooth texture.

Going further

An ice like this is really a dish best served in the heat. The ice crystals make it a textural treat. For a less traditional version, add half of your granita to a cup cool chocolate soy milk and stir vigorously for 1 to 2 minutes.

Orange Sherbet

Sherbet is basically sorbet with a little bit of milk or, in this case, soy milk (but hemp and nut milks also work).

DIFFICULTY

Flavors: Sweet, sour

Equipment: A medium-sized bowl (preferably with a cover; if not, then use a little plastic wrap), hand blender, martini glasses or dessert bowls, and 2 tablespoons

Ingredients

▶ 1 1/2 cup frozen raspberries (you can use fresh, but they'll take much longer to freeze)
▶ 2 tablespoons orange juice concentrate (or limeade if you prefer)
▶ 1 cup vanilla soy milk
▶ 1/4 cup agave nectar (use 1/3 for a sweeter tooth or if you raspberries are particularly sour)
▶ 1/2 teaspoon minced fresh ginger
▶ 1/2 teaspoon orange zest
▶ Pinch of sea salt

Optional: 1/2 teaspoon orange flower water.

Instructions

Add raspberries, orange juice, and agave nectar to the medium-size bowl. Blend with a hand blender. If you like your sherbet around the texture of soft serve ice cream, you can always serve immediately. Otherwise, return to the freezer and chill covered for 30 minutes to 2 hours or longer until you have the texture you like. Unfortunately, this varies by freezer and how cold your raspberries and orange juice are, as well as how frozen you like your sherbet. When ready, scoop some sherbet onto a tablespoon. Cup and smooth the scoop with the other tablespoon. Switch the spoonful into the other spoon and then switch back. Add to the dish. Repeat until you have half of the sorbet in one cup and half in the other. What you're doing with this technique is creating a nice, smooth spoonful for the presentation.

Going further

Sherbet is slightly more complicated in terms of its chemistry than sorbet because of the addition of the soy milk. Refreezing may introduce a little ice (which is fine in a sorbet, but not so much in a sherbet). If you find that that's the case, stir the sherbet with a fork at the 15-minute mark and chill for another 15 minutes. If you use fresh raspberries, plan for about 4 hours, possibly longer.

Citrus Macadamia Gelato

Traditionally, gelato is often made with fruit juices and nuts, although rarely in combination. This version combines lemon, lime, and orange juice, macadamia nut butter, and a little sweetener in a brightly flavored, citrusy, and creamy dessert.

 **DIFFICULTY**

Flavors: Sweet, sour, rich

Equipment: A medium-sized bowl (preferably with a cover; if not, then use a little plastic wrap), martini glasses or dessert bowls, and 2 tablespoons

Ingredients

▶ 1/2 cup macadamia nut butter
▶ 2 tablespoons frozen concentrated orange juice (preferably organic)
▶ 2 cups vanilla soy milk
▶ 1 teaspoon lime juice
▶ 1 tablespoon lemon juice
▶ 1/4 cup agave nectar
▶ 1/4 teaspoon guar gum
▶ Pinch of sea salt

Optional: You can substitute the macadamia butter for tahini if you don't mind the slightly bitter flavor of sesame seeds. You can leave out the guar gum, but you'll have a smoother gelato with it. Add some citrus zest or a little ginger to round out the flavor. If you have a sweet tooth, increase the agave nectar to 1/2 cup.

Instructions

Put your ingredients in a medium-sized bowl and whisk until thoroughly combined. Freeze for at least 3 hours, scraping and mixing with a fork every hour (freezers vary in terms of the length of time required). When well frozen, scoop the ice with a tablespoon, or an ice cream scooper if you have one. If you're using spoons, cup and smooth the scoop with the other tablespoon. Switch the spoonful into the other spoon and then switch back. Add to the dish. Repeat until you have about 1/2 to 1 cup the ice in each cup. What you're doing with this technique is creating a nice, smooth spoonful for the presentation. This yields 3 to 6 dishes, depending on size.

Going further

This is a simple ice with a nice rich flavor and texture. Other nut butters freeze well, as do other juices. Try this with cranberry juice or cherry juice for a different flavor in the high notes. Or try this dish with cashew or almond butter for slight variations in the texture and the underlying flavor of the base.

Chocolate Avocado Fudgesicle Ice

This recipe combines chocolate soy milk and avocados for a simple, rich frozen treat. It was originally titled Chocolate Avocado Gelato, but the testers suggested that it reminded them of Fudgesicles. Either way, it's a nice, dark, chocolaty treat with all those wonderful fatty acids from avocado.

 **DIFFICULTY**

Flavors: Sweet, sour, rich

Equipment: A medium-sized bowl (preferably with a cover; if not, use a little plastic wrap), martini glasses or dessert bowls, 2 tablespoons

Ingredients

- ▶ 2 cups chocolate soy milk (or nut or hemp milk)
- ▶ 1 ripe avocado
- ▶ 1 teaspoon lime juice
- ▶ 1/4 cup agave nectar
- ▶ 2 teaspoons cocoa powder

Optional: 1/4 teaspoon guar gum

Instructions

Put your ingredients in a medium-sized bowl and blend with a hand blender or a whisk. Freeze for at least 3 hours, scraping and mixing with a fork every hour (freezers may vary in terms of the length of time required). When well frozen, scoop the ice with a tablespoon or an ice cream scooper if you have one. Cup and smooth the scoop with the other tablespoon. Switch the spoonful into the other spoon and then switch back. Add to the dish. Repeat until you have half of the ice in one cup and half in the other. The purpose of this technique is to create a smooth texture.

Going further

This is a simple and rich ice. Avocado freezes fairly well and adds all kinds of wonderful fatty acids to any dessert. Feel free to experiment with other flavors, but be sure to always include a little acid (lime juice, lemon juice) to keep the avocado fresh. For a chocolate mint flavor, add 1/4 cup crème de menthe to replace 1 tablespoon of the agave nectar and 1/4 cup the soy milk, or do the same with a coffee liqueur for a mocha version.

Vanilla Ice Cream

This is a simple and straightforward ice cream recipe that will give you a strong basis to make your own ice creams from scratch. The recipe itself is pretty easy, but preparing ice cream is a matter of diligence and knowing your freezer (unless you have an ice cream maker).

Flavors: Sweet, rich

Equipment: A large bowl, a hand blender (a whisk will also do if that's all you have), and an ice cream maker is also nice to have

Ingredients

- ▶ 1 package silken tofu
- ▶ 1 cup agave nectar
- ▶ 2 cups vanilla hemp, soy, or nut milk
- ▶ 1/2 cup macadamia butter
- ▶ 1 teaspoon pure vanilla extract (use real vanilla beans if you can!)
- ▶ 1/4 teaspoon guar gum
- ▶ Small pinch of sea salt

Instructions

Blend everything together in a large bowl with your hand blender. Freeze in a covered bowl or plastic container for at least 6 hours, scraping with a fork every hour or so. If you have an ice cream maker, use that. It's that easy. It's the regular scraping and checking to ensure the right texture that's the hard part.

Going further

The texture of fresh ice cream varies. If you can, make this in the morning on a weekend and freeze over the course of the day, scraping and fussing over it as you can, at least until you have a clear idea of how long it will take to fresh in your freezer using the container that you are using. Now that you have a basic recipe, you can vary it however you like. Use chocolate soy milk for a simple chocolate ice cream. Use the basics of the chocolate and cognac mousse recipe to turn it into a wonderful rich treat. Swap out the macadamia butter for peanut butter and make peanut butter and chocolate ice cream. Replace some of the agave (about 1/4 cup) with 1/4 cup crème de menthe for a chocolate mint. Add some orange extract for an orange creme flavor. Serve fresh-scooped ice cream in a martini glass topped with fresh espresso for a very stylish affogato.

Honeydew, Ginger & Jalapeño Ice

Historically, ices have been used in different ways in coursed meals. Although they're typically desserts, you'll sometimes see ices used to cleanse the palate midway through the meal or, very infrequently, as an opener. This ice brings the wonderful, cleansing flavors of honeydew, singed with a little heat from the jalapeño for a good mid-meal tongue cleaner, or a fiery opener that sets the tone of the meal to follow. But it's still sweet enough to serve as a dessert. This recipe serves 8 as an opener or a mid-meal dish or 4 for a spicy dessert.

 **DIFFICULTY**

Flavors: Sweet, sour, spicy

Equipment: A medium-sized bowl (preferably with a cover; if not, use a little plastic wrap), martini glasses or dessert bowls, and 2 tablespoons

Ingredients

▶ 1/2 cup water
▶ 3 cups honeydew melon
▶ 1/2 teaspoon ginger
▶ 1/2 of a smaller jalapeño pepper, minced (about 1 teaspoon)
▶ 1/4 teaspoon sea salt
▶ 1/4 cup agave nectar

Optional: If you really don't like it spicy, replace the pepper with a little lime juice and zest.

Instructions

Begin by preparing your ingredients. When ready, whisk them together in a medium-size bowl. Cover and freeze 4 hours, scraping with a fork every 30 minutes or so (freezers may vary in terms of the length of time required). When well frozen, scoop the ice with a tablespoon. Cup and smooth the scoop with the other tablespoon. Switch the spoonful into the other spoon and then switch back. Add to the dish. Repeat until you have a several spoonfuls of in each cup. The purpose of this technique is to create a smooth texture.

Going further

This is a great ice and hopefully a good example of just how flexible ice can be, conceptually. A lot of the old rules about what to serve when during a coursed dinner are being reshaped with inventive cuisine. Experiment with the flavors you like. Make a tomato/basil ice. Make a strawberry/chipotle ice. Make pomegranate/walnut. The only real rules are that they should taste good together and they should freeze well. After that, you should be guided by how you're going to use the ice as a part of the meal so that your flavors, colors, and the overall tone of the meal match up well.

Banana & Avocado Brulée

This is a plant-based reinterpretation of crème brulée. You won't need the torch for this version, but it helps if you have one! This is actually a fairly easy recipe to assemble, and much easier than the original recipes, since you're not fiddling with more delicate ingredients. But due to the fire hazard if you do have a torch, I've included instructions for broiling.

DIFFICULTY

Flavors: Sweet, rich

Note: You'll need to get the agave from the HFS

Equipment: A hand blender (a whisk or a fork will do), 4 ramekins and a medium-sized bowl

Ingredients

▶ 4 bananas
▶ 1 ripe avocado, pitted and skinned
▶ 1 teaspoon lime juice
▶ 1 tablespoon macadamia butter
▶ 2 tablespoons agave nectar
▶ 1 teaspoon pure vanilla extract
▶ 4 tablespoons agave nectar (reserved)

Optional: Add a little grated orange zest or replace the banana with roasted and puréed acorn squash if you're brave enough. I'm serious. Puréed acorn squash is creamy and fluffy.

Instructions

Begin by preparing your ingredients. Preheat your oven to 350° F. Add everything to the bowl except for the two reserved tablespoons of agave nectar and blend with a hand blender (or mash with a fork) to thoroughly combine. Add 1/4 of the mixture to each ramekin. Bake about 15 minutes or until heated through. Carefully, with the back of a spoon, smooth out the mixture into the ramekin so that there is a nice, flat surface for your agave nectar. Remove from the oven. Pour 1/4 of the reserved agave nectar over each dessert. Very carefully spread the agave with your spoon. Turn your oven up to broil. When the oven is ready, add the ramekins and broil on the top rack (or an electric oven) or 5 to 10 minutes (this varies a lot by oven), or until the agave nectar has caramelized. Make sure that it has caramelized. If you use a torch, you can skip the broiling. Carefully use the torch to caramelize the agave like you would regular sugar.

Going further

The basic principles behind this dish are its combination of sugar and fat. The sugar caramelizes to make a nice, crunchy texture, while the fat stays nice and rich. Past that, you can vary this recipe in all kinds of ways. Add a little cocoa to the bananas. Add a little rum extract instead of the vanilla. Just remember to keep the proportions similar, and, of course, if you do use a torch, be careful!

Rum Raisin Bread Pudding

Bread pudding is a wonderful, delicious, and simple way to use leftover bread while creating a dessert that's very low-maintenance and not overly rich and heavy.

 **DIFFICULTY**

Flavors: Sweet, rich

Note: You may need to get the agave nectar, the nut butter, or the optional rum somewhere other than your regular grocery store.

Equipment: A sharp knife (preferably serrated), a glass baking dish (3 x 9-inch is fine), a pie wedge, and a hand blender (a whisk or a fork will do)

Ingredients

- ▶ 6 slices whole wheat bread
- ▶ 1 cup dark raisins
- ▶ 2 1/2 cups vanilla soy milk (use 1/4 cup less for a denser, breadier pudding)
- ▶ 1/2 teaspoon vanilla extract
- ▶ 1 teaspoon rum extract (or 1/4 cup rum reduced by 3/4)
- ▶ 1/4 cup nut butter (macadamia or cashew preferred)
- ▶ 3/4 cups agave nectar (use 1 full cup for a sweeter pudding)
- ▶ 1/4 teaspoon cinnamon or cardamom
- ▶ 1/4 teaspoon baking powder
- ▶ 1/4 teaspoon sea salt

Note: Be sure to use pure, nonimitation extracts. Imitation vanilla and other extracts can affect the flavor.

Optional: You can swap the nut butter for 2 tablespoons of margarine. If you'd rather use real rum instead of rum extract, use 1/4 cup dark rum reduced by 3/4 in a saucepan on high heat (it should only take 2 to 3 minutes once the pan is hot and the alcohol starts to boil off). You can use white rum, but you won't get the proper molasses taste. Increase sea salt to 1/2 teaspoon if your nut butter or margarine is unsalted and you like a salty taste with your sweets.

Instructions

Begin by preparing your ingredients. Leave your bread out (preferably for 1 hour, but at least 10 minutes) to dehydrate. When the bread is ready, preheat your oven to 350° F. Whisk together the soy milk, the extracts, the nut butter, the cinnamon, the agave nectar, the baking powder and the sea salt in a medium bowl until combined. If you're using real rum, reduce it, let it stand for 2 to 3 minutes or until cool, and add it to the rest of the liquid ingredients.

Next, slice the bread into 1/2-inch strips width-wise (should yield 6 strips per slice). Pour a small amount of the liquids into the pan and coat the pan thoroughly with it. Add a layer of sliced bread (use 10 to 12 slices) in criss-cross to the bottom of the pan. Pour 1/2 cup liquids over top. Add 1/4 cup raisins. Repeat until you are out of bread. Pour remaining liquids over the top. Add to the oven on the middle rack and bake for 45 to 60 minutes, or until the top is starting to brown like toast.

Remove from the oven and allow to cool at least 30 minutes. Cover with foil and refrigerate overnight or for at least a few hours and serve chilled.

Going further

This is a good desert for coffee. It will make 8 reasonable portions. It also goes well with fruit coulis (see the recipe for Raspberry Coulis, page 50, and use the fruit of your choice) or use the Simple Caramel (page 72) for a nice sauce for your pudding. Or, if you want a sweeter dessert, add 1/4 cup of the Simple Caramel to the liquid ingredients or toss in some chocolate chips instead of the raisins. You could also use minced fig and add a little molasses for a stronger rum taste. This recipe is very flexible.

Simple Blueberry Ice

This is a simple, beautiful, and flavorful ice.

 **DIFFICULTY**

Flavors: Salty, sour, sweet

Equipment: One medium-sized bowl, martini glasses or dessert bowls, and 2 tablespoons

Ingredients

▶ 2 cups frozen blueberries
▶ 1 to 2 tablespoons water
▶ 1 tablespoon agave nectar
▶ 1 teaspoon lemon juice

Optional: If your blueberries are uncooperative, you can add vanilla soy milk 1 tablespoon at a time for a sherbet, or add a combination of 1 tablespoon water, 1/2 teaspoon lemon juice, and 1 teaspoon agave to keep it more like sorbet.

Instructions

Add your blueberries and agave nectar to the medium-sized bowl. Blend with a hand blender. Scoop some of the ice onto one tablespoon. Cup and smooth the scoop with the other tablespoon. Switch the spoonful into the other spoon and then switch back. What you're doing with this technique is creating a nice, smooth spoonful for the presentation. You can chill your spoons for about 10 minutes in your freezer beforehand if you really want to ensure as little melting as possible. When your spoonful is mostly smooth, add it to the dish. Repeat until you have half of the ice in one cup and half in the other.

Going further

Frozen berries and your hand blender are a great way to make quick deserts. Frozen pineapple, mango, raspberries, blueberries, blackberries, and strawberries will also work in this recipe, although depending on the fruit's natural moisture and it's frozen consistency, you may need to add more liquid. If you find the sorbet is a little too melted, just pop it in the freezer for 30 minutes for a slightly firmer texture.

Orange, Cinnamon & Dark Chocolate Mousse

This is an elegant but simple dessert. Most of the work is reducing the liquids, and no double boiling is required. If you're not sure about the orange juice, just use a total of 4 cups soy milk. This mousse is a little denser than a traditional mousse, but you can lighten it a little by using a greater proportion of macadamia butter to silken tofu.

To keep things simple, I buy a 3-ounce bar of Camino brand bittersweet chocolate for this recipe. It's fair trade, organic, and easy.

 **DIFFICULTY**

Flavors: Sweet, rich, green

Note: You may have to go to your local HFS to get the sugar and possibly the chocolate.

Equipment: A pan capable of holding 8 cups liquid, a hand blender, a whisk, a medium bowl, 4 martini glasses or ramekins, and some plastic wrap

Ingredients

- ▶ 2 cups fresh orange juice (the better the orange juice, the better the mousse)
- ▶ 1 1/2 cups chocolate soy milk (hemp or nut milk should also work)
- ▶ 4 tablespoons dark cocoa (the better the cocoa, the better the mousse)
- ▶ 1 teaspoon cinnamon
- ▶ 1/2 cup sugar or agave nectar
- ▶ 1 (12-ounce) package extra-firm silken tofu, drained (use the aseptically packed kind)
- ▶ 1/2 cup macadamia nut butter
- ▶ 3 ounces high-quality semi-sweetened dark chocolate by weight (100 grams, 3 baker's squares or 1/2 cup chips)
- ▶ Small pinch of sea salt

Optional: For a creamier, fluffier mousse, use 1 cup macadamia butter and 1/2 cup silken tofu. You can use other nut butters, but your mousse won't be as light. Also, add a little orange zest for some extra flavor. Swap the cinnamon for ground cardamom for something a little more exotic. Add a little cayenne pepper or chipotle with the cinnamon for a spicy chocolate mousse.

Instructions

Begin by preparing your ingredients. Whisk together the orange juice, sugar, and cocoa. Bring to a simmer on high heat, reduce to medium heat and simmer until reduced by 1/2 (so that you have about 1 cup relatively thick liquid). Be careful not to let it boil over. Add the soy milk and further reduce by 1/3 (so that you have about 1 1/2 cups liquid altogether). This will take about 30 to 40 minutes, but it will vary a little bit depending on the size of your pan and the type of stove. Give it a good stir every 5 minutes or so.

When the mixture is getting close to 1/2 volume, blend the tofu and the macadamia butter in a small bowl until well combined. For a lighter, creamier mousse, use more nut butter, less tofu. Next, prepare your chocolate. If you're using baker's squares, chop your chocolate into chip-sized pieces. Decrease the heat to low and add the chocolate. Stir continuously until fully melted. This should only take a couple minutes. Be very careful not to overcook. Chocolate is traditionally melted in a double boiler in order to prevent exposure to too much direct heat too quickly, which will ruin the setup of this dish.

When the chocolate has melted, remove the pan from heat and add the tofu and macadamia mixture to the pan. Stir until thoroughly combined. Whisk by hand, 100 strokes, and then spoon directly into your martini glasses, ramekins (however you're going to serve the mousse), or a medium bowl. Cover with plastic wrap, poke holes in the wrap with a fork to avoid too much condensation and chill for at least 4 hours, preferably overnight. Serves 4.

Going further

Mousse is wonderful and flexible. Add a little espresso or replace some of the sugar and some of the soy milk with some chocolate liqueur if you prefer. What's important for this mousse to set up properly is the chocolate.

Chocolate & Peanut Butter Pudding

The wonderful flavors of chocolate and peanut butter combine in this creamy, easy-to-make pudding.

 **DIFFICULTY**

Flavors: Sweet, rich, green

Note: You'll probably have to go to your HFS to get at least the agave nectar.

Ingredients

- ▶ 2 cups chocolate soy milk (or hemp or nut milk)
- ▶ 1 package silken tofu
- ▶ 2 tablespoons dark cacao powder
- ▶ 1/2 cup peanut butter
- ▶ 1/2 cup agave nectar (or 3/4 cup if you have a sweet tooth)
- ▶ 2 tablespoons chocolate soy milk
- ▶ 1/4 cup arrowroot powder

Optional: Make it a mocha pudding with 1 shot espresso or 3 tablespoons very strong coffee and 1 extra tablespoon agave nectar.

Instructions

Add all of your ingredients (except for the 2 tablespoons chocolate soy milk and the arrowroot powder) to the pan and whisk thoroughly or blend with a hand blender. On medium heat, bring the mixture to a low simmer. Remove from heat. For the thickener, whisk together the chocolate soy milk and the 1/4 cup arrowroot powder until the arrowroot has been thoroughly dissolved. Add the arrowroot mixture to the other liquid ingredients and stir 1 to 2 minutes until the mixture thickens. Pour the pudding into individual ramekins or a large bowl and let stand for 15 minutes to cool. Then cover with plastic wrap and chill in a refrigerator at least 4 hours, preferably overnight.

Going further

This is a pretty simple pudding. No worries about scalding the milk or a bunch of lumps. Arrowroot works with just about any set of ingredients.

Strawberry Rhubarb Pie

Strawberry rhubarb pie was a frequent and popular part of my childhood. It's a shame that rhubarb has lost some of its popularity in the last couple of decades. It's a very nutritious vegetable and it adds a lot of flavor to this pie. Be sure to see the notes on rhubarb in Preparing Your Ingredients, page 9 (and don't eat the leaves!).

  DIFFICULTY

Flavors: Sweet, sour, rich, salty

Equipment: A pan capable of holding at least 12 cups liquid, a whisk (a fork will do), a 12-inch pie tin, a large bowl, a small bowl, a rolling pin, plastic wrap, and wax paper

Ingredients

- 1 batch Pastry Dough (page 120)
- 2 tablespoons agave nectar (for the dough)
- 1/4 cup vegetable shortening to replace 1/4 of the margarine
- 3 cups rhubarb, trimmed and chopped
- 1 teaspoon lemon juice
- 3 cups strawberries, stemmed and chopped
- 3/4 cup agave nectar (use 1 cup if you have a sweet tooth or if your strawberries are tart)
- 1/2 teaspoon sea salt
- 4 tablespoons arrowroot powder (you can also use cornstarch)

Optional: 1 teaspoon ginger and 1/4 cup rum, reduced by 3/4 in a saucepan on high heat (should only take 1 to 2 minutes once the pan is hot and the alcohol starts to boil off).

Instructions

Begin by preparing your ingredients. Cream together the margarine from the dough recipe, the agave, and shortening. Then cut the mixture into the dough following the basic recipe. When the dough comes together, wrap in plastic wrap and chill in your fridge for 30 minutes. In the meantime, toss your rhubarb, lemon juice, strawberries, agave nectar, and sea salt (as well as the ginger and rum) in the large bowl until everything is well coated. Roll out slightly more than half of your dough into a circle between two sheets of wax paper (aim for about a 12-inch circle) and add to the pie pan. Brush with a little vegetable oil.

Next, add your fruit to the pie. Roll out slightly less than half of your remaining dough into a 10-inch circle. Cover the pie and trim the dough on the edges. Seal with a fork by pressing the dough lightly with the fork tines around the circumference of the pie. Poke small holes into the dough with the fork so that steam can escape. Wrap your pie in foil and bake at 425° F for 15 minutes. Then reduce to 350° F, remove the foil, and bake for another 40 minutes or until the crust is very lightly browned. Remove from the oven and let stand at least 1 hour before cutting to serve.

Going further

Raspberry and rhubarb also makes a nice combination, as do apple and rhubarb. Any fruit that's more sweet than tart or sweetens well with cooking will work with this dish. I like roasted pears and rhubarb and a little white wine and hazelnut butter when I'm feeling gourmet. Serve this with a little vanilla ice cream.

Raspberry, Hazelnut & White Wine Ice

This ice is slightly more complicated but also much richer than the Americano. It combines raspberries, hazelnut butter, and a little white wine for a slightly more adult set of flavors.

 **DIFFICULTY**

Flavors: Sweet, sour, rich

Equipment: A medium-sized bowl (preferably one with a cover; if not, then use a little plastic wrap), martini glasses or dessert bowls, and 2 tablespoons

Ingredients

- ▶ 1/4 cup hazelnut butter
- ▶ 1 cup raspberries
- ▶ 1/4 cup white wine (use a sweeter, fruitier white if you have a choice)
- ▶ 1 teaspoon lemon juice
- ▶ 1/4 cup agave nectar

Instructions

Start by bringing the white wine to a light simmer in your pan on medium heat. Reduce the wine by 1/2 (this should only take a couple of minutes). Add the raspberries and lemon juice, decrease the heat to low, and sauté for 5 minutes. Crush the raspberries with a wooden spoon. Remove from heat and add the raspberries to the medium-sized bowl. Add the remaining ingredients and blend with a hand blender until smooth. Freeze at least 4 hours, scraping and mixing with a fork every hour (your freezer may vary in terms of the length of time required). When well-frozen, scoop the ice with a tablespoon or an ice cream scooper if you have one. Cup and smooth the scoop with the other tablespoon. Switch the spoonful into the other spoon and then switch back. Add to the dish. Repeat until you have half of the ice in one cup and half in the other. The purpose of this technique is to create a smooth texture.

Going further

This is wonderful ice with a more nuanced set of flavors. You can replace the raspberries with strawberries or cherries.

Chocolate & Peanut Butter Cream Pie

I loved chocolate cream pie as a child. This version is perfectly delectable. It builds on the techniques in the mocha pudding and chocolate mousse recipes to make a simple, delicious pie. This is a fairly simple pudding-type approach to pie. If you're not good at baking, no worries. Some premade pie crusts are made without animal ingredients. Most health food stores will have them, as will some grocery stores.

 **DIFFICULTY**

Flavors: Sweet, rich, green

Note: You'll probably have to go to your local HFS to get the agave nectar and possibly the chocolate.

Equipment: A pan capable of holding 4 cups liquid, a pan capable of hold 8 cups, a whisk (a fork will do), a 12-inch pie tin, a large bowl (preferably with a cover), a small bowl, a rolling pin, some plastic wrap, and some wax paper

Ingredients

Dough
▶ 1/2 batch Pastry Dough (page 120)
▶ 2 tablespoon agave nectar

Filling
▶ 6 cups chocolate soy milk (hemp or nut milk should also work)
▶ 1/4 cup dark cocoa (the better the cocoa, the better the filling)
▶ 1 cup sugar or agave nectar (add a little less for more of a dark chocolate flavor, a little more for a sweet tooth)
▶ 2 (12-ounce) packages extra-firm silken tofu, drained (use the aseptically packed kind)
▶ 1 cup unsweetened peanut butter

▶ 6 ounces high-quality semi-sweetened dark chocolate by weight (200 grams, 6 baker's squares or 1 cup chips)
▶ A pinch or two of sea salt (don't use more than 1/4 teaspoon)

Optional: For a slightly fluffier pie filling (or if you don't like peanut butter and chocolate together), use macadamia butter.

Note: To keep things simple, I buy 2 3-ounce bars of Camino brand bittersweet chocolate (or orange, or dark, etc. if you like to mix it up, but be sure to adjust the amount of agave nectar if you need to) for this type of recipe. It's fair trade, organic, and easy to toss in.

Optional: Add a little orange zest for some extra flavor. Add 2 teaspoons dried cinnamon, ground for a little extra spiciness, or swap the cinnamon for cardamom for something a little more exotic. Add 1/2 teaspoon cayenne pepper or 1 teaspoon chipotle with the cinnamon for a spicier, more exotic chocolate pie.

Instructions

Begin by preparing your ingredients. Bring the soy milk to a simmer on high heat, reduce to medium, add the cocoa and sugar/agave, and simmer until reduced by about 1/3 (so that you have about 4 cups relatively thick liquid). Be careful not to let it boil over. This will take about 40 to 50 minutes, but it will vary a little bit depending on the size of your pan and the type of stove. Give it a good stir every 5 minutes or so. Blend with a hand blender to remove any inconsistencies in texture (soy milk makes a slight skin).

When the mixture is reduced by 1/3, blend the tofu and macadamia butter in a medium bowl until well combined. For a lighter, creamier pie filling, use more nut butter and less tofu.

Next, prepare your chocolate. If you're using baker's squares or bars of chocolate, chop or break your chocolate into chip-sized pieces. Decrease the heat to low or, better yet, turn off the burner entirely and add the chocolate. Stir continuously until it is fully melted. This should only take a couple minutes. Be careful not to overcook. Chocolate is traditionally melted in a double boiler in order to prevent exposure to too much direct heat too quickly, which will ruin the setup of this dish.

When the chocolate has melted, remove the pan from heat and add the tofu-macadamia nut mixture to the pan. Stir until thoroughly combined. Whisk by hand, 100 strokes, and then spoon directly into your martini glasses, ramekins (however you're going to serve the mousse), or a medium bowl. Cover with plastic wrap, poke holes in the wrap with a fork to avoid too much condensation and chill for at least 4 hours, preferably overnight. Serves 4.

While your filling chills, make your pie crust following the basic instructions for this recipe, but adding the 2 tablespoons agave nectar to the liquid ingredients. Preheat your oven to 350° F. Once you have the pie dough ready, roll it out between wax paper to approximately 12 inches in diameter. Carefully lay the crust in the middle of the pie tin and let it take the pie tin's shape. Press very gently with your fingers so that there are no air pockets between the pan and the crust. Trim the overhanging edges with a butter knife. Bake the crust for approximately 10 to 15 minutes. It will be golden on the edges when it's done. When done, remove from the oven and let it stand for about 10 minutes. Unwrap your pie filling and pour the filling into the crust. Spread evenly with a spoon if you have to. Cover the pie with plastic wrap and chill for at least 4 hours, preferably overnight.

Going further

You can turn many of the puddings you make into pie, whether it's coconut cream or key lime. Add a little espresso to this pie, or a little liqueur. Serve it with a little vanilla ice cream, or get yourself some plant-based whipped cream and go all out.

Getting Past the Recipes:
Finishing the Meal

So, yeah, I don't really bake (you noticed, right?), unless it's pie, and that's really only baking a dough. Well, that's not entirely true. I do bake, but when I do, I follow other people's recipes. Although there's enormous opportunity to be creative, there's just not a lot of improvisation with most baking and pastry work takes a lot of specialized skill. It's a by-the-rules kind of thing in my experience, although maybe if I did more of it, I'd feel differently. In any case, there are all kinds of really good, plant-based dessert books available, and not without irony, desserts are relatively easy to veganize.

What I wanted to do with this chapter instead was to create some simple, primarily cool recipes that you could adapt to suit yourself. The real question this chapter addresses is how to finish your meal. That's entirely up to you. The most common ways to finish a meal, traditionally, are with sugar, fat, caffeine, and alcohol. I'm not judging. I'm just pointing out that some dessert, a digestif, and some coffee or tea is a great way to round out a delicious dinner!

Chapter 7:
Breakfast, Brunch & Brinner

Breakfast is a wonderful meal. You can eat it any time of the day. Tofu scramble aside, breakfast remains largely the undiscovered continent for a plant-based cuisine. Animal products dominate the international Western breakfast table. This chapter addresses breakfast from a vegan perspective. Breakfast is the meal of the early riser, the gourmand, and the go-getter. It's time vegans take it back! Recipes begin with simple porridges, move to reinterpretations of traditional favorites (e.g., tofu scramble, vegan grits, etc.) and conclude with more elaborate brunches (e.g., Tofu Florentine and "full breakfast" with roasted mushrooms, baked beans, and more). If you're not sure what to feed your remaining guests from last night's dinner party, this is the chapter.

Hot Cereal with Dates,
Figs & Fruit Coulis

Some people prefer something a little more substantial than a smoothie for breakfast. With this recipe, you're just making the warm breakfast cereal of your choice, adding some dried fruit and some fresh fruit sauce. This is a simple way to add fiber and fruit to your diet.

 **DIFFICULTY**

Flavors: Sweet, rich, salty

Equipment: A pan capable of holding at least 4 cups liquid and a hand blender

Ingredients

- 2 cups cooked breakfast cereal
- 1 teaspoon nut butter (your choice)
- 1/2 cup strawberries or other fruit
- Agave nectar or other sweetener to taste
- Sea salt (start with 1/4 teaspoon and add to taste)

Optional: Use 1 teaspoon agave nectar if you have fairly sour fruit. Other fruits will work, but you want to make sure you have enough moisture to do your coulis. If you find that your fruit is too dry, add 1 tablespoon water, 1/2 teaspoon lemon juice, and 1/2 teaspoon agave nectar in proportion until you have a syrupy consistency.

Instructions

Make your oatmeal, cream of wheat, or quinoa flakes as you normally would and add an extra 1/4 cup water. Mix in the dried fruit and nut butter and let stand for 5 to 10 minutes. With a hand blender, blend your fresh fruit until liquid and smooth, adding additional water, lemon juice, and agave nectar as necessary. Spoon the cereal and fruit into bowls. Pour the coulis over your cereal in zigzag or spiral patterns.

Going further

Be sure to pair the nut butter that goes well with your fruit. As a general rule, if you use a strong tasting nut butter, use stronger-tasting fruit. Bananas and peanut butter go together well. Bananas and tahini do not! But tahini goes well with cranberries. To add some sweetness, nutrition, and heft for mornings that require a little more energy. Add some finely chopped dried calimyrna figs or dates. Your mileage may vary if you use figs other than calimyrna. Black mission figs won't be as sweet, and frankly I don't like them!

Figs and dates add a lot of vegan-specific nutrition to a dish, as well as fiber, but you an always branch out into other dried fruits. You can also use dried red currants or raisins, etc. Prunes, cranberries, blueberries, apricots, cherries, goji berries, and all kinds of other dried fruits add wonderful flavor, color, texture, and nutrition to cereal. Try different fruit combinations for the coulis. Raspberries, kiwi, strawberries, and other fruits with a reasonable amount of water work well, but you may need to add a little water, lemon juice and agave nectar for fruits that have a little less water naturally (e.g., blueberries, cranberries, bananas, etc.).

Fruit Salad with Sour Cream

If you have a little more time, combine your fruits into a simple salad and eat them whole instead of puréed. This recipe will get you started. The Sour Cream adds some contrasting flavor and some additional creaminess, but you should consider it optional if you like to keep your fruit salad simple. This is about 5 servings of fruit for 2 people. It may seem like a lot, but it's a great way to start your day!

 **DIFFICULTY**

Flavors: Sweet, sour, rich

Equipment: A hand blender (a whisk or a fork will do), a small bowl, and a large bowl

Ingredients

- ▶ 2 cups berries (your choice)
- ▶ 2 tart apples, cored, seeded, and chopped
- ▶ 2 pears, cored seeded, and chopped
- ▶ 2 bananas, peeled and chopped into 1/4-inch rounds
- ▶ 1/2 cup dried fruit (dates or figs preferred, but any will do)
- ▶ 1 teaspoon lemon juice
- ▶ 1 tablespoons agave nectar
- ▶ 1/2 batch Sour Cream (page 65)
- ▶ 1 tablespoon agave nectar

Instructions

Begin by preparing your ingredients. First, whisk together the lemon juice and the agave nectar. If you use large berries such as strawberries, you should trim them and slice them in half. Prepare the rest of your fruit accordingly, and add it all to the large bowl. Drizzle and toss with the agave and lemon juice until well coated. The lemon juice is important to keeping your fruit from discoloring (so be sure to add it as soon as possible after you've chopped your fruit). Whisk together the Sour Cream with an additional tablespoon of agave nectar in a small bowl. To serve, ladle the fruit into bowls and top with a couple tablespoons of Sour Cream.

Going further

Melon, plums, peaches, and a lot of other fruits make for good fruit salad. Use the fruits you like based on their availability. Add the teaspoon of white miso to your sour cream for a slightly fermented flavor that goes so well with fruit.

Whole Wheat Pancakes with
Raspberry Pomegranate Syrup

Pancakes are a wonderful, filling breakfast. When I was a misunderstood teen, I used to go to a certain popular Midwestern family restaurant chain, the name of which rhymes with Lenny's, and eat pancakes with guacamole and drink coffee, usually in the evenings. This dish adds a little fresh fruit flavor and color to a traditional favorite. Good pancakes are a matter of having the right pan temperature, the right amount of margarine, the right temperature of the margarine when you add the batter, and the right amount of batter added to the pan. You may need to make this recipe a couple of time before you have a clear idea of these. I use a stainless steel pan, although an iron skillet is preferred and the margarine can probably omitted if you use nonstick).

Flavors: Sweet, sour, rich, salty

Equipment: A frying pan (preferably 9 to 12 inches), a large bowl, a small bowl, a whisk, a ladle, a spatula, and some ramekins or a creamer

Ingredients

Pancakes
- ▶ 2 cups whole wheat flour
- ▶ 2 tablespoons baking powder
- ▶ 1/4 teaspoon sea salt (a little more for savory pancakes; a little less if your margarine is salty)
- ▶ 2 1/4 cups vanilla soy, nut, or hemp milk (1/4 cup reserved)
- ▶ 2 tablespoons agave nectar or regular granulated sugar
- ▶ 1 teaspoon apple cider vinegar
- ▶ 1/4 teaspoon pure vanilla extract
- ▶ Margarine as needed (probably not more than 1/4 cup)

Sauce
- ▶ 1 cup pomegranate juice
- ▶ 1 batch Raspberry Coulis (page 50)
- ▶ Reduce to 1/3 (or until you have a nice syrupy consistency).

Optional: This take on pancakes is very Midwestern, where a good pancake is considered to have a thicker, fluffier, and doughier texture (like a little cake!). If you want something that's thinner, and denser, like a thick crepe, add the additional soy milk and reduce the baking powder by half (to 1 tablespoon).

Instructions

Begin by preparing your ingredients. Add your sauce ingredients to the small pan, bring to a simmer, decrease the heat to low, and reduce. In the meantime, combine your dry ingredients for the pancakes (the flour, baking powder, sea salt, etc.) in the large bowl. Only add 1 tablespoon baking powder for a thinner pancake, as discussed above. Whisk your wet ingredients in a small bowl (I just use a measuring glass). Add the extra 1/4 cup soy milk if you prefer your pancakes thinner. Finally, whisk in your wet ingredients with the dry in the large bowl until you have a nice, smooth batter. Thoroughly whisk any remaining lumps.

When your batter is ready, heat your pan. Add 1 tablespoon margarine to the pan and, when hot, ladle or spoon out about a half a cup of batter in an even circle. Use the ladle to smooth out carefully any un-evenness in the circle by pushing batter over the edge of the pancake. Cook for 3 to 5 minutes, or until the pancake is cook-ing through and the top of the pancake is not overly moist. You'll see little bubbles, and then the top will start to look lightly doughy. You're going to flip it. which re-quires that the top not be too runny.

Carefully check that the pancake is lightly browned on the other side by lifting your pancake off the pan with your spatula. If the pancake sticks, either you're not using enough margarine or the pan tempera-ture is wrong (probably not hot enough). If your pancake is burnt, obviously, the pan is too hot. If the pancake comes up and looks nice and brown, add another teaspoon of margarine to the pan and then carefully flip the pancake with your spatula before your margarine overheats. Cook for another 3 to 5 minutes until the pancake is lightly browned on the other side, and repeat until you've used all of your batter. Should make 6 to 8 pancakes depending on the size of your ladle.

To plate, pile the pancakes on plates as appropriate, and add your syrup to an appropriate dish, such as a ramekin for dipping or a creamer for pouring.

Going further

Add a little cocoa to the dry ingredients and use chocolate soy milk for chocolate pancakes. Replace the pomegranate juice with a little frozen concentrated orange juice for quicker sauce. If you want to go savory with your pancakes, add a little agave nectar to the kiwi and jalapeño coulis. No one ever said that pancakes had to be only sweet!

Fresh-Baked Bagels

Bagels are fabulous and easy to make. Traditionally, most bagels are made in a very hot, wood-burning oven, which makes for a very dry heat. Adding a little corn meal to the pan helps, and these bagels are delicious, even if they cheat a little. The day I learned I could make bagels from scratch was one of the happiest days of my life. I once had a friend ask, "Why make your own bagels when you can get them from the store?" Aside from the problem of determining which bagels are properly vegan and which aren't (some mass-produced bagels near you might be, and of course, most small family bakeries will tell you in detail what goes into their bagels), there's nothing like a completely fresh bagel right out of the oven, seasoned just the way you like it. Absolutely nothing.

DIFFICULTY

Flavors: It depends, but mostly sweet and salty

Equipment: A pan capable of holding at least 12 cups liquid, a large bowl, a whisk, a sharp knife, a baking sheet (if you have a pizza stone, use that instead), a pastry brush, and a slotted spoon or spatula

Optional: Add to the dough whatever dry herbs you'd like. If you want to add some minced onion, garlic, and other antifungal flavors, whisk them with some margarine and then fold them in while you're kneading the dough (like you would make pastry dough). Bread dough rises in part because of the gas that yeast microbes produce, so you have to be careful with antimicrobial ingredients and yeast dough. If you want to garnish your bagel with poppy, sesame, or caraway seeds, for example, sprinkle them on top at the end when you brush the bagels with soy milk.

Ingredients

- ▶ 1 batch Basic Yeast Dough (page 118)
- ▶ 1 tablespoon unsweetened soy milk
- ▶ 1 teaspoon corn meal
- One of the following
- ▶ 1 batch Nori Tahini Spread (page 50)
- ▶ 1 batch White Bean and Parsley Spread (page 58)
- ▶ 1 batch Ginger, Garlic, and Tahini Dressing (page 60) with an additional 2 tablespoons nutritional yeast
- ▶ 1 batch Peanut, Chipotle, and Lime Dressing (page 61) with an additional 2 tablespoons nutritional yeast
- ▶ 1 batch Tarragon Aioli (page 64
- ▶ or whatever you want!

Instructions

Begin by preparing your ingredients. If you're making a spread for your bagels, whisk it together (you may have to start earlier if you're making white beans from scratch). Make your dough following the basic recipe and let it rise for at least 30 minutes. When ready, preheat your oven to 450° F and bring the water to a rolling boil. In the meantime, knead your dough for 5 minutes on a floured board.

Break the dough into 4 equal pieces and roll out each piece into a small cylinder about 4 inches long and 1 1/2 inches in diameter. Connect one end to the other and form a small loop with a small amount of hole in the middle (about thumb-sized will do). Repeat until you've used up your dough. If you find there's too large of a hole, just ball back up and reroll. This makes 4 relatively good-sized bagels. Alternatively, you can make slightly smaller bagels and break the dough up into 6 parts (good for company!).

When your water has come to a boil, add 1 bagel at a time and boil for 1 minute (don't over-boil and don't add them all to the water simultaneously). Remove from the boiling water with a slotted spoon or spatula, and place on a dinner plate to dry slightly. Repeat until all of your bagels have been boiled.

Next, sprinkle the baking sheet or pizza stone with a light layer of corn meal. Add each bagel to the baking sheet and bake for 10 minutes. Remove from the oven and brush each bagel lightly with the unsweetened soy milk. Return to the oven and bake for another 5 to 10 minutes or until the bagels are lightly browned. Remove from the oven and let stand for at least 15 minutes to cool.

Going further

As the optional section makes clear, you can add any number of ingredients to your bagels. Or go all out and make your own "everything" bagels. Make one spread that you like, or make a few. Or just eat them with some jam. You can even make them in batches and have them through the week or use them in place of sandwich bread for lunches or burger buns for dinner.

Red Lentil & Amaranth Porridge with
Sun-Dried Tomatoes & Collard Greens

This is a hearty, savory porridge with some wonderful, bright colors and flavors. Amaranth is an ancient grain (technically a seed) that provides complete protein and a wonderful, if slightly unusual texture.

 **DIFFICULTY**

Flavors: Sweet, sour, savory, rich, salty, green

Note: You'll probably have to go to your HFS for the amaranth.

Equipment: A pan capable of holding at least 8 cups liquid, a large bowl, a small bowl, a whisk, and a sharp knife

Ingredients

Amaranth porridge and lentils

▶ 1 cup amaranth
▶ 1/2 cup dried red lentils
▶ 4 cups water, brought to a boil (add an extra 1/4 cup if you like a thinner porridge)
▶ Sea salt (start with 1/2 teaspoon and add more as necessary)

Kale and tomatoes

▶ 2 cups packed kale, stemmed and finely chopped
▶ 1 batch Ginger, Garlic, and Tahini Dressing (page 60)
▶ 1/2 cup sun-dried tomatoes (dry-packed) rehydrated and finely chopped
▶ 2 tablespoons nutritional yeast

Optional: 1 tablespoon white (or red) miso, 1 teaspoon minced jalapeño pepper, or 1/4 teaspoon cayenne pepper.

Instructions

Begin by preparing your ingredients. Soak your tomatoes in 1 cup boiling water for 20 minutes to rehydrate. Drain and chop finely. Add the amaranth, red lentils, and water to the pot. Bring to a boil on high, cover, reduce to low, and simmer for 20 to 30 minutes, or until the amaranth and the lentils have dissolved. Remove from heat when done.

In the meantime, stem the kale 1 inch above where the leaves start to branch out. Discard the stems and chop finely. Whisk the dressing together in the small bowl. Add the kale, tomatoes, and dressing to the cooked porridge at the 20-minute mark and let stand another 10 minutes. Taste and add sea salt as necessary. Ladle into bowls and sprinkle with nutritional yeast. This makes 2 good-sized bowls or 4 smaller ones.

Going further

Complete the flavors of this dish with the optional ingredients and treat yourself to a wonderful, hearty and health, but also remarkably light, breakfast porridge. I like to add red miso to mine, but white has a more subtle flavor. You can add some panache to the presentation of this dish by reserving slices of sun-dried tomato and maybe 1/4 cup minced kale, adding these to the porridge at the end. Add the kale like you would cilantro and the sun-dried tomatoes in thinly sliced spears in a fan on the top of the green field.

Tofu Florentine

This is a simple and elegant breakfast based on a time-honored brunch recipe. If you don't like spinach or béarnaise, you can always add a thin slice of seitan, a seitan sausage patty, or even some salsa. It's all good!

 **DIFFICULTY**

Equipment: A few small bowls, a sauté pan, 2 saucepans capable of holding at least 2 cups liquid, a sharp knife, and a pan capable of holding at least 6 cups liquid

Ingredients

- 16-ounce brick of firm tofu (the squarer, the better)
- 4 English muffins, lightly toasted
- 4 cups packed baby spinach, coarsely chopped
- Sea salt
- 2 cups water, salted
- 1/2 cup vinegar

Optional: 1 pinch of black pepper per slice of tofu, or a few dashes of hot sauce if you like

White sauce
- 1/2 cup Tarragon Aioli (page 64)
- 1 tablespoon water

Yellow sauce
- 1 tablespoon turmeric
- 1 teaspoon cumin
- 1 tablespoon vegetable oil
- 3/4 cup water (1/4 cup reserved)
- 1 teaspoon arrowroot powder
- Sea salt

Instructions

Begin by preparing your ingredients. First, drain your tofu. Prepare your aioli and set it aside.

Slice your tofu by cutting it in half, then quarters, then eighths, and then sixteenths, so that you have 16 equal slices. Bring the water to a boil, and add the white vinegar. Braise the tofu for 10 minutes and drain. Let stand a couple of minutes too cool, and sprinkle each lightly with a little sea salt to taste.

Whisk together the aioli and water. Add to a small saucepan and bring to heat, but don't boil. Remove from heat, taste, and add sea salt as necessary.

Whisk together the yellow sauce except for the reserved water and the arrowroot and it to the second saucepan. Bring it to a low simmer on high, remove from heat. Whisk together the arrowroot and the reserved water until dissolved. When the sauce is at a light simmer, remove from heat and add the arrowroot mixture. Stir until thickened.

Toast your English muffins. Toast them like you normally would. You can add margarine if you like, but you won't really need it for this dish.

Next, prepare your spinach. To cut some of the calories, if you don't want to sauté your spinach, you can always lightly steam it while you braise the tofu. You can also hand wilt it, or wilt it by soaking for 10 minutes in hot water. But to sauté, bring the oil to heat in the frying pan on medium-high and sauté the spinach for 5 minutes until wilted but not overcooked (it should still be bright green). Remove from heat and assemble.

Plate the English muffins, one top and one bottom per plate. Add 1/8 of the spinach to each toasted muffin half. Layer a tablespoon of the yellow sauce on each bottom. Add 1 slice of tofu. Sprinkle with the black pepper or hot sauce if you're using these. Layer a tablespoon of the yellow sauce on top of each slice of tofu. Add an additional slice of tofu on top, rotating the second slice about 45 degrees from the first (so that it doesn't look like a big brick). Add another tablespoon of the yellow sauce. Pour 4 tablespoons white sauce over each English muffin half.

Going further

It sounds more complicated than it is. If you're making this recipe for two, halve the ingredients. To save time, you can always just divide your aioli and mix a little turmeric and cumin into one, if doing multiple sauces is more than you can get up for on a weekend morning. The flavors won't be as discrete, but there's a lot of mixing in this dish anyhow. If you really want to go all from scratch, you can also make your own biscuits using the baking powder dough recipe (page 120). This is a great breakfast no matter how you do it!

Amaranth Cheeze Grits with
Roasted Collard Greens

I'm a big proponent of amaranth and collard greens. This dish is not that close to grits if you're used to big hominy, but it resembles polenta/corn meal grits. Of course, you can always try to make this with regular grits if that's what you would prefer.

 **DIFFICULTY**

Flavors: Sweet, sour, rich, salty, green

Equipment: A pan capable of holding at least 8 cups liquid, a baking sheet (if you plan to roast the collards), a large bowl, a small bowl, a whisk, and a sharp knife

Ingredients

Amaranth
▶ 1 cup amaranth
▶ 3 cups water (1/2 cup reserved)
▶ 1/4 teaspoon turmeric (add more if you like turmeric and want a neon yellow finished color)
▶ 1 teaspoon minced fresh ginger
▶ 1 teaspoon ground cumin

Collards

- 3 to 4 collard leaves, stemmed and minced
- 1 tablespoon extra virgin olive oil
- 1 tablespoon minced fresh garlic

Dash of liquid smoke

- 2 tablespoons white miso
- 4 tablespoons nutritional yeast
- 1 tablespoons nut butter (macadamia, almond, or cashew preferred)
- 1/4 teaspoon ground black pepper

Optional: 1/4 cup cherries, minced; 1 small tomato, cored, seeded, and chopped; 1/4 cup scallions, minced; or 1/4 teaspoon cayenne pepper for a little extra spice.

Instructions

Begin by preparing your ingredients. Add the amaranth and 2 1/2 cups water to the pot. Bring to a boil on high, cover, reduce to low, and simmer for about 15 minutes until the amaranth is starting to dissolve. Cook for another 5 minutes, stirring regularly. If you've never had amaranth, it has a sticky, porridge-like consistency with some grains still intact. Remove from heat when done.

In the meantime, prepare the collards. You can soak or roast (roasting is preferred). Begin by stemming the collards about 1 inch above where the leaves flower out. Discard the stems. If the stems on the leaves bother you, fold the leaves in half and with a knife, carefully slice out the stems. Roll the leaves up width-wise as you would a newspaper. Chiffonade the leaves, slicing in 1/4-inch slices width-wise.

Turn the cutting board or the leaves 90 degrees counterclockwise (whichever is easier) and repeat so that you have finely chopped collards.

If you roast the collards, whisk the garlic, liquid smoke, 1/4 teaspoon sea salt and then dress the chopped collards. Roast on a baking sheet for about 10 minutes at 450° F or until the collards are lightly browning. If you soak, see the instructions in Collard Noodles (page 90) and add the other spices to the amaranth at about the 10-minute mark.

When the collards are ready, add them and any remaining ingredients to the amaranth, stir thoroughly to combine, and then let stand another 10 minutes. If you want a thinner porridge and you find this too thick, add a little of the reserved water. Taste and add sea salt as necessary. Ladle into bowls and garnish with the optional cherries, tomatoes, or scallions. This makes a good-sized bowl for 2.

Going further

Cherries? Really? Of course! What matters is not whether or not the ingredients traditionally go together, but whether or not they taste good. Cherries have a wonderful sour flavor. I roast my cherries a little bit to bring out their sweet flavor. Tomatoes and scallions are more predictable, but they add some beautiful color and texture to this dish. If you really want to get fancy, add some ackee to this dish if you can find it.

The Breaded Biscuit of Seitan!

This is a great, mostly low-maintenance breakfast dish for those weekends when you want something more but don't really want to make a full breakfast.

DIFFICULTY

Flavors: Sweet, sour, spicy, fermented, rich, salty

Equipment: Some aluminum foil, a baking sheet, 3 small bowls, a saucer, a large bowl, a saucepan capable of holding at least 4 cups liquid, and a hand blender or whisk

Ingredients

▶ 1 batch Jalapeño Cheeze Sauce (page 68)
▶ 1 batch Baking Powder Dough (page 120)

Sausage

▶ 1 batch Dark Seitan (page 125)
▶ 1 additional tablespoon agave nectar for the liquid ingredients
▶ 1 additional tablespoon extra virgin olive oil for the liquid ingredients
▶ 1/4 additional teaspoon black pepper for the dry ingredients

Corn meal and spice mixture

▶ 1/2 cup coarse yellow corn meal
▶ 1 tablespoon whole wheat flour
▶ 1 teaspoon paprika (Hungarian preferred)
▶ 1/2 teaspoon ground black pepper
▶ 1/2 teaspoon cumin
▶ 1/4 teaspoon turmeric
▶ 1/4 cup unsweetened soy milk for dipping

Instructions

Begin by preparing your ingredients. Follow the basic recipe for the Dark Seitan, adding the additional ingredients. Add more pepper, whether black, cayenne, or jalapeño, if you really like your sausage spicy. Form the seitan into 4 round patties about 3 inches in diameter instead of 2 cutlets. Roll the dough into 4 equal balls, and flatten with your hand gently into a smooth patty about 1/4 inch thick. Bake as directed. About 15 minutes before your seitan is ready, start your dough. Let it rest for 30 minutes in a cool, dark place while you prepare your sauce.

When the seitan, sauce, and dough are all ready, break your dough into 4 equal pieces. Roll out the dough into circles that are roughly 2 inches wider than your sausages (about 5 inches). Brush the dough with 2 tablespoons sauce in a circle in the middle and smooth to about the size of your sausage. Add the sausage on top of the sauce, and add another 1 tablespoon sauce on top of the sausage. Fold up the edges of the dough and carefully seam them. Shape the biscuit into a small oval carefully with your palms so that the sausage and sauce are seamed in and you have a nice biscuit shape. Repeat with the remaining sausages. When the sausages are ready, bake them on a lightly oiled baking sheet on the middle rack of the oven for 15 minutes. Remove from the oven and let cool for 5 minutes.

Next, add the soy milk to a wide, shallow bowl, and whisk together your corn meal spice mixture on a plate, even plate. Next, dip each biscuit in the soy milk, and then in the corn meal and spice mixture to coat. Don't worry if the biscuit isn't covered head-to-toe in corn meal. The corn meal is really just some added crunch, color, and flavor.

When all of the biscuits are breaded with the corn meal and spice mixture, return them to the oven and bake another 10 to 15 minutes, until the biscuits are browning lightly. Remove from the oven, let stand for 10 minutes until cool and serve.

Going further

You could always add some sautéed greens in with the sausage to make for a more well-rounded biscuit. Or, you could replace the sausage entirely and simply bake in the Tofu Florentine. Otherwise, this dish goes well with a little green flavor on the plate.

Grilled Cheeze Sandwich with
Mushrooms, Arugula & Tomatoes

This grilled cheeze sandwich makes for a rich but no-nonsense brunch and it goes so well with soup! This dish draws on an Irish dish, rarebit, which is really so much more than cheese on toast—really! It also draws on the croque monsieur/croque madame of French brunch, but takes it all American with some arugula, tomatoes, and mushrooms. A brief note of caution: this sandwich is so extremely super-sized with deliciousness, you'll need a knife and fork to eat it. This is also the only dish in this book that really uses all eight flavors at once. The implications of this are left as an exercise to the reader.

 **DIFFICULTY**

Flavors: Sweet, sour, spicy, fermented, rich, salty, green, savory

Equipment: A serrated knife, a small bowl, a pan capable of holding 4 cups liquid, a whisk (a fork will do), and a baking sheet

Ingredients

▶ 1 batch Jalapeño Cheeze Sauce (page 68), without the jalapeño and half the soy milk
▶ 1 additional teaspoon arrowroot powder
▶ 6 cremini mushrooms, thinly sliced
▶ 1/2 cup baby arugula, finely chopped
▶ 1 large tomato, cored, seeded, and finely chopped
▶ 1 teaspoon garlic
▶ 1 tablespoon tamari
▶ 1 teaspoon lemon juice
▶ 1 tablespoon vegetable oil
▶ 4 slices whole wheat bread
▶ 2 tablespoons margarine
▶ Sea salt

Instructions

Begin by preparing your ingredients. Prepare the cheeze sauce according to the original recipe, but reduce by 1/3 (so, cook longer) and then add the additional teaspoon of arrowroot to the thickening process. When the cheeze is ready, remove from heat and sauté your vegetables. Bring the vegetable oil to heat on medium-high in the sauté pan. Add the garlic and sauté for two minutes. Add the mushrooms and sauté for 6 to 8 minutes until the pan starts to brown and the mushrooms are cooked through. Add the lemon juice and tamari to deglaze the pan. Sauté for another 2 minutes. Add the tomatoes and the arugula and sauté until most of the pan's moisture has been absorbed or cooked off, which should take no more than 3 to 5 minutes. Add the tomatoes, mushrooms, and arugula to the cheeze and stir thoroughly to combine. Let stand for about 10 minutes to cool.

Preheat your oven to 350° F. Toast your bread lightly, and let cool. Then, lightly butter both sides of your bread with margarine. Spoon about 4 to 6 tablespoons of the cheeze and vegetables onto the bread open-faced. Bake for 8 to 12 minutes on the baking sheet or until the cheese is starting to brown very slightly. Remove from the oven and let stand for 5 to 10 minutes to cool and solidify. Carefully, close the sandwiches. This can be tricky, since the cheeze will try to get away, and hot faux-cheeze all over your fingers is unpleasant. Set the sandwiches on the plate. Cut in half with a serrated knife and serve with some green salad or a vegetable soup.

Going further

You could always leave out the jalapeño if you don't like spicy for brunch. You could also replace the arugula with a little cilantro if you like. If you really want to get fancy, trade the mushrooms and tomatoes for some Roasted Portobellos with Pears and Onions (page 117). You'll only need about 1/4 to 1/2 of that side dish recipe for this sandwich, or you could just make it more about the mushrooms and pears and only use about half of this cheeze sauce, but then it's not really a grilled cheese anymore, is it? And if it's not grilled cheese, it's lunch, not brunch.

Full breakfast:
Tofu Scramble, Potatoes, Tomatoes,
Mushrooms & Carrot and Kale Slaw

Full breakfast is a wonderful, relaxing way to start a weekend morning, once you've done all the work and can sit down and enjoy it! This is a large breakfast/brunch and should easily provide for 4.

Ingredients

- 1 batch Roasted Potatoes (page 94)
- 1 batch Carrot and Black Kale Slaw (page 96)

Tomatoes

- 2 tomatoes, halved and stemmed (but not seeded and cored)
- 1 teaspoon extra virgin olive oil for each tomato half
- Pinch of salt for each tomato half

Tofu Scramble

- 2 tablespoons vegetable oil
- 4 scallions, trimmed and minced
- 1 brick firm tofu, crumbled (about 2 cups)
- 1/4 teaspoon turmeric
- 1/2 teaspoon cumin
- 2 tablespoons minced fresh garlic (more for a more garlicky flavor)
- 1 teaspoon minced fresh ginger
- 1/2 teaspoon ground black pepper
- 1 green pepper, cored, seeded, and finely diced
- 1 red pepper, cored, seeded, and finely diced
- 2 tablespoons water
- 2 tablespoons nutritional yeast
- 1/2 teaspoon apple cider vinegar
- 1 tablespoon lemon juice
- 1/4 teaspoon sea salt

Optional: Add 1/4 teaspoon cayenne pepper or 1 to 2 tablespoons Mango Chipotle Salsa (page 62) to the scramble to add some spice. Add a tablespoon or two of Sour Cream (page 65) or Tarragon Aioli (page 64) for a richer, softer texture.

Instructions

Begin by preparing your ingredients. Prepare the slaw, the potatoes, and the mushrooms, following their basic recipes. Start with the slaw, then move on to the mushrooms and potatoes.

For the tomatoes, wash carefully, slice in half and rub carefully with the oil. Sprinkle a small pinch of sea salt into the sliced part of the tomato and drizzle lightly with remaining oil. Place it round side down and roast with the mushrooms until lightly browned.

For the scramble, crumble your tofu with a fork, split into 2/3 and 1/3 portions and add each to separate small bowls. Add 1 tablespoon oil to the sauté pan and bring it to heat on medium-high. Add the scallions and sauté for 2 minutes. Add the green and red peppers and sauté for another 5 minutes. Add the apple cider vinegar, lemon juice, water, and black pepper. Stir thoroughly. Add the 1/3 portion of tofu to the pan and sauté for another 5 minutes. Remove from heat and put this tofu in a medium-sized bowl. Taste and add salt as necessary.

Next, add the lemon juice and deglaze the pan if necessary. Add another table-spoon oil, and return the pan to heat on medium-high. Add the turmeric, garlic, ginger, cumin, and cayenne and sauté for 2 minutes. Add the 2/3 portion of tofu and the nutritional yeast, and sauté for another 8 minutes. Whisk together the arrowroot and the water, and then add to the pan. When the sauce thickens, remove from heat. Taste and add salt as necessary.

Add the white tofu to the pan and stir until mottled but not entirely combined. Let stand for 5 minutes to allow the yellow tofu to cool and the white tofu to pick up some ambient warmth. Use tongs to serve with mushrooms, tomatoes, and toast.

Going further

This is a pretty involved brunch! You may not want to make every side dish, and there's nothing wrong with that. You could always make the scramble and the mushrooms and just toss the latter into the scramble. Or you could make the rest and, instead of serving with scramble, you could really go all out and make the Tofu Florentine instead. Of course, you can alter the scramble to include the vegetables you like. Peppers are nice and colorful, but you may prefer red peppers and zucchini for example. Toast is the tra-ditional accompaniment, but you could always wrap everything up in a tortilla for a breakfast sandwich (just be sure to drain the slaw thoroughly if you do).

Getting Past the Recipes:
What Makes for a Good Breakfast?

Breakfast is an important meal; brunch is a time-honored tradition of the leisure class. As a son of the proletariat, I've always leaned more toward a solid breakfast. I'm also a morning person, and although I like to spend time in the kitchen even in the morning, I like to get out and about before 10 a.m. That's a mostly true story. In any case, what makes a good breakfast is whatever you like to eat in the mornings. I drink miso tea with wakame, a smoothie, and espresso in the mornings. But some people like bagels. Some people like toast. I've tried to keep this section either simple (for breakfast) or ridiculously over-complicated (more brunch type stuff). Hopefully, you have enough recipes to get you started in the morning.

Chapter 8:
Entertaining as a Vegan: Brief Notes on Dinner Plans, Booze & Etiquette

So, now you know all the basics to good cooking. You've learned how to combine flavors and textures, how to layer flavors, how to prep someone's appetite and how to address the center of the plate. This concluding chapter tries to address some additional lingering questions, including dinner suggestions, how to move forward in your own cooking with improvisation and innovation, and finally, some notes on entertaining gracefully. You like grace, right?

But the real underlying purpose of this section is to help you navigate the differences between cooking for yourself and preparing a meal to entertain your guests. I think a good cookbook should help cooks to understand how food functions socially, to think clearly about that when planning a shared meal, and to provide a sense of how a cook can pair foods with the right social experience in order to create a meal that their guests will enjoy not just in terms of the food, but in terms of the overall experience. Sometimes people just want to relax and eat noodles. If the food doesn't help them to relax at those times, it's not doing what it should.

Is food entirely subjective? Yes and no, which really means no. There are of course personal tastes and variances by audience. But some ingredients, some food combinations, and some restaurants, for example, are more successful than others for reasons that most people could agree to and explain. Bad service. Poorly prepared dishes that lack flavor. These aren't *just subjective*, even though they may not be as scientifically founded and objective as gravity. Successfully preparing food for your guests is a happy marriage between these two understandings of food: a set of subjective, personal preferences of each guest or the audience; and a set of culturally shared expectations about food should look, taste, smell, feel, and so on, and what foods are appropriate in which situations. So, what do you need to know?

My academic training is largely in cultural arts and anthropology. So, I tend to look at food and all that goes with it from this perspective. There's a reasonable debate in the food community about form and its relationship to function. Is flavor or presentation more important? Is flavor or nutrition more important? These are valid questions with no agreed-upon or absolute right answer. But I do think that food is an art, like painting, writing, or other artistic forms of expression. That doesn't mean I believe that the aesthetic qualities of food should be the determinant factor in what to serve. In fact, I think it's impossible to separate meaningfully form and function in any art.

As the Zen Buddhists say, which is more important: the bowl or the space that the bowl creates? Is there a substantially meaningful difference between social processes and expectations involved with the beautiful pottery that many cultures produce in order to hold their food and the beautiful food they create to put in/on it as a ritualized process that we can shorthand as "making dinner"? Chopsticks, sushi plates, and the sushi itself would be one good example of what I mean. Everything is organized around the preparation of an artful meal, and I don't know what you'd call that except art. Of course, food isn't just something to look at, but then neither is the Roman arch or a Magritte painting.

Food is simply art that I look at (eating with my eyes first), smell, taste, and feel (and some people like to hear the crunch that food makes and some people find it relaxing to each crunchy food), and evaluate along a number of different functional lines. Of course, with food, we can evaluate not just the food itself, but how it functions in terms of nutrition (taking foods that don't taste so good by themselves but are highly nutritious and making them more palatable, visually interesting, etc.), social bonding (e.g., sharing kola nut as a ritual in Western Africa, or breaking bread on American tables), and so on.

For example, in some cases, food should bring everyone to the table. A holiday meal with tiny but elegant portions with ingredients no one has ever heard of, which requires a really sophisticated palate to enjoy probably would fail (unless everyone in the family is a foodie, which is certainly possible). A "fine dining" experience that is meant to provoke the imagination and inspire those who are very serious about food that involves adding avocado to bruschetta probably is also a failure (unless for everyone at the table, this is new and exciting stuff, which is also possible).

Of course, the food may still look, taste, and smell good and have a good texture; it just doesn't meet its social functions as well as it could. Sometimes we want something quick, comfortable, and relaxing for ourselves, and that is largely subjective. But sometimes we want to prepare something that will bring everyone to the table, and in that situation, we should be mindful of the expectations of others. Sometimes we want to make something that will really inspire others when it comes to food, and in those cases we should aim to surprise and delight. As the host, your role is to consider, evaluate, and plan around all of these considerations. It's a lot of work! But hopefully this book has armed you with recipes and examples that are useful across different kinds of social settings, and the following notes on entertaining will help you further.

Dinner Plans: Three- & Five-Dish Dinner Suggestions

This chapter addresses the vegan dinner party, with a set of three-course and five-course dinners. Dinner plans range from a series of simple dishes that marry key flavors to more complex and sophisticated offerings that will allow you to show off your formidable cooking prowess. Not for the meek and mild, this chapter will help you wow your guests but leave your kitchen a serious mess!

Three-dish dinners

The Mediterranean: Orange, Kale, and Kalamata Olive Salad; Lentil and Vegetable Soup; Spinach and Cheeze Tortellini with Spinach, Arugula, and Walnut Pesto.

The Burger Platter: The Basic Garden Veggie with oil and vinegar salad dressing; Chickpea and Coconut Burger; Roasted Red Potatoes with Chives.

My Favorite: Lentil Vegetable Soup; Tortellini with Arugula, Spinach and Walnut Pesto; Chocolate and Peanut Butter Pudding.

Some Like it Fast and Low-Effort: Potato, Scallion, and Kalamata Olive Soup; Tofu and Kale Runza; Raspberry Sherbet.

The Post-Postmodern: Chickpea and Avocado Ceviche; Seitan Florentine with Simple Mornay Sauce; Raspberry, Hazelnut, and White Wine Ice.

The Raw Plate: Carrot and Black Kale Slaw; Collard Noodles with the Ginger, Garlic, and Tahini Dressing (you'll need raw versions of some of these ingredients and, naturally, make sure your water is below 114° F and soak the collards for an hour. If you're not in the mood for collards, shred some daikon noodles instead); Honeydew, Ginger and Jalapeño Ice.

Five-dish dinners

Green All Over: Split Pea and Kale Soup; Roasted Asparagus; Seitan Cutlet with ample mustard glaze topped with Arugula, Spinach and Walnut Pesto, Red Potato/Sweet Potato Mash with Scallions; Chocolate Avocado Gelato.

The Euro: Arugula, Black Lentil and Fig Soup; French-Style Green Beans, Red Peppers, and Onions; Cutlets a l'Orange; Roasted kale; and Vanilla Ice Cream with espresso (affogato) or American Ice.

The "All American": Caesar Salad; Seitan Cutlets with Strawberry Rhubarb or Maple Mustard Glaze; Roasted Button Mushrooms; Roasted Potatoes and Chives; and Raisin Bread Pudding or Strawberry Rhubarb Pie.

The Down-Lo: The Basic Garden Veggie with basic oil and vinegar; Potato, Scallion, and Kalamata Olive Soup; Hot Grilled Portobello Steak Sandwich with Red Lentil and Red Wine Gravy; Roasted Potatoes and Chives; and Chocolate Cream Pie.

The Down-Home: Pumpkin, Tomato and Jalapeño Soup (or Illinois Corn Chowder); Black Lentil and Vegetable Pot Pie; Roasted Asparagus; Midwestern Succotash; and Rum Raisin Bread Pudding with Raspberry Coulis.

Tapas: Serve the Spinach, Arugula, and Walnut Pesto; White Bean and Parsley Dip; the Olive and Pickle Tapenade and any of the other dressings in Chapter 3 with some fresh bread, pita, crackers, and/or crudités.

Veganism & Alcohol:
A Match Made in Heaven

Once you've planned your fabulous dinner, you should consider two additional things. First, if you're serving alcohol, you should consider the relationship of the drinks you're serving to the food you're serving. Some alcohol is produced using animal products, and not all of it goes equally well with any old dish. Second, if you're entertaining nonvegans, there may some small etiquette issues, some sticky situations, and the following section gives you some ideas on how best to handle those.

Aperitifs and digestifs. There are some notes on what these are in Chapter 1. However, some fuller explanation will be helpful. An aperitif opens the meal, and a digestif closes it. At larger dinner parties (e.g., seven courses), it's not unusual to have a middle course of drinks to cleanse the palate (sometimes replaced by an ice), in addition to drinks served with the dinner itself. The aperitif, however, prepares the palate, and as such, it will be alcohols that tend towards a bitter or sour flavor. I prefer Dubonnet, but dry white wine cocktails, and other dry, bitter, or sour liqueurs are also reasonable offerings. Even some nice orangeade or lemonade with a hint of ginger is a good way to start the meal.

In contrast, the digestif rounds out the meal and promotes digestion (in theory!). A digestif will be an alcohol that tends toward a sweet flavor. Grappa, scotch, cognac, ice wines, dessert wines, most whiskeys, limoncello, some bourbons, and most sweet liqueurs in general will provide a reasonable digestif. For a mid-meal drink, serve something clean and fresh-tasting. Grappa, calvados, or other mostly neutral spirits are a good choice.

You may also choose to serve cocktails with hors d'oeuvres, in which case the general rules for aperitifs don't necessarily apply. In short, play it by ear. Match the drink to the food. Just make sure the alcohol isn't produced with animal products! And, of course, be prepared to serve still water, sparkling water, sour juices, and other drinks before dinner, as well as coffee and tea after dinner for those who don't drink at all.

Beer and wine before, with, and after dinner. Individual beers and wines may or may not be made with animal products. If you are a nonvegan host, you should try to determine whether or not what you are serving is vegan as a courtesy to your guests. I try to make sure that the alcohol I serve is appropriate to my guests based on a number of factors. I want people who come into my home to feel welcome.

Past that, beer is fine for an opening drink and can be paired appropriately with appetizers and even entrées. Plant-based food is often very flavorful and rich, and so it often does quite well with beer. As most beer tends to be lightly bitter or lightly sweet, you should pair appetizers that are appropriate complements to the flavor of the beer. Beer tends to go best with spicy, sour, and savory flavors. It can also be much easier to determine whether or not a beer is vegan than a wine. And due to the beer purity laws in many European countries and the long traditions of making beer without animal products, many beers are vegan by default. Certainly, the world's best are.

Wine is slightly more flexible (and more common), but it can be more difficult to determine whether or not a wine is made with animal products. Key things to look for are wines that are either not clarified, filtered, or fined (the only stages at which animal products might be used) or that are clarified, filtered and fined using nonanimal ingredients (e.g., PVPP, bentonite clay). For the most part, better to get nonfined, nonfiltered wines if possible. These tend to be better wines anyhow. When serving, both red and white wine go well with food before, with, and after dinner, depending on the type of wine. There is an outdated sense that plant-based food should be paired with white wine in some circles. This is unfounded, and probably a hallmark of the remarkably bland vegetarian food of previous decades.

Regardless, let the flavor of the food help you to determine what kind of wine to serve. Stronger-tasting foods should get stronger-tasting wines with more body (e.g., Barolo, cabernet sauvignon). Foods with a milder taste should pair with a less robust wine (e.g., merlot, shiraz). But this all varies, and you should follow the notes on the wine itself when making a decision about whether or not to serve it with a specific dish. Having said that, as a general rule, most plant-based foods—because they rely on strong sweet, sour, and green flavors—pair best with bolder, more structured wines. If you are serving wine as an opening drink or with dinner, be sure to have both red and white as a courtesy to your guests. Many guests drink inappropriate wines with their dinner, and there's simply no stopping them. Most guests will want a white wine if they want a dessert wine, but if someone wants red wine as an after-dinner drink, it's only good etiquette to serve your guests.

How Not to Be a Nuisance:
Being a Good Vegan Host

Etiquette is the snare by which the reasonable hold the unreasonable—or worse, the totally willful—at arm's length. There are other books that treat how to be a good guest and how to be a good host, and even books that address this topic from a vegan angle. Nevertheless, I wanted to provide you some closing notes on etiquette in order to help you navigate the delicate nuisances of polite society as a host.

You're the host; they're the guests. When you host a dinner party, it's really about ensuring your guests have a good time, even when they're annoying, boring, or dreary. But, it's your house. Just as you should follow the rules of someone's home when you are invited to get down at their place, you should feel free to set the rules for your guests. Make sure your guests understand what you will or will not brook, and communicate this as politely as possible. If you want no animal foods in your house, just remind them politely as part of the invitation.

If someone brings nonvegan food into your vegan home, don't flip the table. It can be a serious issue when someone brings nonvegan food into a vegan home. Politely remind someone who does so of the instructions you included on your invitation. If they say "But honey's vegan!" just remind them that it isn't. If they say "But it's only a little!" politely remind them that it is not the amount that is the issue. It's not a question or more or less; it's a question of right and wrong. But always be careful to thank a guest for their good intentions in bringing a dish if they do, and clearly explain what makes a dish not vegan; it's about setting an appropriate boundary and educating your guests. Often, people make mistakes, and that's a different problem than someone just behaving poorly.

If someone brings nonvegan alcohol, remind them that it is not vegan and offer them some of your private vegan stash instead. You can avoid this situation altogether by having dry events, or by serving drinks of your choice and discouraging guests from bringing their own alcohol. That can also be expensive. But, still, you may have guests who want to drink alcohol made with animal products in your home. From an etiquette perspective, you are still well within your rights to say no. From an ethics perspective, you should say no (remember, it's not less or more, it's right and wrong). If they have only brought nonvegan alcohol, and you tell them no, you can always politely offer them your own booze.

Answer questions about veganism, but be mindful of the timing. If your guests are nonvegan (and sometimes even if they are), they may have questions about your veganism. You may find this tiresome.

Vincent Guihan | New American Vegan

You may find it invasive. From an ethical position, you should still answer them, so long as the questions are polite. From an etiquette position, either answer the questions politely, or ask to change the subject politely. Occasionally, nonvegans will ask questions while eating about veganism. If it is appropriate to do so, answer the question or politely suggest that you will happily answer the question later. Sometimes it's easier to discuss things when everyone's mouth isn't full.

Jokes about eating family members get the pleather strap (just kidding). Guests who make jokes about eating a companion rabbit, chinchilla, pot-bellied pig, etc., are being profoundly rude, even by the rules of nonvegan society. You are well within your rights as the host to censure them. Furthermore, you have an obligation to your guests not to allow one person who is a crass buffoon to spoil their evening. If you decide not to invite them to leave, politely remind them that your companion is your family member and a refugee, and that if they're nervous, there are plenty of other jokes they could make.

Guests who ridicule veganism also get the pleather strap (also just kidding). Although standard rules of etiquette may dictate otherwise, dinner parties with vegans often have some level of contentious ethical, political, religious, or monetary discussion. As the host, you want to ensure your guests have a good time. If a guest makes more than one quick quip about veganism, politely correct them. If they continue and are upsetting others guests, invite them to change the subject. If that fails, politely ask them to leave. If you take etiquette

seriously, and you should, it is better to get a reputation for being humorlessly polite at the expense of one guest than to get a reputation for being humorlessly rude at the expense of many.

Veganism is about engagement, not separatism. If you have nonvegan guests in your home, you may have to remind your vegan guests to behave. Quips about nonvegan partners, about nonvegan sensibilities, etc., are often misconstrued, and sometimes, rude. You should encourage your vegan guests to remember that they weren't always vegan themselves, and that being a rude oaf to someone who isn't vegan for hipster points does nothing to help nonhuman animals. This is decidedly different from having a polite, sincere even a passionate discussion about the nature of veganism and the reasons for being vegan. Ideological separatism often reflects a lack of political will; it's often a retreat. You should discourage it in your guests for their own sake, and definitely for the sake of encouraging the development of a vegan-friendly community around your table at which nonvegans can learn more about veganism.

Dinner parties are semi-public, semi-private events. There may be times when one guest is offended by the back-and-forth of another set of guests. It's normal in large parties for someone to be offended by something someone says at some point. Ideally, if the first guest is offended, he or she should ignore the exchange—unless it's seriously impolite, in which case, as the host, you should have your say on the matter. More often, however, two guests have had a personal back-and-forth that concerns no one but the two guests involved, and the third guest has taken offense unreasonably. It is impolite to eavesdrop and break in, just as it is impolite to have an impolite, personal back-and-forth that excludes others unnecessarily. In those instances, scold all parties involved gently and remind them that dinner parties are supposed to be fun (for everyone) and that mixing rather than brooding is the key to this.

To act politely is to act well. There will be instances in which you won't know how to handle a situation. Remember three things. It's your home, it's your table, and it's your community around it. That should come before any inclination on your part to be impolite, or to allow any of your individual guests to behave impolitely. Certainly, you should never feel as thought politeness trumps ethics (even if these are not mutually exclusive). If you feel uncomfortable with any guest's behavior in your home, ask him or her to stop. If you feel anything is inappropriate to your specific event, make it clear politely why you feel the way you do. If any impolite behavior infringes on the rights of other guests unnecessarily (or nonhuman animals in your care), curtail it, and if it can't be curtailed, invite the offender to leave politely. But remember that the people around your table form a community and that you behave best as a host when you foster an open, sincere, and meaningful dialogue that resolves disagreements before they become disputes.

In Conclusion:
Improvising & Innovating with Flavors & Textures

When I buy a cookbook, what I'm typically buying is a pique to my own imagination. I'm happy if one recipe in a book I buy really changes the way I looked at a particular dish, ingredient, or flavor. This section is more for folks who are buying the book for the ideas they'll develop from the recipes, more than the specific recipes themselves.

Obviously, not every dish needs all eight of the flavors referred to in this book to be tasty. Vanilla ice cream, for example, doesn't need green, spicy, sour, fermented, or savory to be wonderfully sweet with a great mouth feel in order to make for a satisfying desert. But when you create whole plates of food, your work will be more sophisticated, generally speaking, if you combine a number of these flavors successfully. Your food will taste richer and, generally speaking, you (and your guests) will be more satisfied.

Texture gets a very quick pass in this book, and that's really a shame. But texture is one of those things that is often more personal than flavor. Nevertheless, texture is also a very important part of cooking and I've discussed it in various sections and various recipes. Texture matters a great deal to many eaters, and when preparing food for others you should be mindful of this. Some people, for example, describe wonderful plant-based foods like mushrooms and eggplant as "slimy." I know, deeply misguided. But the truth is that most people also judge their food by its texture. In part, this goes back to mouth feel. When you prepare a dish, you should be mindful of how the textures will work with one another, especially if you're serving picky eaters. Texture, like flavor, is very much a matter of context, and people often have expectations.

217

So, how do you improvise in ways that are innovative rather than just experimentation for experimentation's sake? As a cultural phenomenon, "food" is typically embodied in a set of long-standing traditions. However, it's also very heavily influenced by short-term trends. For example, during the post-WWII period, people valued foods that were mass-produced, mostly bland and "more nutritious than those silly whole foods!" You know, stuff that was "better than nature." Now, the pendulum has swung back the other way and you have people shelling out $50 for a small bottle of olive oil with all of the olives coming from the same grove, or $1000 for an espresso machine. Some things really are difficult to obtain and are pricey as a consequence (e.g., saffron). But there's also a law of limited returns as to the value pseudo-gourmet items really bring to a dish. If you want to innovate meaningfully, you do best to understand tried and true combinations of traditional cuisine first, and then understand what trends are at work on your local table.

You can start by developing a well-rounded understanding of what foods traditionally go well together across different cuisines. Cuisine has been a global or at least a syncretic phenomenon since the sixteenth century, and even before. All those spice caravans back and forth between Europe and Asia long before jet travel are a good example. Saffron is used in different ways in different cuisines, but it is always highly valued. In a sense, this global trade both homogenizes but also diversifies the local cuisines that are part of the trade route, whether that trade was conducted by camel or cargo ship. As a student of cooking, you should pay close attention to both the similarities and differences in terms of texture, flavor, and preparation for an individual ingredient or common ingredient pairs, both the way that they are influenced by short-term trends and what never seems to change.

So, start by looking at what ingredients cuisines outside of North America put together but also how the ingredients are prepared. For example, it's not an accident that zucchini and eggplant are often paired together, and often with tomatoes or peppers and garlic. It's not an accident that green peppers are often paired with mushrooms and onions. And it's no accident that ginger and lemon are commonly paired, and so on. Frankly, I think boiled eggplant is pretty gross, but I love it when it's roasted. Once you have a mental catalog of the specific foods that go well together, think about the preparation, the flavors, and the textures. How do these all complement one another? Eggplant is bitter, and zucchini is sweet. But roasting accentuates the sweetness of both. In terms of their texture, they also provide a beautiful color contrast if they're prepared in reasonable chunks, but if they're puréed, for example, that's lost. If you want to do something new, you must study what others have done, understand why they've done it so, and then think about how you can learn from that without imitating it in a derivative way.

Begin by varying one or two parts of the formula. So, for example, we know that zucchini and eggplant go well together, because sweet, green, and firm goes well with bitter, purple, and moist, and that roasting is a good way to bring out the flavor, texture, and color of these ingredients. You could, for example, roast carrots with the eggplant instead. Carrots, like zucchini, are sweet and firm, but orange. Or, you could roast zucchini and red pepper. Or, we know, for example, that green pepper, mushrooms, and onions go well together. The mushrooms provide a chewy, savory flavor and typically a rich brown color. The green peppers provide a crisp texture with a lightly bitter flavor. The onions provide a wonderful sweet flavor. Swap the green peppers for red or purple peppers. Swap the cremini mushrooms for portobellos. Swap the onions for scallions, or, more daringly, for roasted slices of sweet potato. What's important is to cultivate a sense of the food chemistry as it is embodied in flavor and texture, and the culinary science, as it is represented in the techniques of preparation, all work together to build a successful dish.

There's a wide culinary field still to be discovered with all the rich flavor and texture combinations that plant-based foods provide. Really, who knows how plant-based cuisine should taste? The focus on recreating simulacra of traditional nonvegan meats, cheeses, and other dishes, as well as on cataloguing traditional, mostly plant-based recipes only pushes the boundaries of a plant-based cuisine so far. There's nothing wrong with creating plant-based versions of traditional animal-based dishes (I do a lot of it in this book and for my own meals). And there's certainly a wealth of traditional foods that are plant-based. These all provide a solid bedrock for a new cuisine, but it's not a new cuisine itself. It doesn't take as much knowledge of food to produce knock-offs as it does to really explore what could properly be termed a plant-based cuisine and understand how that should taste. Of course, you can do both, but if you want to create something new, push the boundaries. You can start by pushing your own.

Flavor Index

Index

About PM Press:

PM Press was founded at the end of 2007 by a small collection of folks with decades of publishing, media, and organizing experience. PM Press co-conspirators have published and distributed hundreds of books, pamphlets, CDs, and DVDs. Members of PM have founded enduring book fairs, spearheaded victorious tenant organizing campaigns, and worked closely with bookstores, academic conferences, and even rock bands to deliver political and challenging ideas to all walks of life. We're old enough to know what we're doing and young enough to know what's at stake.

We seek to create radical and stimulating fiction and nonfiction books, pamphlets, t-shirts, visual and audio materials to entertain, educate, and inspire you. We aim to distribute these through every available channel with every available technology, whether that means you are seeing anarchist classics at our bookfair stalls; reading our latest vegan cookbook at the café; downloading geeky fiction e-books; or digging new music and timely videos from our website.

PM Press is always on the lookout for talented and skilled volunteers, artists, activists and writers to work with. If you have a great idea for a project or can contribute in some way, please get in touch.

PM Press
PO Box 23912
Oakland, CA 94623
www.pmpress.org

Friends of PM

These are indisputably momentous times – the financial system is melting down globally and the Empire is stumbling. Now more than ever there is a vital need for radical ideas.

In the three years since its founding – and on a mere shoestring – PM Press has risen to the formidable challenge of publishing and distributing knowledge and entertainment for the struggles ahead. With over 100 releases to date, we have published an impressive and stimulating array of literature, art, music, politics, and culture. Using every available medium, we've succeeded in connecting those hungry for ideas and information to those putting them into practice.

Friends of PM allows you to directly help impact, amplify, and revitalize the discourse and actions of radical writers, filmmakers, and artists. It provides us with a stable foundation from which we can build upon our early successes and provides a much-needed subsidy for the materials that can't necessarily pay their own way. You can help make that happen – and receive every new title automatically delivered to your door once a month – by joining as a Friend of PM Press. And, we'll throw in a free T-Shirt when you sign up.

Here are your options:

- ▶ $25 a month: Get all books and pamphlets plus 50% discount on all webstore purchases
- ▶ $25 a month: Get all CDs and DVDs plus 50% discount on all webstore purchases
- ▶ $40 a month: Get all PM Press releases plus 50% discount on all webstore purchases
- ▶ $100 a month: Superstar – Everything plus PM merchandise, free downloads, and 50% discount on all webstore purchases

For those who can't afford $25 or more a month, we're introducing **Sustainer Rates** at $15, $10 and $5. Sustainers get a free PM Press t-shirt and a 50% discount on all purchases from our website.

Your Visa or Mastercard will be billed once a month, until you tell us to stop. Or until our efforts succeed in bringing the revolution around. Or the financial meltdown of Capital makes plastic redundant. Whichever comes first.

COOK, *EAT, THRIVE*

Vegan Recipes from Everyday to Exotic

JOY TIENZO

978-1-60486-509-7 • $17.95

In *Cook, Eat, Thrive*, Joy Tienzo encourages you to savor the cooking process while crafting distinctive meals from fresh, flavorful ingredients. Enjoy comfortable favorites. Broaden your culinary horizons with internationally inspired dishes. Share with friends and family, and create cuisine that allows people, animals, and the environment to fully thrive.

Drawing from a variety of influences, *Cook, Eat, Thrive* features a diversity of innovative vegan dishes, including well-known favorites like:

- Buttermilk Biscuits with Southern-Style Gravy
- Earl Grey–Carrot Muffins
- Palm Heart Ceviche
- Barbecue Ranch Salad
- Raspberry-Chèvre Salad with Champagne Vinaigrette
- Samosa Soup
- Mofongo with Cilantro Lime Gremolata
- Ras el Hanout–Roasted Beets
- Italian Cornmeal Cake with Roasted Apricots and Coriander Crème Anglaise
- Lavender Rice Pudding Brûlée with Blueberries

With planned menus for all occasions, clear symbols for recipes that are raw, low-fat, soy-free, and wheat-free, and a section on making basics like seitan and non-dairy milks, *Cook, Eat, Thrive* is an essential book for anyone interested in cooking the very best vegan food.

Joy Tienzo loves food, and writing about food. Whether working as a pastry cook, hosting community brunches, or crafting wedding cakes, her purpose in life is to feed as many people as well as possible. When not in the kitchen, Joy can be found on a plane, a yoga mat, or volunteering for refugee and human rights causes.

"*Cook, Eat, Thrive* gives vegans the option of choosing exotic and extraordinary recipes for special dinner preparations, or simpler, yet imaginative creations for day to day meal planning. Whether you're looking for everyday vegan fare, or exquisite vegan dining, Tienzo serves it up with culinary flair!"
—Dreena Burton, author of *Eat, Drink & Be Vegan*

ALTERNATIVE VEGAN

INTERNATIONAL VEGAN FARE
STRAIGHT FROM THE PRODUCE AISLE

DINO SARMA

ALTERNATIVE VEGAN

International Vegan Fare Straight from the Produce Aisle

Dino Sarma

978-1-60486-508-0 • $17.95

Tofu, seitan, tempeh, tofu, seitan, tempeh... it seems like so many vegans rely on these products as meat substitutes. Isn't it time to break out of the mold?

Taking a fresh, bold, and alternative approach to vegan cooking without the substitutes, this cookbook showcases more than 100 fully vegan recipes, many of which have South Asian influences. With a jazz-style approach to cooking, it also discusses how to improvise cooking with simple ingredients and how to stock a kitchen to prepare simple and delicious vegan meals quickly. The recipes for mouth-watering dishes include one-pot meals—such as South-Indian Uppuma and Chipotle Garlic Risotto—along with Pakoras, Flautas, Bajji, Kashmiri Biriyani, Hummus Canapés, and No-Cheese Pizza. With new, improved recipes this updated edition also shows how to cook simply to let the flavor of fresh ingredients shine through.

Explore your inner chef and get cooking with Dino!

Dino Sarma was born in New Delhi, India, and immigrated to the U.S. with his family in 1986. From childhood, cooking has been a passion for him. He draws his influences from his mother and the many hours of food shows on television that he watched.

"This is vegan new school, which is really vegan old school, which draws on traditions that pre-date any of us. Cooking can be empowering, no doubt about it."
—Loren Corman, host of AnimalVoices on CUIT in Toronto

VEGAN FREAK

Being Vegan in a Non-Vegan World, 2nd Edition

Bob Torres and Jenna Torres

978-1-60486-015-3 • $14.95

Going vegan is easy, and even easier if you have the tools at hand to make it work right. In the second edition of this informative and practical guide, two seasoned vegans help you learn to love your inner vegan freak. Loaded with tips, advice, and stories, this book is the key to helping you thrive as a happy, healthy, and sane vegan in a decidedly non-vegan world that doesn't always get what you're about. In this sometimes funny, sometimes irreverent, and sometimes serious guide that's not afraid to tell it like it is, you will:

- find out how to go vegan in three weeks or less with our "cold tofu method"
- discover and understand the arguments for ethical, abolitionist veganism
- learn how to convince family and friends that you haven't joined a vegetable cult by going vegan
- get some advice on dealing with people in your life without creating havoc or hurt feelings
- learn to survive restaurants, grocery stores, and meals with omnivores
- find advice on how to respond when people ask if you "like, live on apples and twigs."

Now in a revised and expanded second edition, *Vegan Freak* is your guide to embracing vegan freakdom.

Bob Torres holds a PhD in Development Sociology from Cornell University. He's the author of *Making a Killing: The Political Economy of Animal Rights* and co-hosts Vegan Freak Radio.

Jenna Torres has a BA in Spanish and a BS in Plant Science from Penn State University, and received her PhD from Cornell University in Spanish linguistics. She is the co-host of Vegan Freak Radio, a podcast about life as a vegan in a very non-vegan world.

"*Vegan Freak* is a witty, helpful, wall to wall look at going vegan. A must read for anyone who's felt like the only vegan freak in the room."
—Sarah Kramer, author of *How It All Vegan*

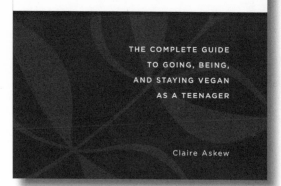

GENERATION V

The Complete Guide to Going, Being, and Staying Vegan as a Teenager

Claire Askew

978-1-60486-338-3 • $14.95

Going vegan is not always easy when you are young. Living under your parents' roof, you probably do not buy your own groceries, and your friends, family, and teachers might look at you like you are nuts.

In this essential guide for the curious, aspiring, and current teenage vegan, Claire Askew draws on her years of experience as a teenage vegan and provides the tools for going vegan and staying vegan as a teen. Full of advice, stories, tips, and resources, Claire covers topics like: how to go vegan and stay sane; how to tell your parents so they do not freak out; how to deal with friends who do not get it; how to eat and stay healthy as a vegan; how to get out of dissection assignments in school; and tons more.

Whether you're a teenager who is thinking about going vegan or already vegan, this is the ultimate resource, written by someone like you, for you.

Claire Askew was born in 1990 and went vegan a few days after her 15th birthday. After growing up in the Midwest, she is currently studying English and gender at a small liberal arts college in Portland, OR.

"An essential guide that covers all bases... this first effort is a welcome surprise"
—VegNews

Cook Food

a manualfesto for
easy, healthy, local eating

Lisa Jervis

COOK FOOD

A Manualfesto for Easy, Healthy, Local Eating

Lisa Jervis

978-1-60486-073-3 • $12.00

More than just a rousing food manifesto and a nifty set of tools, *Cook Food* makes preparing tasty, wholesome meals simple and accessible for those hungry for both change and scrumptious fare. If you're used to getting your meals from a package—or the delivery guy—or if you think you don't know how to cook, this is the book for you.

If you want to eat healthier but aren't sure where to start, or if you've been reading about food politics but don't know how to bring sustainable eating practices into your everyday life, *Cook Food* will give you the scoop on how, while keeping your taste buds satisfied. With a conversational, do-it-yourself vibe, a practical approach to everyday cooking on a budget, and a whole bunch of animal-free recipes, *Cook Food* will have you cooking up a storm, tasting the difference, thinking globally and eating locally.

Lisa Jervis is the founding editor and publisher of *Bitch: Feminist Response to Pop Culture*, the founding board president of Women in Media and News, and a member of the advisory board for outLoud Radio. Her work has appeared in numerous magazines and books, including *Ms.*, *The San Francisco Chronicle*, *Utne*, *Mother Jones*, *Body Outlaws*, and *The Bust Guide to the New Girl Order*. She is the co-editor of *Young Wives' Tales: New Adventures in Love and Partnership*, and *Bitchfest: Ten Years of Cultural Criticism from the Pages of Bitch Magazine*. She's currently working on a book about the intellectual legacy of gender essentialism and its effect on contemporary feminism.

"*Cook Food* is what you would get if you combined CliffsNotes of Michael Pollan's foodie insta-classic *The Omnivore's Dilemma* with the vegan parts of Mark Bittman's *The Minimalist* cooking column in the *New York Times*, added a healthy pour of DIY attitude and ran it all through a blender. The book's subtitle calls it a 'manualfesto,' and that's just about right—it's a nitty-gritty how-to with a political agenda: to give those of us with good intentions but limited budgets, skills, confidence, or time a chance to participate in the burgeoning local food revolution."

—Salon.com

LICKIN' THE BEATERS 2

Vegan Chocolate and Candy

Siue Moffat • Illustrated by Celso and Missy Kulik

978-1-60486-009-2 • $17.95

The beaters go on—in *Lickin' the Beaters 2: Vegan Chocolate and Candy*, the second of Siue Moffat's fun vegan dessert cookbooks.

Themed around the duality of desert—an angel on one shoulder and a devil on the other—Siue takes chocolate, candy, and even ice creem (vegan alternative to ice cream) head-on with quirky illustrations, useful hints, and a handy "Quick Recipe" indicator to make using this book simple and amusing. With an understanding that dessert should be an indulgence, Moffat provides vegan renditions of tantalizing delicacies, both traditional and original.

Recipes include old favorites such as Caramel Corn, Salt Water Taffy, Pralines, Cookies, Cakes, and Fudge, as well as some brave new recipes like Fabulous Flourless Chocolate Torte and Toll-Free Chocolate Chip cookies.

Siue Moffat puts things on paper and film. She loves making vegan candy (she has started a chocolate truffle business) and inspecting beat-up film collections. Radical politics make her eyes light up and *Peanuts* comics make her giggle. Siue lives here and there and has a love/hate relationship with sugar and punk rock.

LICKIN' THE BEATERS

Low Fat Vegan Desserts

978-1-60486-004-7 • $10.95

Don't pass up dessert! If you're vegan or trying to eat healthy, there's no reason to deny yourself sweet treats. Lickin' the Beaters brings you over 80 fabulous low-fat, dairy-free desserts where even the second helping is guilt-free. Breads, cakes, donuts, candies, cookies and bars, pies, ice creams, puddings, toppings, fruity stuff, drinks, and a whole lot more. Illustrated with beautiful linocuts and zany cartoons, you'll find the recipes fun, easy to follow, and so good you'll eat half the batter.

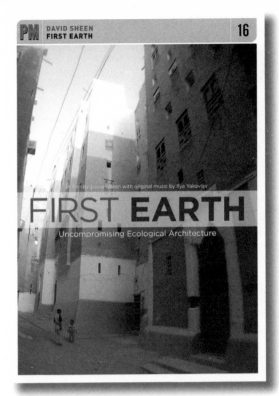

FIRST EARTH

Uncompromising Ecological Architecture

David Sheen

978-1-60486-199-0 • $19.95

A manifesto filmed over four years and four continents, this proposal contends that earthen homes—those made from cob, straw, clay, adobe bricks, and rammed earth— are the healthiest and best houses in the world. Also posing that suburban sprawl should be transformed into eco-villages, this discussion provides evidence of the benefits of this lifestyle in every cultural and socioeconomic context, from countrysides to urban jungles, third-world countries to tribal communities. Beautiful scenes of a myriad of cultures—curving art-poem dwellings in the Pacific Northwest, thousand-year-old Pueblo architecture in New Mexico, centuries-old and contemporary cob homes in England, thatched huts in West Africa, and Moorish-style skyscrapers in Yemen—make this global trek a testament to both the spiritual and material benefits of building with the earth.

This documentary film features appearances by renowned cultural observers and activists Derrick Jensen, Daniel Quinn, James Howard Kunstler, Richard Heinberg, Starhawk, and Mark Lakeman as well as major natural building teachers Michael G. Smith, Becky Bee, Joseph Kennedy, Sunray Kelly, and many more.

"This evocative and beautiful documentary shows why building with earth works well structurally, compels the eye and heart, is healthier for builders and dwellers than most other construction methods, and feels good to live in."
—Diana Leafe Christian, author of *Finding Community*

STUFFED AND STARVED

Raj Patel

978-1-60486-103-7 • $14.95

How can starving people also be obese?

Why does everything have soy in it?

How do petrochemicals and biofuels control the price of food?

It's a perverse fact of modern life: There are more starving people in the world than ever before (800 million) while there are also more people overweight (1 billion).

On this audio CD lecture, Patel talks about his comprehensive investigation into the global food network. It took him from the colossal supermarkets of California to India's wrecked paddy-fields and Africa's bankrupt coffee farms, while along the way he ate genetically-engineered soy beans and dodged flying objects in the protestor-packed streets of South Korea.

What he found was shocking, from the false choices given us by supermarkets to a global epidemic of farmer suicides, and real reasons for famine in Asia and Africa.

Yet he also found great cause for hope in international resistance movements working to create a more democratic, sustainable and joyful food system. Going beyond ethical consumerism, Patel explains, from seed to store to plate, the steps to regain control of the global food economy, stop the exploitation of both farmers and consumers, and rebalance global sustenance.

Raj Patel is a writer, activist and former policy analyst with Food First. He has worked for the World Bank, the WTO, and the United Nations, and has also protested them on four continents. He is the author of *Stuffed and Starved: The Hidden Battle for the World Food System*.

> "For anyone attempting to make sense of the world food crisis, or understand the links between U.S. farm policy and the ability of the world's poor to feed themselves, *Stuffed and Starved* is indispensable."
> —Michael Pollan, author of *The Omnivore's Dilemma* (on the book)